CHINA'S CONTINGENCIES AND GLOBALIZATION

CHINA'S CONTINGENCIES AND GLOBALIZATION

Editor

Ferdinand David

Socialy PRESS

AN IMPRINT OF SCITUS ACADEMICS

China's Contingencies and Globalization
Edited by **Ferdinand David**

This Book is Printed on Acid-Free Paper. ♾

ISBN: 978-1-68117-779-3
Library of Congress Control Number: 2017938803

Socialy Press
(An Imprint of Scitus Academics),
616, Corporate Way, Suite 2, 4766,
Valley Cottage, NY 10989

www.scitusacademics.com

Notice

Printed in United States of America.

Preface

As China has become an increasingly important part of the global trading system over the past two decades, interest in the country and its international economic policies has increased among international economists. There is no considerable account of China that doesn't mark major contingencies. China's development has been significant, yet its further course hinges on challenges across many terrains. Since this concerns the world's largest economy and a fifth of humanity, the stakes are large and China's contingencies take on a dramatic character. The contingencies have been shaped by globalization; how China meets these challenges shapes globalization in turn. The globalization speedily driven by the world economy has been shaping the world in a profound way. With this mega trend, China was able to break the bondage of the Cultural Revolution. It has taken a historical step to initiate a set of policies conducive to reform and liberalization, with modernization as its mission. Such a move has transformed China from a planned economy into a socialist market economy. It leads China in further opening up and integrating with the global economy, which will in turn speed up the progress of modernization in the country. Over the past 20 years, China achieved significant economic growth. If China failed to make such a decisive move, China would miss the golden opportunity to advance its economy. In absence of such a sound external environment created by economic globalization, the effectiveness of China's open door policy would have been lackluster.

This Book, China's contingencies and globalization, presents an emphasis on the major constraints and transformations that China faces, primarily on the basis of policy discussions in China. It discusses how these constraints and China's rebalancing policies narrate to globalization dynamics.

China has moved on from its growth and survival stage to its transformation stage. The keynotes of China changing its model of development in the post-crisis era are its transformation from a production power to a consumer power; the notion that consumption-driven growth best embodies equitable and sustainable growth; and the belief that urbanization, the integration of urban and rural areas, along with institutional innovation, are the best avenues to accomplish these transitions. Implementing this will slow growth rates and run counter to powerful elite interests, so it is a long and winding road.

Table of Contents

1

CHAPTER

Globalization, Culture and ELT Materials: a Focus on China

Zhichang Xu

Monash University, Melbourne,, Australia

ABSTRACT

In this paper, I shall discuss issues regarding globalization and culture in the context of English language teaching (ELT), with a particular focus on Chinese ELT materials in secondary schools in China. Globalization has a far-reaching impact on the foreign language education industry in China. Chinese learners of English view globalization positively as opportunities for geographical and social upward mobility. In addition, Chinese learners adopt a pragmatic approach to Chinese and foreign cultures in terms of negotiated multiculturalism based on a *Yin Yang* principle (Fang 2011, p. 34) of co-existence, mutual reinforcement and paradoxical unity. This paper reviews Chinese conceptualizations of globalization and culture as well as English as an International Language (EIL), and analyses ELT textbook materials for secondary schools in China. The analytical framework is based on current EIL principles and criteria for ELT materials (Sharifian 2009, McKay 2012, & Matsuda 2012). Chinese secondary school English textbooks have been collected as data, and their analysis shows that 1) texts about cultures other than English (COTE) co-exist with texts of traditional

Inner-Circle (Kachru 1982) cultures, 2) cross-cultural perspectives are represented in current secondary school English texts, 3) multiculturalism has been incorporated in the texts, 4) explicit efforts have been made in the compilation of text materials and relevant learning activities to cater for the needs of Chinese secondary students for learning English in the Chinese context, 5) texts that help raise awareness of world Englishes and local functionalities of English are included in the textbooks, and 6) the teachers' and students' relevant personal experiences and schemas are utilized and activated in the choice and design of the main and supplementary texts and related activities. I conclude the paper by arguing that the ongoing globalization and multicultural awareness, alongside the paradigm shift to teaching EIL in the Chinese context have engendered desirability for incorporating multicultural and multimodal ELT materials in China. It is, therefore, not only feasible but also natural and timely to focus on the local functionalities, i.e., local needs, functions and purposes, in the ELT materials, and this has significant implications for Chinese learners and teachers of English.

Keywords: Globalization, Culture, English as an International Language, ELT material, Chinese English learners

INTRODUCTION

In China, the notion of globalization (*quanqiuhua*) has been embraced since the 1970s when China proposed and implemented economic reforms and open-door policies. This was a time when concepts of 'global village', 'future shock' and the 'third wave' (c.f., Toffler 1970, 1980) were popular both domestically in China and overseas. Since then, China has been seeking to revitalize its 'global village' membership. Against this backdrop, English began to be extensively taught in schools replacing Russian and Japanese in their school curricula as a major school subject for 'foreign language' (*waiyu*) education. Earlier texts for learning English are either localized, including slogan-like texts of 'Long live Chairman Mao', or imported texts, e.g., the Aesop's Fables, and the Million Pound Note. In the 1980s and 1990s, the English textbooks that were commonly used in China mainly included texts written in the so-called 'standard' English expressing the cultural values of Americans or British. As a result of this, Chinese students were exposed to linguistic and cultural expressions and values that they did not have first-hand experiences with, and they could not have the opportunity 'to challenge the knowledge or put it to use in their immediate contexts' (Xu 2010, p. 176). Xu (2004, p. 68), therefore, proposes that textbooks in China should consider why Chinese students learn English, how they use English, and whom they should regard as language models.

Since the beginning of the century, Chinese ELT materials for secondary schools have been developed to incorporate both global and local Chinese cultures, specifically designed for Chinese learners of English. This new dimension in ELT material development is aligned with Chinese conceptualizations of globalization, culture and the changing profile of the English language, and the emerging Chinese variety of English (Xu 2010). In this paper, I shall analyse a new series of English textbooks adopted nationwide for senior secondary schools in China. The textbooks include five volumes of 'New Senior English For China' (Second Edition). These books are written and edited for secondary school students across China by the 'course book research team' affiliated to the People's Education Press. This paper analyses the texts included in the 'New Senior English for China' series from the perspective of Chinese conceptualizations of globalization, culture, and the emerging paradigm of EIL. Major research questions include whether the texts expose the Chinese secondary school English learners to diversities of English and cultures; what cultures are represented; and whether the texts help engage the Chinese students in using English, and provide opportunities for the students to associate their own Chinese cultures with other cultures. This paper shall start with a review of the conceptualizations of globalization, culture, and EIL. It shall then propose an analytical framework, followed by text analysis. I shall conclude the paper by arguing that the ongoing globalization and multicultural awareness, alongside the paradigm shift from teaching English as a foreign language to teaching EIL in the Chinese context have engendered desirability for incorporating multicultural and multimodal ELT materials in China. It is, therefore, not only feasible but also natural and timely to focus on the local functionalities, i.e., local needs, functions and contexts, in the ELT materials, and this has significant implications for Chinese learners and teachers of English.

CURRENT CONCEPTUALIZATIONS OF GLOBALIZATION, CULTURE AND EIL

In this section, I shall review the current conceptualizations of globalization, culture and EIL, in particular how Chinese conceptualize these notions in relation to the spread of English in China, and the development of Chinese ELT materials.

Globalization

Globalization is an ongoing process that permeates almost all societies. Many scholars (e.g., Blommaert 2010; Eriksen 2007; Garrett 2010; McKay 2002; McKay & Bokhorst-Heng 2008; Mufwene 2010; Schneider 2011; Scholte 2000) have explored the meanings and implications of 'globalization'. It is essential to understand the process of globalization in order to examine cultures and ELT materials in China, where an increasing number of people learn and use English for both intra- and inter-cultural communication. Globalization has been closely associated with global communication and mobility. However, people from different cultures conceptualize globalization differently, and their attitudes towards globalization also change over time.

One of the connotations of globalization, to an average Chinese, is Americanization. Since late 1970s, when English was re-introduced into the Chinese school curricula, Chinese learners of English have been increasingly influenced by American cultures, and become one of the major consumers of American cultural products, including Hollywood movies, Radio and Television programmes, fast food chains, American English teaching materials, and American English speakers as language instructors. Garrett's research (2010, p. 456) on the East-West contrastive analysis of globalization shows that people from different nations hold different views towards globalization, with China and the USA leaning towards more 'positive orientations' while the UK, New Zealand and Australia leaning towards more 'negative orientations'. According to Garrett (2010, p. 458), while people from the UK, Australia, New Zealand and Japan perceive globalization as 'global unity', Chinese tend to see it primarily as 'opportunity' coupled with 'cooperation' and 'change'. To a certain extent, the Chinese conceptualization of globalization as opportunity renders an explanation to the Chinese craze for English. English learning in China implies opportunities for geographical (going overseas) and social upward mobility (i.e., professional development and promotion), and it also symbolizes the removal of imposed territorial and ideological restrictions in the sense of 'liberalization' as defined by Scholte (2000, p. 16). Globalization as opportunity for a Chinese is also closely associated with progressiveness, modernity, and positive changes at an individual level and that of China as a developing nation.

Current literature on globalization reveals a wide range of connotations, including mobility (i.e., the flow of populations, commodities, and ideologies) (Blommaert 2010; Eriksen 2007; Garrett 2010; Mufwene 2010); blending and mixing of local, translocal and global cultures (Blommaert 2010; Eriksen 2007; McKay and Bokhorst-Heng 2008); 'local functionality' (Blommaert 2010, p. 44), 'super-diversity' (Blommaert 2010, p. 7), 'polycentricity' (Blommaert 2010, p. 60), and 'micro-hegemonies' (Blommaert 2010, p. 62); and the paradox of standardization

(Eriksen 2007). I shall review these major connotations with a focus on Chinese cultures and ELT materials in China.

1. Globalization as mobility

Mobility has been identified as one of the key features of globalization by Eriksen (2007). Migration, tourism, domestic and international conferences have thrust people to move around and settle either temporarily or permanently in new communities. Although these people bring with them their own languages and cultures, they also adjust themselves both linguistically and culturally in order to survive and thrive in the host communities. Blommaert (2010, p. 6) views migration as a 'change in the spatial organization of one's life in an enduring way'. It is 'enduring' in the sense that the nature of migration (i.e., the separation from the land of origin and one's own linguistic and cultural belongings) is likely to 'bring pressure to accommodate to the host society'. What adds to the endurance nature of migration is that in the context of globalization, according to Blommaert (2010), language forms are more mobile than before, patterns of use become less predictable, and all of the processes of mobility appear to display complex connections with language.

English learning in the context where English is not widely used is comparable to embarking on an enduring journey of migration. It is common for a Chinese to conceptualize globalization as mobility. To an average Chinese, 'mobility' that is associated with English learning may not exclusively mean migration, but it also means social or professional upward 'mobility' in terms of joining social elite groups, or seeking political, administrative and academic promotions. 'The Chinese, especially educated adults and university students, are motivated to learn English because they believe it will enable them to join an educated elite group and to have access to better jobs, more opportunities, and a wider world' (Xu 2010, p. 172). This connotation of 'globalization' also reflects Blommaert's ideologically 'acquirable imagery of the self as being in the world', because English learners in China are not simply learners of English, but symbolically they add a global element to their Chinese identities and become Chinese 'global' citizens.

Another aspect of mobility is closely related to the notion of space and time, which is subsequently related to issues of cultural 'dis-embedding' and 're-embedding' (Eriksen 2007, pp. 8-9), 'deterritorialisation' and 'territorialisation' (Blommaert 2010; Scholte pp. 45-46; Scholte 2000, pp. 15-17), and 'supraterritoriality' and 'transnationalism' (Garrett 2010, p. 449). Cultural 'dis-embedding' and 're-embedding' are two of the key features of globalization identified by Eriksen (2007, pp. 8-9). Dis-embedding 'includes all manners through which social life becomes abstracted from its local, spatially fixed context', while re-embedding is a countervailing process to territorialize a mix of local and global cultures through 'strong networks of moral commitment, concerns with local power and community integration, national and sub-national identity politics' (Eriksen 2007, pp. 8-9). Cultural dis-embedding and re-embedding processes are also closely related to deterritorialization and territorialization. The former stands for 'the perception and attribution of values to language as something which does not belong to one locality but which organizes translocal trajectories and wider spaces', while the latter refers to 'the perception and attribution of values to language as a local phenomenon, something which ties people to local communities and spaces' (Blommaert 2010, pp. 45-46). With globalization, the notion of language (de)territorialisation can become relative and fluid due to the increased velocity of movement of people and the unprecedented engagement of people in the virtual online world. 'Interaction across large distances enters into a complex relationship with local activity', therefore, the local has never been more closely connected to the global through the 'compressed time and space' in terms of 'supraterritoriality and translationalism' (Garrett 2010, p. 449). In the Chinese context, Xu's research (2009, pp. 123-124) shows that it can be hypothesized that there are varying 'micro-linguistic markets' co-existing in China, including a 'global linguistic market' where English is used for transnational communication; a 'supra-local market' where cosmopolitan Mandarin Chinese (often code-mixed with English) is used for trans-regional interaction among Chinese elite groups, and a 'local linguistic market' where dialects and vernacular Chinese are used in local communities. It should be noted that the 'micro-linguistic market' is not a geographical concept, but a conceptualization in relation to mobility, and dynamic communities of multiple language users in contemporary China. One implication of globalization as mobility for learning and using English in China is that ELT materials should reflect the dynamic linguistic and cultural complexities of a mobile world both in a global sense and the local reality. In other words, ELT materials should facilitate Chinese learners of English to raise their awareness that English has increasingly been used as an international language, and to cater for their needs of using English both locally and globally for intra- and international communication.

In addition, it should be noted that 'mobility' does not necessarily imply global symmetrical flow of populations and commodities. According to Mufwene (2010, p. 31), 'the players or partners involved in the relevant world-wide networks of interconnectedness and interdependence do not hold equal economic powers; it is the more powerful who control which populations and commodities (including languages) are transported more freely, and in which directions'. ELT materials as a carrier of cultures and ideologies play a crucial role in China, as learners of English generally have undiscerned access to English and its associated cultural content in their ELT classroom. The cultures and ideologies that the learners are exposed to may well determine how they perceive the language they learn. If the cultures are exclusively about the Inner Circle (Kachru 1982), then the learners tend to view English as a 'foreign' language. On the other hand, if the ELT materials are inclusive of a variety of cultures, and the texts include a variety of Englishes, then the learners may increase their awareness of EIL. In other words, English can be utilized as a tool to express different cultures and enhance multicultural identities of the learners. Eriksen (2007, pp. 8-9) points out that one of the consequences of globalization is the vulnerability in terms of protecting certain communities of people against unwanted flows. In the Chinese ELT context, English learners may not be empowered if they are only exposed to 'foreign' cultures and non-local linguistic forms through their ELT material. Such unwanted 'flows' of linguistic items and ideologies may demotivate the learners, and put them in a vulnerable position both as learners and users of English. To cater for the needs of Chinese learners of English, it is essential to be aware of the Chinese conceptualization of globalization as mobility.

2. Globalization as cultural blending

Blommaert (2010, p. 60) points out that 'an important feature of globalization processes is the fact that they blend the local and the translocal in complex networks'. This blending involves both language and culture. In terms of language blending, people code-switch and code-mix when they communicate with others. In addition, they also transfer linguistic forms from their local languages to English. Cultural blending results from the increasing 'mutual dependence and transnational connections' and the 'instantaneous exchange of messages characteristic of the information era' (Eriksen 2007, pp. 8-9). McKay and Bokhorst-Heng (2008, p. 2) view globalization as a 'reformulation of social space in which the global and local are constantly interacting with one another'. They also argue that 'neither one should be afforded a dominant position'. This globalization as cultural blending implies that the English-speaking world that the ELT materials present should contain a blending of cultures, both local and international, so that learners can naturally blend their local experiences and cultures with those that are presented in the ELT materials.

3. Globalization as local functionality

It cannot be assumed that globalization is about everything-going-global. There has also been a concurrent localization process focusing on how a language operates at a local level. According to Blommaert (2010, p. 44), a language functions in a community precisely because it 'provides local meanings: meanings that provide frames for understanding the local environment, to categorize and analyse the (strictly) local world.' Even deterritorialized languages, e.g., English in China, should adapt to local functionalities. Blommaert (2010, p. 45) argues that 'when another language is introduced in a particular environment, it may as well be dysfunctional for it does not articulate the particular local meanings required for the sustenance of this environment'. If English in China is viewed exclusively as a 'foreign' language, then local cultures can hardly be encoded in English, e.g., using English in its Anglo-American sense to encode the *Duanwu* Festival, commonly known as the Dragon Boat Festival, and its associated cultural activities including making *zongzi* (angular rice balls wrapped in reed or bamboo leaves), drinking *xionghuang* (realgar) wine, and racing dragon boats. This conceptualization of globalization as local functionality implies that ELT materials should be developed to provide sufficiently localized English input to enable Chinese learners of English to function locally, e.g., describing and expressing their own local cultures and experiences for intra- and intercultural communication.

Mufwene (2010, p. 47) argues that localization can be regarded as globalization at a local or a regional level. He argues that 'however global the English language has become – in the sense of being a language that is spoken almost anywhere on our planet and permeates so many diverse domains of modern life – it will continue to indigenize everywhere, acquiring local characteristics in the same way it has done to date'. To incorporate texts of local cultures in local varieties of English into ELT materials is aligned with the process of globalizing English at the local or regional level. This localization process can sometimes go so far as to adopt local linguistic forms as in the case of McDonald's going local to adapt to local taste buds and using local languages for product marketing.

4. Globalization as super-diversity

Globalization is the driving force for a global lingua franca, and English has been widely adopted as one. However, globalization does not necessarily lead to monolingualism or a monolithic 'global English'. Instead, Mufwene (2010, p. 50) argues that 'the differential evolution of English appears to be substituting a new form of diversity for an older one'. This new form of diversity also includes blended linguistic forms and cultures. Blommaert (2010, pp. 7-8) points out that 'super-diversity poses descriptive as well as theoretical challenges'. The descriptive challenge involves the spatial reconfiguration of the local and translocal, as well as real and virtual. 'All of this has effects on the structure and development of language repertoires and patterns of language use'. The theoretical challenge involves the stretching of 'the limits of existing frameworks for analysing and understanding multilingualism and the dynamics of language change'. In the context of ELT in China, this conceptualization of globalization as super-diversity can also be interpreted as the diversity in the needs of the learners, the demands for a variety of teaching pedagogy, e.g., grammar translation, communicative teaching, bilingual education and immersion, and the diverse ELT materials both for classroom use and extracurricular utilization, e.g., textbooks by different publishers, various reading and multimedia English learning materials, and super diverse preparation materials both in terms of quantity and quality for public tests, e.g., College English Test (CET) Band 4 and Band 6, Test for English Majors (TEM) Band 4 and Band 8, IELTS, TOEFL, and GRE.

The notion of super-diversity is also closely connected to micro-hegemonies, poly-centricity, and normative complexes. Blommaert (2010, p. 62) defines 'micro-hegemonies' as a notion of 'restricted, niched hegemonies that co-exist with others in polycentric environments'. Taking the Chinese linguistic market (Xu 2009) as an example, the local, supralocal and global markets operate in a way that certain varieties of language(s) evolve and co-exist in super diverse communities in China. A localized variety of English co-exists with cosmopolitan Chinese in the global and supralocal linguistic markets, formulating micro linguistic and cultural hegemonies in relation to polycentric environments. Within these micro-hegemonies, certain beliefs, values and norms are shared and practiced. An example of such a micro-hegemony is the Chinese white-collar community in major cities such as Beijing, Shanghai and Guangzhou, where 'white-collar workers actively utilize resources from multiple languages (such as Standard English, Standard Mandarin, Chinese regional dialects, and Internet language), and the multimodal functions of the digital technologies' (You 2011, p. 409). The existence of micro-hegemonies implies poly-centricity. A polycentric context, according to Blommaert (2010, p. 61), is a 'context in which multiple normative complexes are simultaneously at work, but are of a different order'. Chinese ELT context is polycentric in the sense that English learning and teaching in China are contextualized in a heterogeneous society comprising multiple 'normative complexes' including local cultural norms, norms of the greater Chinese diaspora, and norms that have been introduced through ELT materials and other media forms. Blommaert (2010, p. 60) points out that 'given the intense polycentricity of learning environments and the fact that globalization processes develop at several different scale-levels, the issue of normativity becomes quite complex'. This suggests that ELT materials should not be oriented towards a monolithic norm mindset, but raise the awareness of the learners that multiple normative complexes have become the norm.

5. Globalization as heterogeneity

Another connotation of globalization is standardization. A common misperception about globalization and standardization is that globalization has led to a global village with a global English, and that commercial products and manufacturing processes have to go through various forms of standardization in order to achieve uniformity. To some extent, this can be true, because globalization entails a wide spread of English, and other notions, including 'internationalization' (the growth of international exchange), 'universalization' (the spreading of common objects and experiences to everyone) (Scholte 2000, pp. 15-17), and 'comparability and shared standards' (Eriksen 2007, pp. 8-9). However, Eriksen (2007, p. 10) also points out rightly that 'globalization does not entail the production of global uniformity or homogeneity. Rather, it can be seen as a way of organizing heterogeneity.' Indeed, in World Englishes, standardizing (or codifying) different varieties of English has been operating as a counteracting process leading to the heterogeneity of English . According to Mufwene (2010, p. 50), the heterogeneity resulting from the changing ecology of English features in: '1) the extent of the interactions the new speakers have had with speakers from the Inner Circle; 2) the specific languages English has come in contact with; and 3) the particular uses to which it has been put'. This conceptualization of globalization as heterogeneity enables Chinese to understand that the spread of English in China does not necessarily produce Chinese communities of uniform speakers of RP (Received Pronunciation) or GA (General American). Instead, it enables the local variations of English in China to continue to thrive. English is increasingly seen as either a 'local practice' or a language for 'translingua franca' communication (Pennycook 2010, pp. 682-684). The 'worldliness of English', in Pennycook's terms (2010, p. 681), may not simply be 'a matter of grammatical or lexical variation', but of 'cultural and ideological difference'. As far as ELT materials are concerned in the Chinese context, pluralizing cultures and Englishes can only be the first step towards addressing issues of super diversity under new conditions of globalization. A further step will have to be considered in terms of how the teachers and learners make use of the ELT materials so that their own language ideologies, cultural identities and local language practices also play an integral part in decoding and encoding the additional language of EIL both locally and globally. Situated and contingent ways of compiling ELT materials to address the heterogeneous nature of Chinese learners, teachers, and ELT pedagogy are what globalization as heterogeneity implies for English language education in China.

Cultures, ELT materials and English as an International Language

Globalization has various connotations, as discussed in the section of 'Globalization as mobility', however, according to Garrett (2010, p. 457), 'it is the culture category that is the most salient'. Byram (1988, p. 82) defines culture as knowledge which is 'shared and negotiated between people', and 'much of that knowledge is symbolically expressed in artefacts and behaviours and is formulated as rules, norms, expectations, as moral and legal codes, as proverbs, as parental injunctions to children'. Sharifian (2011, pp. 8-11) interprets culture in terms of schemas, including 'event', 'role', 'image' 'proposition' and 'emotion' schemas. Event schemas are abstracted from our experience of certain events, e.g., funerals and weddings; role schemas include knowledge about social roles which denote sets of behaviours that are expected of people in particular social positions; image schemas are iconic images that are readily imagined in relation to physical or social experiences, e.g., the image schema of a 'building' associated with the 'foundation of a nation', or the 'path' image associated with a straight path mapped onto ideologies as in 'the path to God'; proposition schemas are abstractions which act as models of thought and behaviour, e.g., marriage is enduring; and emotion schemas are complex configurations of feeling states and scenarios by reference to certain events or situations, e.g., 'shame' and its associated circumstances can be culturally specific. This notion of culture as schema renders a practical framework for textbook material analysis.

Fang (2011, pp. 27-31) has reviewed different paradigms of culture including 'static' and 'dynamic' paradigms. The 'static paradigm' assumes that 1) the complex phenomenon of culture is captured through simplification; 2) nationality or nation state is adopted as the basic unit of analysis; 3) cultural differences, cultural clashes, and cultural collisions are seen essentially as a problem; 4) cultures can be analysed in bipolar cultural dimensions along which each national culture is given a fixed indexing; 5) value is the most crucial component of culture, and 6) culture is conceptualised as stable over time. Fang (2011, pp. 28-29) points out that this static paradigm is essentially a 'pre-globalization and pre-Internet phenomenon', and it is incapable of capturing cultural dynamics in a globalizing society or dealing with intra-cultural diversity as well as cultural change over time. The 'dynamic paradigm' of culture centres around intercultural interaction, and it focuses on 'negotiated culture', and 'multiple cultural identity' (Fang 2011, p. 29). In the dynamic paradigm, cultural differences are seen essentially not as a problem but as an opportunity for learning and knowledge transfer, in which cultures are 'negotiated, compromised, embraced, and transferred' (Fang 2011, p. 30).

In light of the dynamic paradigm, Fang (2011, p. 31) has also proposed a Chinese 'Yin Yang' perspective on culture.

According to the Yin Yang philosophy, all universal phenomena are shaped by the integration of two opposite cosmic energies, namely Yin and Yang. Yin represents the 'female' energy, such as the moon, night, weakness, darkness, softness, and femininity; while Yang stands for 'male' energy, such as the sun, day, strength, brightness, hardness, and masculinity. The white dot in the black area and the black dot in the white area connote coexistence and unity of the opposites to form the whole. (Fang 2011 *, p. 31)*

The Yin Yang principle suggests the underpinnings of 1) co-existence, 2) mutual reinforcement, and 3) dynamic and paradoxical unity (Fang 2011, p. 34). The implications of the Chinese notion of culture as yin and yang for ELT materials for Chinese learners are likely to be that 1) texts about different cultures can co-exist; 2) they can be used locally to the advantage of the Chinese learners to reflect on their own cultures; and 3) they provide Chinese learners and teachers opportunities to reinforce their dynamic multi-cultural awareness and identities.

There are two views regarding the impact of globalization on culture. One is the homogenization and the other is hybridization of cultures. Garrett (2010, pp. 448-449) associates cultural homogenization with 'cultural imperialism, westernization, or Americanization'. He summarizes that some scholars hold the view that the global distribution of television programs, cinema, and other western cultural media products 'carry and spread the ideology and values of their creators and will ultimately replace the cultures in which they are distributed', while other scholars hold the view that western cultural commodities become 'localized or hybridized, and adapt to local tastes' so that their associated ideology and cultural value systems can be ignored or perceived differently in their new contexts. Over the past three to four decades, Chinese ELT materials have been developed to reflect the homogenization view, with a recent propensity towards the hybridization of cultures in the English texts for Chinese learners.

Taking culture as 'an endlessly recursive process of meaning making and meaning taking', Gray (2010, p. 715) views ELT textbooks as 'cultural artefacts', which serve to make English mean in particular ways. Gray (2010, p. 730) also points out that 'as with all cultural artefacts, textbooks are products of the cultures which produce them'. Yuen categorizes cultures that are represented in ELT material into four aspects, including products, practices, perspectives, and persons. 'Language can be considered an artefact or a system of code (products) used, to signify thoughts (perspectives), for communication (practices), by different people (persons)' (Yuen 2011, p. 459).

English has evolved into different varieties, and it has become distinctly English as an International Language. According to McKay (2002, p. 5), EIL is 'a language of wider communication both among individuals from different countries and between individuals from one country'. McKay (2006, pp. 120-121) points out further that 'cultural knowledge often provides the basis for the content and topics that are used in language materials and classroom discussions. Which culture to use in instructional materials needs to be carefully considered in reference to the teaching of an international language'. Sharifian (2009b, p. 2) regards EIL as 'a paradigm for thinking, research and practice' and he emphasizes that 'as a paradigm, EIL calls for a critical revisiting of the notions, analytical tools, approaches and methodologies within the established disciplines such as sociolinguistics of English and TESOL.' Matsuda (2012, p. 7), on the other hand, conceptualizes teaching EIL as 'preparing English learners to become competent users of English in international contexts.'

As far as the shift from teaching EFL to teaching EIL is concerned in the Chinese context, Xu (2002, pp. 233-237) proposed six changes over a decade ago regarding Chinese ELT perceptions and practices. These include (1) EIL should equally be associated with the cultures of all speakers of English; (2) Chinese English learners should incorporate their own Chinese norms and values and use EIL for local as well as international communication; (3) multilingual competent users should be regarded as models in the Chinese ELT classroom; (4) Chinese learners and teachers should be exposed to varieties of English to raise their awareness of EIL; (5) Chinese ELT classroom should be closely connected to the Chinese societies in terms of the use of English; and (6) Professional ELT teachers of multilingual backgrounds, both local and international should be employed for classroom teaching. Some of these changes have already taken place in the classroom. In terms of ELT materials for Chinese learners of English, the current textbooks that are used in senior secondary schools have shown new tendencies of involving Chinese learners as integral participants of a global EIL community, but in its virtual (imagined) sense. A number of scholars, e.g., Matsuda (2012), McKay (2012), have researched on the EIL teaching materials, curricula and principles. In terms of ELT material development for TEIL, the following criteria have been discussed, (1) the localization of English materials for local learners; (2) the exposure of the learners to different varieties of English, (3) the intercultural awareness of the learners in relation to the use of English and the learners' needs for English; (4) the promotion of multiculturalism; (5) the opportunities provided for the learners to associate their own needs and cultures. The following section will adopt the conceptualizations of globalization and culture that have been outlined above, and the criteria for EIL material development to analyse the current Chinese senior secondary school English textbooks. The main purpose of this analysis is to find out whether currently adopted English textbooks reflect the current conceptualizations of globalization and culture, and whether they meet the criteria for EIL material development.

CHINESE SENIOR SECONDARY ELT TEXTBOOK DATA ANALYSIS

For this paper, I have collected a full set of textbooks that are currently used in the Chinese nationwide secondary schools. The books include five volumes of 'New Senior English For China'. They were published by the People's Education Press of China in 2007. The books under investigation are their 10th impression, published in July 2011. Each volume contains five major units. Within each of these units, there are separate sections including functional items, structures, reading, writing, and workbook. All the texts in the five volumes, including supplementary reading texts and text-based activities have been thoroughly investigated. The main focus is on how these texts and activities reflect on current conceptualizations of globalization, culture and EIL. In particular I have looked at how the texts cater for the needs of Chinese secondary school English learners, in terms of whether the texts enable them to associate their own daily life activities and cultures.

In the following section, I shall analyse the texts based on the observations and themes I have developed while processing the data. These observations include: 1) texts about cultures other than English (COTE) co-exist with texts of traditional inner-circle cultures, 2) cross-cultural perspectives are represented in English textbook series under investigation; 3) multiculturalism has been incorporated into the texts, 4) explicit efforts have been made in the compilation of text materials and relevant learning activities to cater for the needs of Chinese secondary school students for learning English in the Chinese context; 5) texts that help raise awareness of world Englishes and local functionalities of English are included in the textbooks; and 6) the teachers' and students' relevant personal experiences and schemas are utilized and activated in the choice and design of the main and supplementary texts and related activities.

Co-existence of cultures other than English (COTE) and Inner-circle cultures

Globalization instantiates itself in cultural blending, and this coincides with the Chinese Yin-Yang cultural perspective. In the five volumes of the textbook series, the majority of the texts, i.e., over 80%, serve as examples where different cultures as reflected in the texts co-exist. For example, Book 1 unit 5 contains a text in the form of a personal account by Elias, describing how Nelson Mandela helped him deal with issues in his personal and professional life with regards to the equal rights between black and white people. Apart from Nelson Mandela, other 'heroes' including both Chinese and other nationalities have also been included in the pre-reading activity. These include William Tyndale of Britain, Norman Bethune of Canada, Sun Yat-sen of China, Mohandas Gandhi of India, and Neil Armstrong of the USA. Another example of cultural blending is Book 2, Unit 1. It deals with cultural relics. The images of 'cultural relics' as shown in the text include a Chinese Ming Dynasty vase, the Indian

Tah Mahal, an ivory dragon boat, and the Chinese Mogao Caves. The text is 'in search of the amber room', known as a joint effort of German and Russian craftsmen. This unit is a case in point regarding the co-existence of cultures that do not originally belong to Inner-circle English-speaking cultures, e.g., China, India, Russia and Germany.

Similar examples also include Book 2, unit 5, where the text introduces western music (band) culture to Chinese learners. The first paragraph of the text poses a number of questions, e.g., Have you ever wanted to be part of a band as a famous singer or musician? Do you sing karaoke and pretend you are a famous singer like Song Zuying or Liu Huan? The text involves Chinese learners and their music cultures, although the main body of the text introduces Monkees, which is an American music band.

Book 3, Unit 1 is also a good example of the co-existence of global cultures in English texts. The text is about 'festivals around the world'. The festivals that have been discussed include 'Festivals of the Dead' (including the Japanese Obon, the Mexican Day of the Dead, and the Western holiday of Halloween), 'Festivals to Honour People' (including the Chinese Dragon Boat Festival, the American Columbus Day and the Indian national festival to honour Mohandas Gandhi), 'Harvest Festivals' (including the Western Harvest and Thanksgiving festivals, the European traditions of celebrating harvests, and the Chinese and Japanese moon-associated mid-autumn festivals), and not surprisingly 'Spring Festivals' (including the Chinese Spring Festival, and western carnivals, Easter, and Japan's Cherry Blossom Festival). The supplementary reading is more of a 'manifesto' of the co-existence of Chinese and Western cultures, in which a 'sad love story' was depicted, about a Chinese girl who missed her date on a Valentine's Day evening making the boy frustrated. The text encourages cross-cultural comparison in that this modern day Valentine story is interwoven with a classical Chinese love story about two traditional Chinese lovers being cruelly separated by the

Milky Way, meeting each other only once a year by crossing the River on a bridge constructed by magpies with their wings.

Even when traditional and modern cultures that are commonly classified as belonging to the Inner-circle English speaking countries are presented, there are always explicit efforts either in supplementary reading or follow-up activities to involve the Chinese learners and their own cultures. For example, Book 3 unit 3 comprises of two scenes of Act I of the play based on a short story by Mark Twain, 'the Million Pound Bank Note'. This text presents certain cultural conflicts between two of the main Inner-Circle countries about a bet between two wealthy brothers, Roderick and Oliver, with a young American businessman from San Francisco, Henry Adams, involved, who at the moment was lost in London. The text reveals some of the traditional, and also stereotypical, cultural values about class, wealth, and how the British and Americans see each other (e.g., the British restaurant owner says 'it is well-known that Americans like to eat a lot'). One of the follow-up tasks for the Chinese learners is to work in pairs to continue writing the play. This task is designed in such a way that it involves the learners' own cultural values in relation to the cultures that are reflected in the text.

The above examples show that it is common in the Chinese English textbooks to have different cultures co-existing in the texts. This also conforms to the Chinese conceptualizations of globalization as cultural blending, and culture as co-existence in their Yin-Yang cultural philosophy. In addition, these texts also confirm McKay's (2002, p. 128) notion of 'a sphere of interculturality', in which Chinese learners learn about other cultures as a basis for reflecting on their own.

Fostering cross-cultural and global perspectives of the Chinese learners of English

Globalization also means mobility and opportunities for Chinese learners of English to become global citizens. Chinese learners see cultural differences as opportunities. The textbook series offers cross-cultural and global perspectives, and embraces cultural differences as opportunities for cross-cultural understanding. The texts are often narrated from a Chinese perspective, engaging Chinese learners in the interaction between global and local cultures. For example, Book 2 Unit 2 contains a significant text in terms of cross-cultural communication. It is about an 'imaginary' interview between Pausanias (a Greek writer about 2,000 years ago) and Li Yan (a Chinese volunteer for the 2008 Olympic Games). It is an interesting text cross-culturally, because the 'interview' text is not just between two characters from different cultural backgrounds, but also across time about 2000 years apart. Another example is Book 3 Unit 5 about Canada as a country of the 'True North'. Even if this text is exclusively about the Canadian landscape and cultures, it is narrated by two Chinese school girls, who were visiting Canada, and travelling on the 'True North' cross-Canada train. In this case, the Inner-Circle cultures have been (re)presented from a cross-cultural (i.e., Canadian and Chinese) perspective.

Book 4 Unit 4 is about variations in 'body language' across cultures. The text is presented in a first person perspective of a Chinese university student about meeting International Exchange Students at the Beijing Capital International Airport. They meet and observe different customs for greeting each other. The international students are from Columbia, Britain, Japan, Canada, Jordan, and France. The text has also explicitly discussed practices of body language, and concluded by saying that 'studying international customs can certainly help avoid difficulties in today's world of cultural crossroads'. This reinforces the Chinese learners' willingness to embrace cultural differences as opportunities for cross-cultural understanding.

Incorporation of Chinese variety of English (Chinese English) into the texts

One of the EIL material development criteria, as discussed earlier in the paper, is the localization of English materials for local learners. This localization of English also means the use of Chinese English in the texts by the Chinese writers for the Chinese English learners. For example, Book 1 Unit 4 is about 'earthquakes'. The text 'a night the earth didn't sleep' is a good example of using English to describe a Chinese past event. The text is not written in the first person Chinese perspective, but it is in Chinese English, because of the Chinese event, image, and emotion schemas. There is also some 'proposition' schema, e.g., even after describing 'one of the greatest earthquakes of the 20th century' in which 'the number of people who were killed or seriously injured reached more than 400,000', the text writer proposes that 'all hope was not lost', and 'the army organized teams to dig out those who were trapped and to bury the dead', and 'slowly, the city began to breathe again.' What is worth noticing here also includes the Chinese People's Liberation Army (PLA) 'image' schema, as great rescue fighters, under Chinese government leadership, in coping with natural disasters of such scales.

Another example of the incorporation of Chinese English into the texts is Book 4 Unit 2. The text is 'working the land', and it introduces 'a pioneer for all people', Dr. Yuan Longping, who worked and researched for 5 decades trying to grow super hybrid rice that has a high output. This text is a typical example of Chinese English, showing the Chinese learners how English can be used by Chinese to describe Chinese people in the Chinese context without reference to other non-Chinese cultures and role schema.

Book 5 Unit 4 is another example of Chinese English. The main text 'My first work assignment' is a 'dialogue' between a Chinese graduate (Zhou Yang) and his new boss from China Daily (an English newspaper based in Beijing), about his first job assignment as a reporter. This dialogue, inauthentic as it were, shows that English is not only just a 'written' language in the Chinese context, but also a 'spoken' one. In addition, the interaction is between two Chinese English speakers, without other non-Chinese involved, demonstrating that English can be used for intra-cultural/national communication for exclusive 'local' purposes. The supplementary text shifts from the dialogue in the main text to a third person descriptive story about how the protagonist in the main text had his first front page news article published. This text is localized in that English is used exclusively in a local Chinese professional setting. Sharifian's (2009a, pp. 249-250) research shows that there are advantages of using local culture content as ELT materials, because 'it minimizes the potential of marginalizing the values and lived experiences of the learners', and more importantly, 'source culture content does not place local teachers in the difficult position of trying to teach someone else's culture'.

Catering for the needs of Chinese secondary school English learners

Secondary school English learners in China age between 12 and 18, and they learn English as a school subject. They may also have extracurricular activities or tutorial classes for improving their English proficiency, but the English classroom is the main venue where they are exposed to English. At teenage years, these secondary school students are usually curious about the English-speaking world. They have an imagined community where English is used, and they also enjoy reading stories in English that are of an imaginary nature. The textbook series has a considerable number of texts that are specifically selected or written to cater for the needs for Chinese teenage readers. For example, Book 1 Unit 1 'Anne's Best Friend' is about a teenage girl, Anne, and her Jewish family hiding from German Nazis during WWII. The whole story is about Anne living in her imaginary world of making a 'friend' with her own diaries, named 'Kitty'. The supplementary text of Book 2 Unit 2 is the 'story of Atlanta', a Greek princess, and how a young man, named Hippomenes had won her love through a 'race' (a theme related to the main text about Olympic Games). Such texts present the students a mobile world where English can be used to describe things in the past, at present and in the future, with interactions between Chinese and people of non-Chinese backgrounds. Another example is Book 2 Unit 3 about 'computers'. This topic is nothing new to Chinese teenagers. However, it is written as a narrative from the perspective of a personified character of a 'computer' about its development from a 'calculating machine' to a modern-day personal computer. There is no explicit cultural perspective in the text, but the text has been made interactive with Chinese teenage readers.

The power of 'imaginary' world also plays a huge part in the supplementary reading text in Book 2 Unit 5, where a music band called Freddy the Frog getting all the fame and popularity and then decided to leave Britain and return to the lake. In this case, English is used in a fantasized world, and this helps the Chinese teenagers learn and use the language in an imagined community. Another example of an imagined world where Chinese teenagers are involved is the text of Book 5 Unit 3 entitled 'Life in the future'. It is about 'First Impressions' of a Chinese school boy, Li Qiang, travelling in a time capsule to a world of AD 3005, writing to his mum and dad about his first impressions of the future world. The supplementary reading, also using first person voice, describes an amazing imaginary world of a space station in which alien creatures live, work and interact with human space scientists. Here, English is taught to and learned by Chinese learners, not just for getting acquaintance with the outside world, both English speaking and non-English speaking, but also for associating the learners' own lives in an imaginary world. It makes the Chinese learners implicitly feel that English can be bended to their own needs, and it is not explicitly attached to any specific English speaking cultures. The texts as discussed in the above examples show the flexibility that cultures can be disembedded and re-embedded in the imaginary world to cater for the needs of Chinese teenage learners.

Awareness of world Englishes, and global variation and change of cultures

Another criterion for EIL text development is whether the learners are exposed to different varieties of English, and whether they are made aware of the superdiversity of cultures. A case in point in the textbook series regarding awareness of world Englishes is Book 1 Unit 2. This unit deals with the topic of 'World Englishes' explicitly, with a title of 'English around the world'. The reading is a brief historical account of the development of English, which touches upon topics of English change and variation, with explicit mention of British English, American English, Australian English, as well as Englishes in South Asia, including India, Singapore, Malaysia, and countries in Africa such as South Africa. This reading ends with a statement and a question, i.e., 'Today the number of people learning English in China is increasing rapidly. In fact, China may have the largest number of English learners. Will Chinese English develop its own identity? Only time will tell'. One claim in the reading is worth rethinking, that is, 'native English speakers can understand each other even if they don't speak the same kind of English' (Book 1, p. 10). The example that is provided is 'British Betty: Would you like to see my flat? American Amy: Yes. I'd like to come up to your apartment', and this example seems to be insufficient to support the above claim. However, in the supplementary reading 'Standard English and Dialects', the proposition that 'Believe it or not, there is no such thing as standard English' reflects the paradigm shift of English.

It is sensible to include a text (i.e., Book 1 Unit 2) to introduce to Chinese learners the concept of World Englishes. However, it may take more than a simple text to raise the students' awareness of World Englishes. The textbook series has made a good effort to include texts of Chinese English and a considerable number of texts about other cultures. This may implicitly help Chinese students to be aware of the different varieties of English. At this stage, it appears that focus has been laid on the different expressions between British

English and American English. For the students to gain a better awareness of the variation and change in World Englishes, more texts about different cultural schemas (e.g., event, role, image, emotion and proposition), cultural metaphors and cultural categories (Sharifian 2011) should be selected or written for the revised editions of the series.

Relevance to the students' own Chinese experiences, and local functionalities

The textbook series has done well in relating the texts to the Chinese secondary school learners' own experiences, and local functionalities. At the very beginning (i.e., Book 1 Unit 1) of the series, it has been very clear that learners are provided with opportunities either through texts or text-related activities to associate with their own personal experiences, e.g., one of the 'reading and writing' tasks in Book 1 Unit 1 is that the students are instructed to write a reply letter to a student from Huzhou Senior High School about his 'problem' of not being able to communicate with his peers, and feeling lonely. The role schema as set out in the task projects local characters such as 'Miss Wang' and 'Xiao Dong'. This helps students compose situated responses in relation to their own cultural experiences using English as a medium for written communication.

Another example of students associating their own cultures and practices is that the text of 'Standard English and Dialects' is immediately followed with a pair-work discussion task, e.g., 'The Chinese language also has many dialects. Work in pairs and make a list of the ones you and your partner have heard'. In Book 1 Unit 3, there is a small section of 'Reading for Fun' towards the end of the unit. It is an English translation of a well-known Chinese classical poem by Li Bai. To Chinese learners, it serves as an immediate trigger to activate their Chinese poem schema, as part of their first language literacy practices is to memorize classical Chinese poems, particularly those that were written in the Chinese Tang and Song dynasties.

Other examples involving the Chinese learners' own schema and experiences include Book 2 Unit 4. The text is about 'wildlife protection'. The warming up activity is a closely relevant task, as it is about a 'report on some endangered wildlife in China', including Panda, Milu deer and South China tiger. In addition, the text Book 3 Unit 2 deals with the competition between two Chinese restaurants (one serving barbecued mutton kebabs, roast pork, stir-fried vegetables and fried rice, and the other serving plain rice, raw vegetables, fruit and water). The two restaurant owners met and discussed their menus and they decided to serve a balanced menu with food full of energy and fibre. This text appeals to Chinese learners because the food items that are included in the text relate to Chinese food, and the students can easily associate their own diets with the menus described in the text, and also activate their restaurant schema based on their dining out experiences.

What the above analysed texts have in common is that they all have an explicit focus on local functionalities. English fulfils multiple functions in the Chinese context, with regards to Chinese learners of English. These functions include: 1) a tool for Chinese learners to improve their 'foreign language' literacy; 2) a language through which Chinese learners gain access to other cultures and worlds beyond their local premises; 3) a language that can be fully adopted and bended to serve their own purposes of describing their own life events, in the past, at present, and in the future; 4) a language that can be used in professional settings in the Chinese context; and 5) a language to extend their world from realities to imaginations.

IMPLICATIONS AND CONCLUSION

The review of the meanings of globalization and culture, and the analysis of the textbook data have implications for ELT textbook writers as well as teachers and learners of English in a global EIL context.

As far as ELT textbook writers are concerned, it is important to be aware that the notions of globalization and culture can be interpreted differently in different cultures. The selection and composition of English texts for EIL instruction should be based on the current conceptualizations of globalization and culture. A wide range of texts should be selected or composed to reflect the current scenarios of mobility, cultural blending, local functionalities, super-diversity, and heterogeneity in the globalized EIL paradigm.

It is also essential that ELT teachers be aware that the cultural paradigm is not static. Teachers may avoid linearizing a language-nation-culture perception. In classroom teaching, it can be suggested that English teachers customize ELT materials so as to direct learners to understand that cultures co-exist, and that cultural differences are opportunities for raising cross-cultural awareness. In addition, there has been a paradigm shift from TEFL to TEIL in the Chinese and other Expanding Circle ELT context. It can also be suggested that teachers make an explicit effort to associate teaching and learning content and activities with the students' own experiences and cultural schemas.

As far as learners of English are concerned, it can be suggested that their own experiences and schemas be always made relevant to English learning. English, in the Chinese context, may not have to be learned exclusively for use in the future to interact with native speakers of English. Therefore, it is essential that learners associate with their own cultural schemas actively in the learning process, and focus on the use of English in local settings as well as for international communication.

It is worth pointing out that there are limitations of this textbook study in that it analyses only one textbook series among a number of others used in China. In addition, this study focuses primarily on what is in the textbook itself. To find out how the textbook materials are actually used and implemented in the classroom in China, it can be anticipated that classroom based research regarding the relationship among globalization, culture, and Chinese ELT materials should be conducted in due course.

In conclusion, throughout the paper, I have explored meanings of globalization and culture in relation to ELT and Chinese learners of English, with a particular focus on ELT materials in secondary schools in China. Chinese learners of English perceive globalization and the spread of English in China positively as opportunities for geographical and social upward mobility. In addition, Chinese learners adopt a pragmatic approach to the co-existence of Chinese and non-Chinese cultures. Taking Chinese conceptualizations of globalization and cultures, and EIL as frameworks, I have analysed ELT textbook materials for secondary schools in China. The data analysis shows that 1) texts about cultures other than English (COTE), including Chinese cultural texts, co-exist with texts of traditional inner-circle cultures, 2) cross-cultural perspectives are represented in current secondary school English texts; 3) multiculturalism has been incorporated in the texts, 4) explicit efforts have been made in the compilation of text materials and relevant learning activities to cater for the needs of Chinese secondary students for learning English in the Chinese context; 5) texts that help raise awareness of world Englishes are included in the textbooks; and 6) the teachers' and students' relevant personal experiences and schemas are utilized and activated in the choice and design of the main and supplementary texts and related activities. The ongoing globalization and multicultural awareness, alongside the paradigm shift to teaching EIL in the Chinese context have engendered desirability for incorporating multicultural and multimodal ELT materials in China. It is, therefore, as the current secondary English textbook data analysis testifies, not only feasible but also natural and timely to focus on the local learners as the legitimate users of English in the ELT materials, and this has significant implications for textbook writers and editors, as well as learners and teachers of English.

ACKNOWLEDGEMENTS

I wish to acknowledge the constructive comments provided by Prof. Farzad Sharifian and Prof. Sandra McKay. All remaining inadequacies in the paper are my own responsibility.

COMPETING INTERESTS

The author declares that he has no competing interests.

REFERENCES

1. Blommaert J: *The Sociolinguistics of Globalization*. Cambridge: Cambridge University Press; 2010.
2. Byram M: *Cultural Studies in Foreign Language Education*. Clevedon, Philadelphia: Multilingual Matters; 1988.
3. Eriksen TH: *Globalization: the key concepts*. Oxford, New York: Berg; 2007.
4. Fang T: Yin Yang: A New Perspective on Culture. *Management and Organization Review* 2011, 8(1):25–50.
5. Garrett P: Meanings of 'Globalization': East and West. In *The Handbook of Language and Globalization*. Edited by: Coupland N. Maldden, Oxford, West Sussex: Wiley-Blackwell; 2010:447–474.
6. Gray J: The Branding of English and The Culture of the New Capitalism: Representations of the World of Work in English Language Textbooks. *Applied Linguistics* 2010, 31(5):714–733. 10.1093/applin/amq034

7. Kachru BB (Ed): *The Other Tongue: English across Cultures*. Urbana: University of Illinois Press; 1982.

8. Matsuda A: Introduction: Teaching English as an International Language. In *Principles and Practices of Teaching English as an International Language*. Edited by: Matsuda A. Bristol, Buffalo and Toronto: Multilingual Matters; 2012:1–14.

9. McKay SL: *Teaching English as an International Language: Rethinking Goals and Approaches*. Oxford, New York: Oxford University Press; 2002.

10. McKay SL: EIL Curriculum Development. In *English in the World: Global Rules, Global Roles*. Edited by: Rubdy R, Saraceni M. New York: Continuum; 2006.

11. McKay SL: Teaching materials for English as an international language. In *Principles and practices of teaching English as an international language*. Edited by: Matsuda A. Bristol, Buffalo, Toronto: Multilingual Matters; 2012:70–83.

12. McKay SL, Bokhorst-Heng WD International English in its Sociolinguistic Contexts: Towards a Socially Sensitive Pedagogy. In *English in an era of globalization*. New York: Routledge; 2008:3–17.

13. Mufwene SS: Globalization, Global English, and World English(es): Myths and Facts. In *The Handbook of Language and Globalization*. Edited by: Coupland N. Maldden, Oxford, West Sussex: Wiley-Blackwell; 2010:31–55.

14. Pennycook A: The future of Englishes: One, many or none? In *The Routledge Handbook of World Englishes*. Edited by: Kirkpatrick A. London and New York: Routledge; 2010:673–687.

15. Schneider EW: English into Asia: From Singaporean Ubiquity to Chinese Learners' Features. In *Contours of English and English Language Studies*. Edited by: Adams M, Curzan A. Ann Arbor: University of Michigan Press; 2011:135–156.

16. Scholte JA: *Globalization: a critical introducation*. Hampshire and New York: Palgrave Macmillan; 2000.

17. Sharifian F: Cultural Conceptualizations in English as an International Language. In *English as an International Language: Perspectives and Pedagogical Issues*. Edited by: Sharifian F. Bristol, Buffalo and Toronto: Multilingual Matters; 2009:242–253.

18. Sharifian F: English as an International Language: An Overview. In *English as an International Language: Perspectives and Pedagogical Issues*. Edited by: Sharifian F. Bristol, Buffalo and Toronto: Multilingual Matters; 2009:1–18.

19. Sharifian F: *Cultural Conceptualizations and Language (Vol. 1)*. Amsterdam, Philadelphia: John Benjamins Publishing Company; 2011.

20. Toffler A: *Future Shock*. New York, Toronto, London, Sydney, Auckland: Bantam Books; 1970.

21. Toffler A: *The Third Wave*. New York, Toronto, London, Sydney, Auckland: Bantam Books; 1980.

22. Xu Z: From TEFL to TEIL: Changes in Perceptions and Pactices: Teaching English as an International Language (EIL) in Chinese Universities in P. R. China. In *Englishes in Asia: Communication, identity, power and education*. Edited by: Kirkpatrick A. Melbourne: Language Australia Ltd; 2002:225–244.

23. Xu Z: From English to Englishes: Changes in College English Textbooks for Chinese Students. In *The Proceedings of the 9th English in Southeast Asia Conference*. Edited by: Alip F. Yogyakarta, Indonesia: Sanata Dharma Unversity Press; 2004:57–69.

24. Xu Z: Linguistic, cultural and identity issues in Englishization of Putonghua. In *Englishization in Asia: Language and Cultural Issues*. Edited by: Tam K-k. Hong Kong: Open University of Hong Kong Press; 2009:119–139.

25. Xu Z: *Chinese English: Features and Implications*. Hong Kong: Open University of Hong Kong Press; 2010.

26. You X: Chinese white-collar workers and multilingual creativity in the diaspora. *World Englishes* 2011, 30(3):409–427.

27. Yuen K-M: The representation of foreign cultures in English textbooks. *ELT Journal* 2011, 65(4):458–466.

2

CHAPTER

The Cause, Features and Effects of Current Policy mix of Opposing Fiscal and Monetary Policies

Wei Liu

Beijing University, Beijing 100871, China

ABSTRACT

Currently, China's expansionary fiscal policy and tight monetary policy have formed an opposing policy mix. This is due to the imbalanced macro-economy, which suffers from the pressures of inflation and slow growth. In response to economic changes, China adjusted its monetary policy as the real economy has a weak demand for money. In its reactions to the financial crisis, China adopted a series of policies different from those implemented in European and American countries. For this mix of opposing fiscal and monetary policies to be effective, three conditions should be met: the adjustment of direction should fit the real imbalanced economic situation, financing and investing mechanisms should be market-based, interest rates and exchange rates should gradually become market-determined.

Keywords: ***Macro-control, Fiscal policy, Monetary policy, Mix of easing and tight policy***

CAUSES FOR THE MIX OF OPPOSING POLICIES

The mix of opposing policies refers to the combination of proactive (expansionary) fiscal policy being implemented in pllel with prudent (tight) monetary policy. This combination was put in place in China between 2003 and 2007 before the 2008 financial crisis broke out. From 1999 to 2007, China had proactive fiscal policies and prudent monetary policies. Yet, before the fourth quarter of 2003, the monetary policies had not imposed much of a tightening effect as the required reserve ratio was kept at a relatively low level of 6% to 8% and was decreasing year by year from 1999 to 2003. From the fourth quarter of 2003 onwards, monetary policy was tightened with an increase in required reserve ratio. Required reserve ratio increased from 6% by the end of 2003 to 17.5% by the third quarter of 2009. In the period from 2003 to 2007, fiscal policy and monetary policy had been a sharp contrast. The main reason lies in the fact that in the imbalanced macro-economy in China, there was an overheated demand for investment yet an overcapacity in producing consumer goods. The opposing trends in investment and consumption made neither an expansionary nor a tight policy kit possible. An expansionary policy kit would help to boost consumption and digest extra productivity but would create even more demand for investment. Likewise, a tight policy kit would help to strike a balance between demand and supply in the investment market but would make things worse in the consumption sector. A sector-specific adjustment in structure that aimed to discourage investment and encourage consumption would lead to little policy effect as a result of the offset. This is because a conservative investment market with little expansion would end up with little increase in salaries and funds for consumption and thus end up reducing consumption. Similarly, if it were to encourage consumption, demand for investment would rise, as there would be a need to increase productivity. Facing imbalances in investment and consumption, it would be immature to stick to a single policy direction before figuring out which imbalance would pose the primary threat. Under this situation, it is plausible to have a policy combination of expansionary fiscal policy and tight monetary policy to greatly reduce policy risks, though the effect might be undermined.

When the 2008 financial crisis lashed China's economy, China opted for an overall expansionary economic policy, i.e. a more proactive fiscal policy and a relatively loose monetary policy, switching the policy mix to the expansionary direction. For a year's time from the third quarter of 2009, the required reserve ratio dropped from 17.5% to 15.5%. It was more than 2 years until October 2010 when the macro-economic policy changed again. From that time onwards, expansionary macro-economic policy changed to an opt-out-when-appropriate direction. Facing pressures of inflation and slowing economic growth, China again adopted a mix of proactive fiscal policy and prudent monetary policy. Compared with the 'more proactive fiscal policy' in the past that aimed at cushioning the impact of the financial crisis, this time the policy was still an expansionary policy, even though it placed controls on the fiscal deficit and government debt. At the same time, a prudent monetary policy that put inflation prevention as its priority replaced the easing policy of the past. By using monetary instruments such as the required reserve ratio and central bank bills, the policy tightened the control of the money supply. As a result, the required reserve ratio grew from 15.5% in 2009 to 20.5% in the second quarter of 2011, and the interest rate for central bank bills grew from 1.5% in July 2009 to 3.5% in 2011 (Yao and Tan 2011).

The root cause for the mix, though, was different from that in 2003 to 2007. Then, the combination of opposing fiscal and monetary policies was adopted to tackle the structural imbalances in investment and consumption. The policy combination implemented since late 2010 is due to the overall imbalance at the macro-economic level. As the economy had undergone 2 years of general expansion, by late 2010, inflationary pressures accumulated significantly for the following four reasons. First, after more than 2 years of expansion, in 2010, significant, lagging inflationary pressure began to influence the economy by creating demand in the market. Second, China's economy entered the middle-income stage and saw cost pressures booming. Third, as China's economy has become more closely linked with the world economy, inflation coming from the international market has become more visible at home. Lastly, the imbalance in the international balance of payments severely impacted domestic money supply. The yuan equivalent of foreign exchange holdings caused by the continued increase in foreign currency reserves became the biggest reason for the increase of money supply.

As inflationary pressures have intensified, the general economy has been under a growing threat of a downturn for the following four reasons. First, the lack of motivation for technological innovation in companies has weakened domestic demand and intensified already severe domestic contradictions. In particular, large and extra-large state-owned enterprises (SOEs) have not made sufficient technological advances, leaving little room for industrial upgrading and few opportunities for investment. Suffering from a systemic bottleneck, SOEs have been protected from market competition and unwilling to develop their own new technologies. Second, market-oriented reforms have lagged, and there has been little progress in systemic innovation. Companies in the market, especially private medium- and small-size companies, find it hard to get funding from the monetary or capital markets even through normal market channels. Third, there are contradictions in income distribution. On the macro-level, resident income growth has long lagged far behind government and corporate income growth. The ratio of resident income to the general income decreases annually, leaving resident income growth sluggish compared with general economic growth. On the micro-level, the income gap has widened between individuals, between residents of the city and those of the countryside, and between those in different industries and areas, undermining overall appetite for consumption. Moreover, a feature of China's current economic mechanism is its strong power to stimulate investment. When domestic demand needs to be boosted, investment is the first stimulus to be introduced, which in turn hinders the growth in consumption. According to estimates, since the reform and opening, China's fixed-asset investment has grown by approximately 13.5% annually (excluding price factors) with an 11% standard deviation. If the fixed-asset growth rate is below 24.5%, the growth rate in consumption demand slows by over 0.5% for every 1% growth in fixed-asset investment. If the growth rate is over 24.5%, the growth in consumption demand slows by over 0.8%. If the rate is over 30%, the consumption demand shrinks as fixed-asset investment rises (Liu 2011). Fourth, the world economy has had a sluggish recovery coupled with occasional protectionism. China's exports have faced challenges in the international economy, politics, culture and other areas. From 2000 until the outbreak of the global financial crisis, China's export growth rate stood at over 20% for most of the time and accounted for 2% to 3% of gross domestic product (GDP) growth. So when the export growth rate fell or exports contracted (as in 2009), the overall economy suffered. The policymakers need to, on one hand, avoid inflation and, on the other hand, avoid economic downturn, but neither target seems to have had absolute priority over the other. A combination of expansionary fiscal policy and tight monetary policy became a natural choice.

FEATURES OF THE CURRENT MIX OF OPPOSING POLICIES

The current policy mix of expansionary fiscal policy and tight monetary policy has the following characteristics:

1. In adjusting the policy mix, policymakers changed the direction of monetary policy and kept the expansionary fiscal policy unchanged. The change of direction in monetary policy was not due to a sudden demand for money from the real economy, but was the result of a change in the reasonable supply of money. After the financial crisis, in order to better respond to the crisis, in the case of deflationary pressure, monetary supply should have increased. But

as inflationary pressure gained intensity, the rate of increase of the money supply should have been controlled.

In the academic literature on economic thinking and policies, there are severe differences in answers to the question of whether monetary policy or fiscal policy is more important. The various schools of economics - Keynesianism, Monetarism, New Classical Economics, New Keynesianism and Rational Expectation - all have their own interpretation. From the 1950s to 1970s, Western developed countries advocated Keynesianism, believing that 'fiscal policy is the most important, but monetary policy is important too', and enjoyed over two decades of healthy economic growth. With the emergence of new problems such as 'stagnation' after the 1970s, Keynesianism seemed to have failed. In practice, expansionary monetary policy was deployed to intensify demand, particularly to change the low-efficient demand into valid demand for funding expansion. This expansionary monetary policy was also meant to reduce costs, especially corporate financing costs, and thus boost the economy. It thus relieved inflationary pressure caused by costs so as to solve the problem of stagnation.

However, the expansion came at the expense of lower efficiency and competition standards. Seemingly, monetary tools that reduced interest rates for financing companies helped to reduce financing cost, relieve inflation pressure, stimulate investment demand and finally boost economy and solve stagnation. But in reality, the mode of undermining long-term efficiency was unsustainable. The 2008 world financial crisis was the result of 'bubbles' caused by such a low-efficient, expansionary monetary policy.

Facing economic recession, monetary policies such as pricing tools could hardly stimulate the economy, and officials turned to expansionary fiscal policy, especially expansionary government expenditure policy, leaving monetary policy at a subordinate position. America's so-called quantitative easy monetary policy was actually meant to set its money supply based on the policy requirements of fiscal stimulus. In other words, in reacting to the financial crisis, American and European countries focused on their fiscal policies whilst putting monetary policy relatively unchanged or slightly changed to cater for the fiscal policy.

Things went differently in China. In the second half of 1998, China began to enact proactive fiscal policy to cushion the impact of the Asian financial crisis. From 2003 to 2007, to balance its economic structure, China employed a combination of proactive fiscal policy and prudent monetary policy. From 2008 to 2010, in reaction to the global financial crisis, China made its fiscal policy more active and opted for a moderately loose monetary policy. From the second half of 2010 to today, after multiple rounds of stimulus, China moved back to a proactive fiscal policy and prudent monetary policy. During all these times, the expansionary direction for fiscal policy remained unchanged. Only the degree of expansion changed before and after the crisis. Nevertheless, monetary policy changed direction twice. Over the crisis, prudent (tight) policy changed to easing (expansionary) policy and then to prudent (tight) policy. Expansionary fiscal policy drove up the money supply. Easing monetary policy in Western countries did not restrict their fiscal policy deployment. However, tight monetary policy in China did.

1. Compared with monetary policies of the rest of the world, especially Western countries, policy in China changed more rapidly and significantly, as reflected in the following features.

First, at the beginning of the financial crisis, China adopted a macro-economic policy that was the opposite of those in Western countries. Breaking out in the USA in 2007, the crisis spread across the world in 2008. Most countries opted for expansionary macro-economic policy as a response. In contrast, by the beginning of 2008, China was employing an overall tight macro-economic policy that aimed to avoid an overheated economy and inflation. Tight monetary policy was set to cool down overheated demand for investment triggered by the fast economic growth between 2003 and 2007 (the growth rate over this period was over 10%). Only 6 months after the policy was set, the financial crisis started to take its toll on China's economy. After June 2008, the target of macro-economic policy was to 'maintain growth, control prices, and optimise the structure', with economic growth set as the top priority and price control as the second. Therefore, expansionary macro-economic policy replaced tight policy. As the financial crisis worsened, by the end of 2008, the general target was to 'maintain, expand domestic demand, and optimise structure'. Inflation prevention was no longer one of the macro-economic goals and an expansionary policy was in full swing. The question is, in the first half of 2008, should China have opted for tight policy instead of the expansionary policies chosen by Western countries?

Second, because China took action later than Western countries, its expansionary policy was strong once announced, which was known as 'a more proactive fiscal policy and a relatively loose monetary policy'. The powerful expansionary policy was best reflected in the investment expenditure plan of 4 trillion RMB of investment in 2 years. The loose monetary policy could be seen in the growth rates of M2 and in monetary instruments such as banking loans. Fiscal deficit skyrocketed from a few hundred billion RMB to 950 billion, approaching the red line of 3% of GDP[a]. In terms of money quantity, in 2008, newly issued loans amounted to 4.6 trillion RMB and were mostly issued in the second half of the year. In 2009, the figure doubled to 9.6 trillion RMB. For the first half of 2010, similar to the previous year, 4.6 trillion RMB more loans were issued, leaving the growth rate of M2 as high as 27% in 2009. Should expansionary policy have been so strong in such a short time? As for tackling the financial crisis in the short run, the expansionary macro-economic policy brought considerable growth. In 2008, China's economy grew by 9%. In 2009, it grew by 8.7% against the global downturn and over 10.3% in 2010 and 9.2% in 2011. In the long term, however, the policy aggravated a series of hidden contradictions by creating significant inflationary pressure and undermining efficiency brought by market competition. If this continues, the sustainability of the economy will suffer. As the imbalances have different root causes, similar policies could bring different results.

Third, the imbalances in the supply and demand for money in the market have different root causes, and employing the same policies can have different effects. At the outbreak of the financial crisis, China had abundant money supply while Western countries were short in money supply. In Europe and America, the crisis stemmed from the financial sector, not the real economy. In the capital markets, the real economy had a need for money, and the need became direr as financial institutions such as banks increased their reserves. Unfortunately, banks and financial institutions were in deep crisis due to their own fragile capital chains, and their money supply (loans) and money mobility were weak. In other words, the demand for money increased at a time when there was a shortage of supply. This was the after-effect of the previous expansionary monetary policy, which interfered with the normal operation of the money supply mechanism as the bubble burst. Before Western financial institutions returned to normal operation, the money supply mechanism could not meet the demand for money from the real economy.

The supply–demand imbalance urged the government to drive money supply through macro-level policy, for instance, by providing funding to banks so that banks could give out loans or by providing funding directly to the real economy to ease the thirst for money. For China, however, the financial crisis came as an external factor. The world economy went into recession as the financial crisis took its toll. Part of China's real economy was first directly affected by the financial crisis. Gradually, general economic growth slowed. For various reasons including mechanism-related ones, financial institutions of China were not affected by the world financial crisis at first. Besides, Chinese citizens have long had a strong willingness to save. Therefore, China's banking system was steady and with good money mobility. This can be proved by the fact that by the end of 2009, the difference between savings and loans in China's banks was

19 trillion RMB (Su et al. 2009). In contrast to the situation in Western countries' money supply and demand situation, China's real economy could not form enough demand for capital even though its banks were abundant in money supply.

Due to insufficient technological innovation and systemic reform, lack of demand for investment capital has long been a problem in China's real economy and became even worse as financial crisis struck. To solve this contradiction, the government should focus on boosting concrete demand for investment in the real economy, rather than increasing money supply as in Western countries. Concrete demand for investment capital lies in technical and institutional innovation, especially in pushing forward the marketization of the financial system and production elements, in deepening the reform of SOEs and breaking up monopolies, and in developing small and medium enterprises by creating a friendly business environment. The short-term policies should, on one hand, encourage investment and, on the other hand, help companies to upgrade technology, improve efficiency and reduce costs. But in reality, China's government opted for an expansionary policy that increased the money supply. Though this brought obvious growth, the price was high. In the long term, proactive fiscal policy cannot introduce more investment demand into China's real economy.

Fourth, China 'withdrew' its monetary policy first. After October 2010, China stopped its overall expansionary policy and 'opted out' for a 'proactive fiscal policy and prudent monetary policy' earlier than Western countries did. The reasons were that China's economy still enjoyed quick growth under the financial crisis and that expansion brought with it significant inflation pressure. In 'opting out', monetary policy was the first to change. Its direction changed from 'loose' to 'tight'. This directional change occurred because China suffered from heavy inflationary pressure from tackling the financial crisis with an expansionary policy. The policy set at that time did not ease the supply–demand tension but worsened it. China changed its expansionary monetary policy earlier than Western countries. In October 2010, Western countries started to further stimulate their economies through expansionary fiscal policy. At this time, China had already employed a tight monetary policy and lowered the degree of expansion in its fiscal policy.

THE EFFECT OF A MIX OF OPPOSING MONETARY AND FISCAL POLICIES

There are generally two circumstances under which opposing monetary and fiscal policies will create the desired effect. First, when the imbalance in the macro-economy is unclear or the degree of imbalance is not completely clear. In this case, if fiscal and monetary policies are both expansionary or both tight, the macro-economy would be subject to great ups and downs and suffer from instability; in the case where there was imbalance in different areas (e.g. investment and consumption) and regions (developed and undeveloped regions), if fiscal and monetary policies are both expansionary or tight, the structural imbalance would become worse; in the case where the economy is facing a stagnation threat, and the culprit of the threat is unclear, a combination of expansionary or tight fiscal and monetary policy would ease one conflict but intensify the other.

As so, a mix of expansionary fiscal policy and tight monetary policy reduces the policy risk and may help to rebalance economic growth. The other case where a reversed policy mix may be applicable is where the national economy and international balance of payments both suffered from imbalances and require policies with opposite directions. The policies are tailor-made according to the requirements of the national economy and international balance of payments respectively and have their own features.

It needs to be said that in the two cases described above, for an expansionary-tight mix to work, prerequisites must be met.

46 The effect of a mix of opposing monetary and fiscal policies

1. When the general imbalance is not clear, or the economy may suffer from stagnation, the government should consider the features of both fiscal policy and monetary policy and their long-term and short-term effects respectively before implementing a combination and make infrequent adjustments to the combination. Generally speaking, when facing economic downturn caused by financial crisis, monetary policy is used to control the short-term prices and fiscal policy to keep the economy growing. Evidence shows that the 'monetary policy index (MPI) is a positive factor in lowering inflation during a crisis and the year after, but no statistical significance is found for the third year after a crisis.' 'MPI does not significantly affect the statistics of economic growth during and after the crisis.' 'The fiscal policy index (FPI) has a significant positive impact on the lowest GDP growth rate and average GDP growth rate during a crisis', and 'FPI does not significantly affect the statistics of inflation levels after a crisis.' However, 'after a crisis, the positive impact upon the economy from expansionary fiscal policy would not last long; the deficit that came alone with the policy would start to take its toll around three years after the crisis.'

In short, in reaction to crisis, a change in monetary policy would quickly be reflected in prices and relief from deflation, but the effect would diminish as time passed. If faced with concurrent pressures for stagnation and inflation, expansionary monetary policy would only worsen the inflation but fail to power economic growth. Short-term growth stimulated by expansionary fiscal policy needs to be paid for in the years to come as inflation would gradually appear. Moreover, expansionary fiscal policy cannot guarantee growth in the long term; it even hinders growth. Tight fiscal policy, although it might undermine growth in the short run, would help to control post-crisis inflation. Facing dual threats of stagnation and inflation, fiscal policy could be resorted to as a temporary solution to stimulate growth with caution in order to relieve the inflationary pressure that comes after the crisis. In short, under the threats of inflation and economic downturn, the policy mix should basically consist of moderately expansionary fiscal policy and moderately tight monetary policy. It should be noted that expansionary policy should not last too long and while it is in effect, monetary policy should not be highly expansionary so that short-term inflation can be avoided. When crisis has passed, expansionary fiscal policy should be withdrawn on time; otherwise, lagging inflation will increase and drag down growth.

In the battle against this financial crisis, China had an expansionary (more proactive than before) fiscal policy and an expansionary (moderately loose) monetary policy. However, facing crisis, the government should have avoided highly expansionary monetary policy, especially at a time when it came with a threat of 'stagflation', as it was unlikely to stimulate growth in the short term. At the same time as stimulating short-term growth, this formed significant inflationary pressure and forced the government to withdraw monetary policy at an early date. After the policy was withdrawn in the second half of 2010, fiscal policy was still in line with the expansionary direction whereas monetary policy was placed once again in the prudent direction. But if expansionary fiscal policy continued, it would harm rather than benefit long-term economic growth. Expansionary monetary policy would not bring notable impact on the long-term price level. That said, with stagflation hovering, normally the government should have employed a moderately loose monetary policy and moderately tight fiscal policy as a combination, instead of the other way round. Why has China adopted a proactive fiscal policy and prudent monetary policy? The main reason is that the usage of a mix of opposing fiscal and monetary policy should go together with the market on the micro-level. When the market failed to function in the crisis, especially when investment demand from the market was weak and dragged the economy down, the market needed governmental stimulus through fiscal policy. In the following recovery, the timing of the withdrawal of expansionary fiscal policy should depend on the performance of the market. If the market is not mature enough to create concrete demand, expansionary fiscal policy is needed. If that were the case, a long-term expansionary fiscal policy would harm the economic growth and be bound with significant inflationary pressure.

2. Facing imbalances in the domestic economic environment and in the international balance of payments, a mix of opposing fiscal and monetary policy may help to strike a balance in both fields. This is because fiscal policy is more closely related to national economy while monetary policy is more related to the external economic environment. When the economy suffers from unemployment and sluggish growth domestically with a deficit in the international balance of payments, expansionary fiscal policy would help to stimulate general demand and create jobs. Although enlarged demand might drive up imports and increase the deficit in the international balance of payments, fiscal policy would affect the national economy more than the international economy. Logically, it would boost general demand (national income) first and then be reflected in the international balance of payments. The job opportunities created by new demand could more than offset the international deficit it brings. On the other hand, tight monetary policy that pushes up interest rates and welcomes capital inflow would help to rebalance the international balance of payments but suppress demand and worsen the unemployment situation. If one considers the short-term impact only, monetary policy would affect the international environment more than the domestic environment.

Tight monetary policy does less harm in terms of demand suppression than the good it does in bridging the deficit. In this case, a combination of expansionary fiscal policy and tight monetary policy can help to achieve the targets of stimulating general demand and reducing the international deficit. Following the same logic, when domestic demand is booming with inflation and good international savings, a tight fiscal policy helps to cool down demand and an expansionary monetary policy keeps interest rates low and urges capital outflow so as to nudge international payments to a balance. Of course, while a tight fiscal policy cools demand, exports would increase while imports drop, and thus, the international account would see more savings. But fiscal policy works better internally than externally. While increasing capital outflows, an expansionary monetary policy also stimulates aggregate demand and worsens inflation. But monetary policy has more salient effect on the outside environment than on the national economy. With this said, a mix of opposing fiscal policy and monetary policy would work.

However, there are two conditions under which such a mix can work effectively.

First, the direction of the opposing mix should be in line with the situation. Either domestic demand needs to be boosted and there is a significant deficit in the international balance of payments or domestic demand needs to be cooled down and there is a significant surplus in the international balance of payments. For the former, a combination of expansionary fiscal policy and tight monetary policy is feasible; for the latter, the opposite is true. Currently, China has a shortage of demand but runs a surplus in its international balance of payments, so it meets neither of these conditions. The opposing combination of policies has done little to change the status quo in China, but nor has it produced significant unwanted effects. An important reason is that the capital account is not yet fully convertible, and the current account is more sensitive to the exchange rate. Tight monetary policy does not impose significant appreciation pressure upon the RMB but rather affects exports. The international surplus would not accelerate its rise, then, but rather slow its growth. However, as the market increasingly sets interest rates and the capital account enjoys more and more convertibility, the current opposing policy mix would take its toll on the national economy and international balance of payments over time. To be more specific, the long-term expansionary fiscal policy slows economic growth and worsens the inflation, while tight monetary policy suffocates the economic growth and increases the international surplus.

Second, to rebalance the national economy and international balance of payments by an opposing policy mix requires a change to the mechanism. Marketization of interest rates and the exchange rate has to be stepped up. If not, interest rates cannot react quickly and sensitively to changes to demand and supply in the market, rise to attract capital when monetary policy tightens or fall to push capital out when monetary policy expands. As required for interest rates, the exchange rate should be freer and more subject to changes in the market. With fewer non-market uncertainties and risks, capital would enjoy a faster inflow and outflow. Otherwise, monetary policy would do little to balance international payments. Obviously, we are still some time away from truly market-oriented interest rates and the exchange rate in China. It is too early to say if the current market mechanism meets the conditions for an opposing policy mix to attain the targets of balancing the national economy and international payments.

CONCLUSION AND THOUGHTS

The root cause for an opposing policy mix lies in the particularities of the imbalance in China's macro-economy, which faces the dual threats of inflation and economic downturn. This is the difference with the proactive (expansionary) fiscal policy and prudent (slightly tight) monetary policy employed from 2003 to 2007 when investment demand was overheated and there was insufficient consumption. Today, however, the risk is stagflation.

Second, China chose a different macro-economic direction during the financial crisis compared with Western countries. First, in adjusting the direction of policy, China shifted expansionary monetary policy to a tight one while maintaining and stepping up expansionary fiscal policy. Western countries, however, made fiscal policy their primary tool with monetary policy as only a supplementary tool. Second, China's policy changed at a quicker pace. From the second half of 2007 to the first half of 2008 when financial crisis was budding, China adopted an all-tight (dual prevention) policy mix. During the peak of the crisis, China deployed highly expansionary fiscal and monetary policies. In a capital market that had a different imbalance from Western countries, inflationary pressure was increasing, forcing China to withdraw expansionary policies sooner than other countries. By the end of 2010, when others were still expanding their economies, China 'withdrew when appropriate' and resorted to an opposing policy mix. Third, China's real economy did not have enough demand for money, which set it apart from Western countries. If China chose to increase the supply of money, it could trigger short-term demand and economic growth but would likely result in serious inflation.

Third, given that the macro-economy was under the threat of stagflation, a working opposing policy mix was an expansionary fiscal policy (to cushion the impact of the crisis) and a moderately tight monetary policy. When the crisis had passed, a mix of a moderately tight fiscal policy and a moderately loose monetary policy seemed more appropriate as the government gradually shed of the role of stimulating the economy. However, to achieve this directional transition, investment and financing activities should have been conducted under a market-led mechanism rather than a government-led mechanism. If not, market forces would never be able to take over the role of expansionary fiscal policy in influencing the market, even in prosperous times. Given imbalances in the national economy and the international balance of payments, an opposing policy mix that aims to solve both problems at once can only work with market-set interest and exchange rates. If this prerequisite cannot be met, macro-economic policy adjustment cannot touch upon the international balance of payments. As the above mechanism condition could not be met, China adopted an opposite policy mix from Western countries. The policy mix resulted in considerable short-term growth, unfortunately, at high long-term cost.

Clearly, when under the threat of stagflation and expansionary policy is forced 'to be withdrawn when appropriate', the following issues should be properly dealt with for sustainable and balanced economic growth to be achieved: (1) In matching fiscal and monetary policies, avoid long-term highly expansionary fiscal policy and try to employ a moderately loose monetary policy to the extent possible rather than the other way round. (2) In adjusting the economy on macro-level, focus on the management of demand as well as supply. Macro-economic policy affects both demand and supply. If supply continues to be ignored, rebalancing the economy, corporate efficiency, productivity, industrial restructuring and innovation can never make progress. (3) In terms of setting policy direction, policymakers should fine tune the direction in a timely manner as the contradictions of the macro-economy change. When making major decisions, policymakers should follow a more democratic, law-based and procedure-abiding method so that the conflicts of interests between central and local governments, governments and enterprises, fiscal and financing bodies, banks and companies, and SOEs and private companies can be coordinated and well balanced. In fact, adjustment of macro-economic policy is always aimed at protecting the interest of one party in the economy and depriving another. If the interests cannot be well balanced between parties, conflicts will surely become more intense. (4) When talking about mechanism innovation, we should continue to deepen reforms for a socialist market economy and work intensively on the marketization of elements such as land, labour, capital and foreign currencies and on building a market competition mechanism. Without proper marketization, macro-economic policy can hardly realise its desired effect and working fiscal and monetary policy mix, and supply management and balance of interests will be difficult to achieve.

ENDNOTE

[a]According to the *Maastricht Treaty* (formally the *Treaty on European Union*), member states' deficits should be lower than 3% of the GPD and debt lower than 60% of the GDP.

AUTHOR'S INFORMATION

Wei Liu, born in 1957, is the Vice President of Peking University, the Vice Chairman of the Steering Committee for Economics under the Ministry of Education, a member of the Theoretic Economics Division of the Academic Degree Committee of the State Council, a member of the Standing Committee of the Beijing Municipal Committee of the Chinese People's Political Consultative Conference and the Vice Chairman of the Chinese Finance Society. He is a holder of government allowance, a member of the first batch of Trans-Century Talents (Arts) for the State Education Commission, one of the State Class Persons of National Talents from the Ministry of Personnel and six other ministries, and a Distinguished Professor of Peking University from the Chang Jiang Scholars Programme under the Ministry of Education.

DISCLOSURE

This is an interim report of 'Study on China's Mid-long Term Economic Growth and Structural Transition' (Project Code: 09AZD013), a key project of the National Social Science Foundation, published in Economics Perspectives, 2010, No. 7.

COMPETING INTERESTS

The author declares that he has no competing interests.

REFERENCES

1. Liu W: *Economic growth in transitive economy (转轨中的经济增长)*. Beijing Normal University Publishing Group (北京师范大学出版社), Beijing; 2011.

2. Su J, Lin WB, Ye HY: **Difference of the economic situation in China and the U.S amidst the financial crisis and choice of monetary policies (金融危机下中美经济形势的差异与货币政策的选择).** *Econ Perspect (经济学动态)* 2009, **9:** 57–63.

3. Yao YD, Tan HM: **Central bank bill interest rate can act as a comprehensive indicator of monetary policy (央票利率可以作为货币政策的综合性指标).** *Economic Research Journal (经济研究)* 2011., **2:**

3

CHAPTER

An Empirical Study on the Factors of Chinese Urbanization Process and Policy Proposals about the "New-Type" Urbanization

Qinhua Pan, Ruofan Xu

Schools of Economics and Management, Tongji University, Shanghai, China

ABSTRACT

First of all, this thesis will compile negative effects of this process since the reform and opening-up policy was enacted. And then the policy background, the connotation and the main function of new-type urbanization will be introduced. Followed by an empirical study, this thesis will also analyze the main factors of traditional urbanization and make corresponding policy proposals for modern urbanization nowadays.

Keywords: The Factors of Urbanization, the New-Type Urbanization, Empirical Study

1. INTRODUCTION

With the adjustment of national economic structure, the momentum of Chinese economy is changing from relying on export and investment to domestic demand. Meanwhile urbanization is the most powerful weapon to en-hance internal demand. Prime minister Li Keqiang points out that, as the law of modernization development, the urbanization ratio of China will improve continually in future ten or twenty years. A considerable amount of rural remaining labor force and population will transfer to cities each year, which will lead to rapid increase in investment and consumption, and also more kinds of human resources for city development. Some scholars argue that urbanization is one of the three engines of Chinese economic transition: according to the data provided by McKinsey & Co, the urbanization ratio of China is now at 52.6% (2013), and will be up to 70% in 2020. More people transferring to cities means more consumption and more opportunities for employment.

So, this thesis aims to find out the key factors in the process of urbanization in a way of empirical test and analyze the results in order to make some corresponding policy proposals for the new-type urbanization. The structure of this journal is about 4 sections: Firstly, the problem of Chinese urbanization; Secondly, the introduction of so-called "new-type" urbanization; Thirdly, the empirical study of urbanization; Last but not least, the corresponding policy proposals.

2. THE PROBLEM OF CHINESE URBANIZATION

Lengthways from 1978 to 2011, the urban population of China went from 172 million to 690 million; the ratio was from 17.9% to 51.3%. Although the level of urbanization was seemingly near to the average of the world, the conflicts and contradictions were more and more non-neglectable.

1) Low-cost and predatory mode

Low-cost way of urbanization, which accelerated the process of population migration, left some problems. The worst one may be urbanization lagged behind industrialization, neglecting the importance of population ag-glomeration except economy agglomeration. Take the rate (urbanization ratio: industrialization ratio) in 2011 for example, it was 1.1 (51.3%:46.8%) compared with 1.95, the average level of the world.

2) For rural residents, the real right of land performs practically no function This problem included that farmer's land rights was impaired in the past 30 years; the local government finance relied on auctioning lands; the efficiency of land utilization was low; the framework of land law was imperfect.

3) The Urban and rural household registration system

In China, Urban population refers to all people residing in cities and towns including 160 million rural migrant workers (or peasant-workers). However because of the hinder of registration system these workers were not treated equal to other citizens.

4) The imbalance and inharmony of urbanization development

Compared with the west, the east areas were overburdened by rapid urbanization, causing resources of economy and society mismatch. As population was over-intensive, metropolis like Beijing, Shanghai and Guangzhou had a lot of troubles such as water, air, education, healthcare and so forth.

On the other hand, the similar structure of regional economy and the convergence of industrial structure bringing excessive competition lead to lower utility.

5) High level of energy dependence

In future decades, the need for urbanization of iron, copper, chromium, sylvite, oil, natural gas and so on will be rigid, the bulk mineral imports will ascend consistently. Thus the degree of foreign-trade dependence will also become higher.

3. THE INTRODUCTION OF NEW-TYPE URBANIZATION

3.1. The Policy Background

In the Central Economic Working Conference Dec. 16th 2012, the conclusion of discussion indicates that urba-nization is the historic mission of Chinese modernization development and also the way to expand domestic demand, so it's vital and urgent to make urbanization develop in a healthy and ordered way. Meanwhile, the National Planning to Promote the Healthy Development of Urbanization (2011-2020), which is the master planning outline of national urbanization, has already finished and will be published soon.

3.2. The Connotation and Function of New-Type Urbanization

1) The connotation

Until now, there are no standard definitions of new-type urbanization. Generally speaking, the new-type urbanization contains four aspects: a) coordinated with the development of industrialization and agricultural modernization; b) adapted to population, economy, resources and environment; c) having equal opportunities for all kinds of cities (Large, medium or small) and towns to blossom; and d) with population aggregation, citizenization and the coordinated development of public service. All in all, the characteristics of new-type urbanization are urban-rural overall development, urban-rural integration, production-city interaction, economization and intensification, ecological and livable, harmonious progress.

2) The function

Firstly, in the macro level of nation, the new-type urbanization is the engine of economic growth.

International experience shows that domestic demand is the endogenous power of economic growth, especially for large countries. It's essential to convert the growth pattern from relying on investment to consumption. But there should be a stage of transition, which means investment and consumption have the same privilege to boost growth in this time. The new-type urbanization will be the key to this kind of transition.

Then, in the meso level of industry, the new-type urbanization will impulse industrial accumulation and up-grade.

As the advantage (compared with rural areas) of capital technique, transportation, living conditions, human resources, communication etc., a large number of labor force and production activities converge on urban regions. Thus the scale of the urban market increases rapidly, impulsing industrial upgrade continually.

Lastly, in the micro level of economic entity, the process of the new-type urbanization has benefit to improve residents' income, especially for rural residents.

Those people who migrate from countryside to city mostly go in for secondary and tertiary industry, with higher level of salary than what they have earned in rural areas; for citizens, their income can also be improved, as investment and consumption was boosted by those immigrations.

4. THE EMPIRICAL STUDY OF URBANIZATION INFLUENCING FACTORS

Past empirical studies on urbanization [1]-[3] were mostly based on the analysis of time-series, and the data covered both national level and some specific administrative districts' level.

While, this thesis will use the panel data with the model of two-way fixed effect [4]. Based on the existing achievements by other scholars, this paper will take a further step to analyze the specific factors of Chinese ur-banization, will explain the outcome and will make some policy proposals for the way of future development (the new-type urbanization).

4.1. Selecting Data

Considering the availability, the data of this thesis include 28 provinces of China (excluding Chongqing, Hong Kong, Macao, Hainan and Xizang) from 1987 to 2008. The independent variables (explanatory variables xi) are listed in the following Table 1.

The dependent variable (explained variable yi) is the urbanization ratio, the ratio of urban population to total population [5].

4.2. The Outcome of Regression

As the result indicates, we find that the significant factors of Chinese urbanization include: GDP per capita of provinces, the provincial tertiary industrial structure, household registration system, the way of land-expansion urbanization, economic openness and rural income level of provinces (Shown in Table 2).

4.3. Analysis of the Outcome

For the proxy variable of household registration system: peasant-workers (migration), the coefficient of it is significantly positive, which means the increasing number of peasant-workers in cities boost the economic development of cities leading to improve urbanization level, but also they are counted as temporary alien workers of the nominal urban population. This is because hindered by the household registration system, they cannot gain the permanent urban residence certificate (in Chinese it calls: hukou) easily.

The variable of the areas of city (land) represents the way of land-expansion urbanization, the coefficient of it is significantly positive proves that land-expansion was one of the ways to improve urbanization level. Generally speaking, one of the prominent problems or "features" in the process of Chinese urbanization is that the growth of urban built up area is much faster than the gather of urban people apparently. The result of this thesis, the coefficient of land is small but significant, proves this point of view.

The coefficient of GDP per capita (GDPpercapita), one of the four variables of economic development, is significantly positive. So it means increasing the average (not only the aggregate) income level of one region can enhance the urbanization level truly, which fits our instinct.

However, the coefficient of tertiary industrial structure (third_second) is significantly negative, which means at present the tertiary industry in our country hasn't absorbed rural surplus labor force adequately. As many regions of high level tertiary industry in China are the developed areas such as Shanghai, there may be some certain rejective intention against immigrations. At the same time, the primary industrial ratio is not significant.

The economic openness of one region represents the development level and the geographic position of provinces (in China, east areas near the sea are considered more exoteric and developed) indirectly. The coefficient of it (iexport_ ra tio) is significantly negative reflects the problem of rejection of outsiders, because rejection of outsiders may downgrade the level of urbanization to some extent.

Table 1: Selected variables of the factors of urbanization

Factors of Urbanization	Specific Index & Variable Name	Explanatory of Index
Economic development	GDP per capita: GDPpercapita	GDP per capita of provinces
	Logarithmic GDP of primary industry: ln 1stGDP	The development of provincial primary industry
	Logarithmic GDP of secondary industry: ln 2ndGDP	The development of provincial secondary industry
	Logarithmic GDP of tertiary industry: ln 3rdGDP	The development of provincial tertiary industry
Industrial structure	The added value of the tertiary industry/The added value of the secondary industry: third_second	The provincial tertiary industrial structure
	The added value of the primary industry/The added value of the secondary industry: first_second	The provincial primary industrial structure
Household registration system	Peasant-workers: migration	The proxy variable of urban and rural household registration system
The areas of city	Built-up urban area: land	Represents the way of land-expansion urbanization
Economic openness	Value of provincial imports and exports/GDP (converted to dollar): iexport_ratio	Reflects the openness, economic level and geographic position of provinces (in China, east areas near the sea are considered more exoteric)
Income level	Logarithmic urban income: lnurbanincome	The absolute urban income level of provinces
	Logarithmic rural income: lnruralincome	The absolute rural income level of provinces
	Rural income/urban income: incomeratio	The relative income level of provinces
Population growth (control variable)	Logarithmic natural population growth rate: populationgrowth	The growth of provincial population
Education level (control variable)	College and high school students per ten thousand people: college & highsch	Represents the stock of provincial human capital
	Average education years: education	Represents the knowledge level of provinces
Government expenditure (control variable)	Agricultural expenditure: ariexp	Represents the support of provincial agriculture
	Fiscal expenditure / GDP: govexpense	Represents the proportion of provincial fiscal expenditure
Infrastructure (control variable)	Capital stock: capital	Represents the capital level of provinces
	Length of high way: highway	Represents the road construction of provinces and the convenience of the connection between cities and country sides
	Fixed investments: invest	Represents the investment level of provincial infrastructure
Employment (control variable)	Employee of primary and secondary industry: primaryworker & secondaryworker	Represents the employment distribution of provinces

Table 2: The result of the two-way fixed effect modela (The dependent variable is urban ratio).

	Explanatory Variables (x_i)	Coefficient
Economic development	GDPpercapita	0.00189*
	ln 1stGDP	−0.01106
	ln 2ndGDP	−0.02909
	ln 3rdGDP	0.03954
Industrial structure	third_second	−0.06682***
	first_second	0.01593
Household registration system	migration	0.00003***
The areas of city	land	0.00002***
Economic openness	iexport_ratio	−0.03387***
Income level	lnurbanincome	−0.15328
	lnruralincome	0.07139*
	incomeratio	−0.05330
Control variables: agriexp capital highway govexpense college highsch primaryworker		
Dummy variables of year: yes		
R^2 (within) = 0.991 Number of obs: 173		
R^2 (between) = 0.0357 Number of groups: 26		

a. The significance testing used robust standard error. As some observations were missing, the number of obs was low and 2 groups were missing. *represents that the estimation is significant at 10% level, **represents 5% and ***represents 1%.

In the three variables of income level, the coefficient of rural income level (lnruralincome) is significantly positive indicates improving rural income can boost the urbanization ratio. While neither the urban income level (lnrubanincome) nor income gap between urban and rural area is significant.

5. THE CONCLUSION AND PROPOSALS

The result of regression based on the panel data of 28 provinces from 1987 to 2008 finds out the influencing factors of traditional urbanization to some degree. The main factors are the household registration system, land- expansion mode, GDP per capita of provinces, the tertiary industry ratio, the rejective intention of developed regions and the rural income level. Based on these findings, the following policy proposals are made:

5.1. Lead by Metropolis, Boosted by Urban Agglomerations and Avoid Relying on Land-Expansi on

Taking advantage of the lead of metropolis to boost the development of urban agglomerations is designed as one of the principle thinking of urbanization. It aims to use urban agglomerations to drive large, medium and small cities and towns to develop coordinately. At the same time, by improving the structure and scale of cities, controlling the number of metropolis and giving priority to developing small towns, satellite towns, towns w ith professional characteristics, economic growth and urbanization development can be realized.

When it comes to selecting the way of urban pullulation, it's necessary to avoid traditional expansion mode of enclosure. As is analyzed before, land-expansion did play a vital role in the past process of urbanization. How-ever, with the severe lack of land resources and agricultural land this extensive form of enclosure movement needs to be reformed immediately. The goal of urbanization should be changed from expanding the land of cities to improving the hardware and oftware facilities in city areas, optimizing the urban layout and creating characteristic cities.

5.2. To Reform the Household Registration System

In our empirical outcomes, one of them with Chinese characteristics is the peasant workers who truly have in-creased the nominal urbanization level (by 2011, the real ratio of urbanization is about 35% to 36%, far less than the official statistics: 51%) but were not considered as citizens (of course they didn't have the same rights and protection as city people had). Some scholars argue one of the crucial points of new-type urbanization is to ensuring the peasant-workers both the urban residence certificate (hukou) and the equal treatment of urban citizens.

5.3. To Reform the Scale of Cities and to Increase the Number of Medium and Small Cities

The outcome above indicates metropolis may have rejective intention against immigrant people from developing regions whose economy level and income level are far less than the big ones. Given this, increasing some medium and small cities moderately can narrow the gap of different regions, and also promote the citizenization of peasant-workers orderly. Thus the real urbanization ratio can be improved.

New medium and small cities should embrace the centre city or metropolis positioned them as satellite cites with complementary function to form urban circle and create economy of scale jointly.

5.4. To Narrow the Income Gap between City and Country Side and to Improve the Rural Income

As is proved above, the increase of rural income can enhance the level of urbanization. With the economy of scale brought by the process of urbanization, the added value created by peasant workers is also counted as the increment of cities' net profit. So, the local governments should not only consider immediate rewards but also put the task to improve rural income into the development of new-type urbanization.

REFERENCES

1. Wang, Z.P., Zhang, C. and Guo, L.M. (2013) Chongqing's Urbanization Rate Changes Influencing Factors-Based on Regression Analysis. Liaoning Agricultural Sciences, 5, 33-37. (in Chinese) http://www.cqvip.com/QK/94904X/201305/47558605.html

2. Wu, J. and Shen, L.J. (2012) An Empirical Analysis of the Factors in the Route Choice of New Urbanization in

Chongqing. Journal of Southwest University (Social Sciences Edition), 38, 151-155. (in Chinese)

3. http://www.cqvip.com/QK/81271A/201202/41383543.html

4. Guo, C.X. (2009) An Empirical Study on the Development of Urbanization and Tertiary Industry in Our Country. Special Zone Economy, 12, 290-291. (in Chinese) http://www.cqvip.com/QK/96767X/200912/32623365.html

5. Wooldridge, J.M. (2008) Introductory Econometrics A Modern Approach. 4th Edition, Cengage Learning, 473-478

6. Chenery, H.B. and Syrquin, M. (1975) Patterns of Development: 1950-1970. Oxford University Press, USA, 68-70.

4
CHAPTER

China's Latent Human Capital Investment: Achieving Milestones and Competing for the Top

Amelie F. Constant , Bienvenue N. Tien , Klaus F. Zimmermann & Jingzhou Meng

[1] Professor at the Elliott School of International Affairs and the Economics Department at George Washington University,

[2] Migration at the Institute for the Study of Labor (IZA, Bonn). Bienvenue N. Tien is Research Assistant at DIWDC.

[3] Klaus F. Zimmermann is Professor at the University of Bonn and the Director of IZA, Bonn.

[4] Country Assistance and Technical Support Team at the International Monetary Fund in Washington, DC

ABSTRACT

In this paper we provide an overview of China's human capital strategy and educational achievements over the last two decades. While everyone acknowledges China as an economic superpower, very few are aware of or realize China's notable achievements in education as well as its internationalization of education. Since 1978, the landmark for the foundation of the Chinese modern higher education system, China has made tremendous strides in education both domestically and internationally. While China maintains 10%

growth in GDP, albeit with a GDP per capita at a low level for a developing country, it is also producing serious scholars and a tremendous amount of scholarly output; more and more Chinese students are seeking higher education abroad; and international students are showing a rising interest in receiving education in China.

Science has no boundaries. China's endeavors in science and technology need to be more integrated with those of the world, and the world needs a China that is vibrant and able to deliver more in science and technology. Just as collisions generate sparks, exchange and communication enrich imagination and creativity. (Premier Wen Jiabao)1

INTRODUCTION

China is known, acknowledged and revered because of its strong economic ascension. In 2010, China became the second largest national economy and the second largest exporter.2 It also has the world's largest current account surplus and foreign exchange reserves, thus being 'far more deeply integrated into the world economy than either of the economic superpowers'.3

While achieving the title of economic superpower is impressive, combining it with the status of being a cocoon of innovation and information technology and of incubating human capital is even more striking. Fewer people, however, are aware of China's impressive strides in human capital investment and its notable achievements in education. Currently, China is spending, on average, more on research and development than any other major developed economy in the West. It is becoming an attraction pole for expatriates and international students alike and a pioneer in producing scientific papers in natural sciences and engineering. In 2007, 59% of the scientific papers published by Chinese scholars were in natural sciences. In its twelfth five-year plan for 2011–2015

China revealed that it is attempting to become, by 2050, the world champion in science and research.

In this paper we document the notable achievements that China has made in accumulating human capital. We further seek to identify the strategy which China wishes to follow in order to close the gap to the USA, Japan and Germany's human capital production. We suggest that capacity building by internationalization is the core of the Chinese science policy. We start by providing an overview of China's human capital strategy and its painstaking commitment to fostering and speeding up the progress of science and technology. We continue with China's internationalization of education and its evolvement over the last 30 years. The following section looks at China as a magnet for international talents. In the final section we summarize the milestones that China has achieved and conclude with possible implications for the twenty-first century.

INVESTING IN HUMAN CAPITAL AND CONQUERING THE WORLD

China's tumultuous love affair with education

Access to higher education was not open to ordinary people until late into the nineteenth century, when the first modern Chinese higher institution was established during the Qing Dynasty (1871–1908).4 During the Republican Era of 1912–1949 and with the newly founded higher education system, Western university models began to gain in popularity, and Chinese students were sent abroad to learn advanced technologies. By 1949, 205 universities had been founded in China.5 The beginning of the People's Republic of China (PRC) in 1949 heralded an end to the educational expansion; and by 1953 the number of comprehensive universities had fallen from 49 to 13. Only colleges specializing in applied subjects such as medicine and agriculture were spared as they were regarded as vital for economic development.6 During the Cultural Revolution of 1966–

1976 China's higher education system suffered further in the hands of political meddling. Many universities were forced to close between 1966 and 1971. Shortly after they were allowed to reopen, but the emphasis was to be on political studies rather than a standard college curriculum.7

Meng and Gregory8 studied the educational cost of the large-scale school interruptions due to the Chinese Cultural Revolution. They estimated that those who did not obtain a university degree, because of the Cultural Revolution, lost an average of more than 50% of potential earnings. Men and women alike suffered reduced attainment of senior high school certificates and more than 20% prematurely stopped their education at the junior high school level. Interestingly, these educational responses do not appear to have commanded lower earnings. While at each level of educational attainment most of the cohort experienced missed or interrupted schooling, the authors found that, once they controled for the education certificate attained, the impact on earnings of these missed years of schooling or lack of normal curricula was small.

Deng Xiaoping's renowned Gai Ge Kai Fang, or ‘opening-up policy’9 in the late-1970s brought about many reforms, which put education back on course. Human capital was deemed to be of paramount importance as education could turn China into a global, economic power. In a concerted effort, the Chinese government took concrete steps to protect it and advance it. A two-way street approach was to be implemented: that of learning from the West and that of attracting the West to China. In 1977, China resumed the National College Entrance Examination, granting more people the opportunity of higher education.10 The academic system was based on British and American models, with associate degrees offered by short-cycle colleges, and bachelor's, master's and doctoral degrees granted by standard institutions of higher education; a post-doctoral research system was also enacted, all of which signaled a new phase in modern Chinese higher education.

The Chinese government had also been encouraging students to study abroad, with the availability of various scholarships. However, recipients had to return to China after graduating and work for at least two consecutive years, or face a severe penalty. In addition, the quota that stipulated the number of students studying abroad who financed their own studies and supported themselves was relaxed by the end of 1986. The government even pledged to 'support students and scholars studying abroad, encourage them to return to China after their completion of studies and guarantee them the freedom of coming and going'.11

China's domestic education and the internationalization of education

By the 1990s China had made tremendous strides in advancing its education system and in educating its people. Still, using 1995 data on public expenditures on education as shares of GDP, Heckman12 found that China had only spent about 2.5% of its GDP on human capital investment. In stark contrast, China had devoted roughly 30% of its GDP to physical capital investment. The resulting ratio of annual investment in physical capital to human capital was much higher than in most other countries in the world. Heckman heavily criticized China's underinvestment in human capital at the expense of over-investment in physical capital. This imbalance, he said, was 'symptomatic of a serious distortion in current policy that serves to retard economic development in China'.13

Nonetheless, China continued on its strategic course of expanding higher education as prescribed. Employing newly available Chinese micro-data, Heckman and Li14 estimated the returns to college education in China in 2000. They found substantial heterogeneity in returns to schooling: people sort into schooling according to their comparative advantage. This finding has become an empirically important phenomenon in modern Chinese labor markets. The authors found that the effect of college attendance on a randomly selected person is an 11% annual increase in earnings in urban areas; the effect on those who go to college is actually higher (13%). They concluded that China's economic reform with pronounced market-orientated economic directives over the past 20-plus years has significantly increased returns to education in the 2000s.

Moreover, the Chinese directive on education affected the education opportunities of various population groups and the labor market. Based on 2005 Census data, Li and Xing15 found that higher education expansion increased the probability of going to college for some groups. While minority females, those from the central-western region and those from rural areas were less likely to benefit from it, one-child families were more responsive to this policy. Education expansion decreased the within-sector inequality of those with above high school (inclusive) education, mostly because of the increase in the income level for high school graduates.

After the return of Hong Kong to mainland China in 1997, China's higher education system entered a new phase of internationalization. Chinese and Western universities started cooperating, and a growing number of Chinese students went abroad to study. In 2003, the Chinese Government started offering scholarships to outstanding students who were financing their own studies.16 These scholarships were open to all Chinese citizens who had shown excellent academic performance and respected the recipients' choice after graduation in case they wanted to stay abroad. However, scholarships were only given for doctoral programs, and the US$5,000 grant could not be awarded to the same recipient twice.17 By 2007 China had established educational relationships with 188 countries and regions all over the world, and agreements on the mutual recognition of academic degrees had been signed with 32 countries and regions in the world.18 Further steps to strengthen international ties resulted in the establishment of Confucius Institutes, which are centers for the promotion of Chinese language and culture. By the end of November 2009, the number of such centers had reached 282 and they could be found in 84 countries and regions abroad, with 94 in Europe and 87 in America.19

China and the international circulation of students and scholars

Since 1978, the number of higher education institutions has increased from 600 to more than 2,000 in 2008, accompanied by an even more dramatic increase in student enrollment to 20 million in 2008.20 At the same time, the body of students and scholars studying abroad—called 'expatriate brains'—as well as the body of international students studying in China—called 'lured in brains'—have witnessed rapid developments.

Trends and distributions of Chinese students abroad

Depending on the type of funding they have, Chinese students studying overseas can be broadly put into two categories: those officially sponsored by the government and those who support themselves. The first category can be further divided into two groups: state-sponsored students, sent overseas by the Ministry of Education (MoE); and organization-sponsored students, supported by provincial governments or companies.21 In the beginning of the opening-up reform era, most Chinese students overseas were officially sponsored, as they lacked financial resources to support their studies abroad. However, the introduction of the loose policy in 1986 and the fast economic growth in the twenty-first century reduced limitations for self-supported students.

In 2000, 38,989 Chinese students22 went overseas. The majority of them were self-supported (82.8%), followed by those who were financially supported by organizations (10.0%) and by the government (7.2%). In 2008, the number of Chinese students who went abroad was 179,800; a more than a fourfold increase. Self-supported students accounted for a whopping 89.9% of the outgoing students. The percentage of students receiving organizational support was 4.8% and 6.2% of the students were financially supported by the government. With the year 2000 as the reference year, Figure 1 illustrates the overall number of Chinese students overseas since 2000 by type of financial sponsorship. While the number of self-supported students is clearly above the others and keeps increasing, it is the number of government supported students that exhibits the fastest pace, especially after 2005. This affirms the Chinese government's continual effort to support students going abroad. However, the number of students supported by organizations has been dwindling from 2005 onwards.

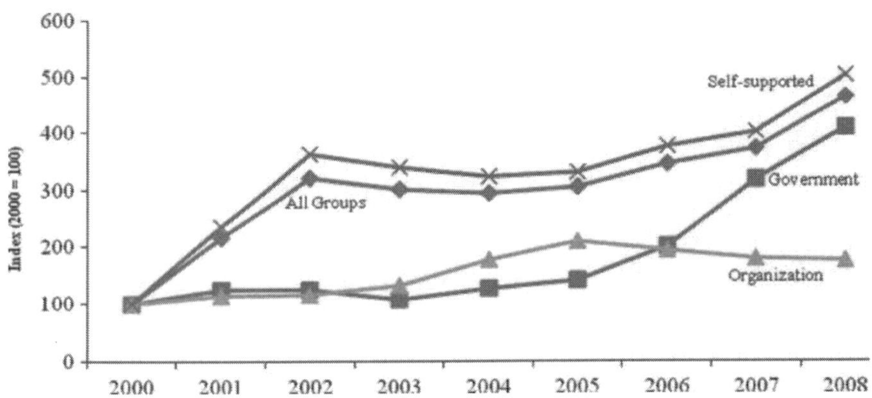

Figure 1. Evolution of Chinese overseas (post-)graduate students by sponsorship status. Note: Data for 2008 are from Ministry of Education of the People's Republic of China. Sources: China Education Yearbook, 2001–2008 edns; own calculation.

Not only has the number of Chinese students studying abroad increased, but Chinese students are now to be found in 108 countries and regions all over the world.23[23.] MoE, *Work Related to Students and Scholars Studying Abroad.*View all notes While their preferred destinations vary with time, they mostly favor Western countries, especially English-speaking ones. Table 1 documents that the top five destinations of Chinese students in 2008 were the USA, the UK,

France, Australia and Germany. The USA is by far the most popular destination for Chinese students. In terms of absolute numbers, in 2008, 419,109 Chinese students went abroad for tertiary education. Out of the five preferred destination countries, higher education institutions of the USA alone received 110,246 Chinese students, followed by Australia (57,596), the UK (45,356), Germany (21,977) and France (20,852). That makes about 26.3% for the USA, 13.7% for Australia, 10.8% for the UK, 5.2% for Germany and 5.0% for France relative to the entire Chinese students' population going abroad. However, examining the presence of Chinese students from the host country perspective, one observes that out of the entire foreign student population in the United States, they represent about 18%, 25% in Australia, 13.7% in the UK, 11.6% in Germany and 8.6% in France. So Chinese students are largely in the USA, but among the foreign students they have their strongest relative presence in Australia.

Table 1. ***International flows of students at the tertiary level—matrix of the top five host and home countries in 2008***

	Host country						
	The USA	The UK	France	Australia	Germany	Other countries	Total number of native students abroad
Home country	1	2	3	4	5	6	
1 China	110,246	45,356	20,852	57,596	21,977	163,082	419,109
2 India	94,664	25,901	1,038	26,520	3,257	13,700	165,080
3 Republic of Korea	69,198	4,031	2,292	6,270	3,929	25,683	111,403
4 Germany	8,917	13,625	6,918	1,934	–	46,857	78,251
5 Japan	34,010	4,465	1,908	2,974	1,858	3,623	48,838
6 Other countries	307,439	248,413	210,428	135,341	158,326	660,351	1,720,298
Total number of foreign students in the host country	624,474	341,791	243,436	230,635	189,347	913,296	2,542,979

Note: Tertiary education refers to ISCED 5 and 6.
Sources: UNESCO Online Education Database, available at: http://stats.uis.unesco.org; own presentation.

Figure 2 (assuming 1999 = 100) depicts the flow of Chinese students at the tertiary level by the top five destination countries24 over the period 1999–2008. While the flow of students to the USA has remained almost constant, there has been a rapid increase of between ten- and twelvefold of students going to the UK, France and Australia. First, it is interesting to note the UK's dominant role as a top five destination country. The impressive increase in the number of students going to the UK reached a maximum in 2005; it has been slowly decreasing since then. Nonetheless, the UK is still a favorite destination because of its—perceived by the Chinese—prestigious and high quality education. According to the British Council's *Vision 2020*,25 Chinese students will be the UK's number one source of international students after 2010, with an annual growth rate of 11.4%.

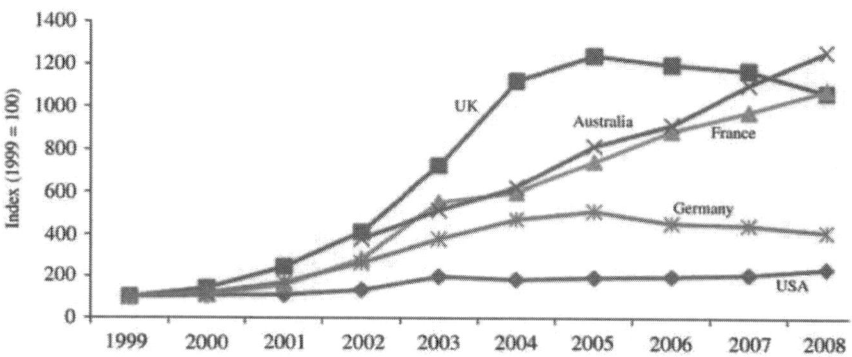

Figure 2: Flows of Chinese students at the tertiary level to some selected host countries: 1999–2008. *Note:* Data for Australia in 2001 were not available in the UNESCO database. *Sources*: UNESCO education online database; own presentation.

Second, Figure 2 shows that the number of students going to France has followed an impressive up-sloping curve: while only 2,000 Chinese students chose France in 2000, 12,000 went in 2004 and 21,000 in 2008. Burgeoning bilateral agreements between French and Chinese institutions and universities to support the international exchange of students between the two countries have certainly contributed to this trend. Australia is the present and future favorite of Chinese students, as flows have been rising steeply since 2002. Lastly, the promising rise in the number of students going to Germany has been short-lived. Undoubtedly, the number of

Chinese students enrolled in tertiary education in Germany has tripled from 2000 to 2008. While flows have been increasing since 2000, albeit at a rather slow pace, they reached a maximum in 2005 and started decreasing after 2005. As German policymakers debate about charging higher tuition fees to international students,26 Chinese students are clearly showing that they prefer to go to other countries to study.

Figure 3 illustrates the portions of graduate and undergraduate students from mainland China who were enrolled in American schools juxtaposing the academic years 2006/2007 and 2008/2009. It is clear that the number of students enrolled in graduate education is the highest in both academic years, supporting the perception that graduate education obtained in Western universities is very prestigious in China. However, comparing the percentage change of graduates to that of the undergraduates in these two academic years, Figure 3 shows that while the graduates increased by 17%, the undergraduates increased by 62%. Put differently, while the share of graduate students as a percentage of the entire Chinese student body fell from 70.83% in 2006/2007 to only 58.48% in 2008/2009, the share of undergraduates as a percentage of the entire Chinese student body increased from 14.7% in 2006/2007 to 26.7% in 2008/2009. Therefore, while the total number of undergraduates is far smaller than the total number of graduate students, these statistics indicate strong demand for American education at the undergraduate level. Equally notable is the number of Chinese students with Optional Practical Training (OPT) status.27 While in 2006/2007 2,573 Chinese students who graduated from American colleges and universities stayed to work for a year in the USA, their number almost quadrupled in 2008/2009 to 8,212.

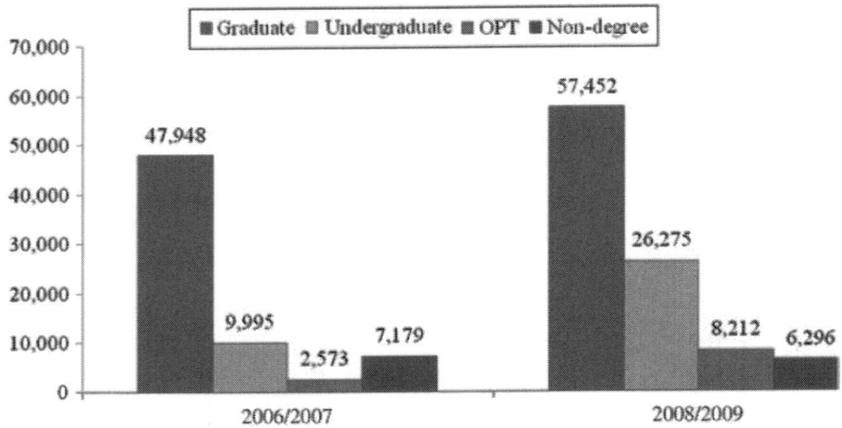

Figure 3 Number of Chinese students in the USA by academic levels. *Note:* OPT stands for Optional Practical Training. *Source:* Institute of International Education.

How China deals with its talented students going abroad

It is said that whoever wins the battle over talents will be the victor in the twenty-first century. The statistics presented above allude to some kind of brain drain for China. The pertinent question is, then, how does the Chinese government deal with this possibility? This section documents the systematic steps taken towards the return of talented Chinese living abroad.

Acknowledging a looming brain drain, China's Premier Wen Jiabao said that the

future of China's science and technology depends fundamentally on how we attract, train, and use young scientific talents today. Thus, at the core of our science and technology policy is attracting a diverse range of talents, especially young people, into science and providing them with an environment that brings out the best of their creative ideas.28

Since 1990, the Chinese government and the MoE have initiated, sponsored and carried through various programs to encourage highly talented Chinese expatriates to return and contribute to the country's economic reform and human capital. These programs have a wide range, covering young students and middle-aged scholars alike, and short-term visits or permanent stays. The most famous among them is the Chunhui Program (literally, Spring Bud), which—by the end of 2003—had funded more than 8,000 individuals and 90 groups of scholars and researchers who returned on a short-term visit.29 Table 2 lists the main programs in the 1990s and early 2000s.

Table 2. ***Main official programs to fund Chinese returnees***

Program name	Starting year	Targeted group	Incentives
The Fund for Returnees to Launch Science and Technology Researches	1990	Returnees with doctoral degree who work at education and research institutes[a]	Provide funds for purchasing equipments and books, doing on-site research, and attending conferences
Program for Training Talents toward the 21st Century	1993	Outstanding young teachers returning from overseas	Provide 200,000–300,000 yuan annually for doing research in major topics
The *Chunhui* Program (literally, Spring Bud)	1996	Returnees with doctoral degree and outstanding achievements in their fields	Cover travel expenditure to attend conferences and academic exchange programs
Changjiang[b] Scholar Incentive Program	1998	Young and middle-aged leading Chinese scholars who have experience studying abroad and are invited by HEIs as visiting professors	The program provides 100,000 yuan annual incentives, and the HEIs offer the salary, insurance and other social welfares during the visit
Program of Academic Short-return for Scholars and Research Overseas	2001	Outstanding Chinese scholars who come back to China in short breaks to give lectures or do research in 28 key Chinese HEIs[c]	The Ministry of Education covers travel expenditures, and HEIs pay salaries, provide accommodation and health insurance

Notes: [a]For detailed information, refer to: http://www.moe.gov.cn/edoas/website18/level3.jsp?tablename = 12632606 67176395& infoid = 1263277716024458 (in Chinese).
[b]It is also called the 'Yangtze River', literally translated as the 'Long River'. It is the longest river in China and Asia and the third longest in the world.
[c]The list of 28 key Chinese Higher Education Institutes (HEI) is available at: http://www.moe.gov.cn/edoas/ website18/level3.jsp?tablename = 1305&-infoid = 12200 (in Chinese).
Source: Ministry of Education of the People's Republic of China, available at: http://www.moe.edu.cn/english/ international_2.htm.

In December 2008 the Chinese central government set the bar higher in terms of attracting la crème de la crème by launching the 'One Thousand Talents Scheme'. This scheme aimed at attracting three groups of the most talented, Those who (1) have an academic title equivalent to professor in internationally well-known universities and institutions, or (2) work as senior managing staff within a well-known international company or banking institution, or (3) have developed technologies and patents and established their own business abroad.30

It is worth mentioning here that there is a division of tasks between the central and local governments in terms of attracting the most talented people to China. While the central government has indeed placed priority on recruiting top scientists and academics, local governments are more active in attracting high-tech entrepreneurs.31

These great efforts to attract expatriates along with the 'China opportunity theory', which results from China's continual double-digit GDP growth and its recent growing global influence, have enticed more and more Chinese students overseas to return and live their 'American dream' in China. Figure 4 depicts the ratio of the annual flow of Chinese returnees to the flow of students leaving to study abroad in reference to GDP per capita (in Yuan). The positive co-movement between economic development and the Returnees–Student Abroad ratio is striking. Over the last ten years, although the number of Chinese students studying abroad is higher than those who return home, the ratio of those who returned to those going abroad to study has been increasing. It has also been exactly following the GDP per capita evolution of the country. For instance, in 1999, 32.6% or almost one in three Chinese students returned home, with a GDP per capita for about 7,000 Yuan. In 2008, China's GDP per capita was about 22,000 Yuan, and the ratio of Returnees to Students Abroad has dramatically changed to 38.5% or almost four in ten students leaving have returned home. Nonetheless, the dip around 2003 was mostly due to SARS.

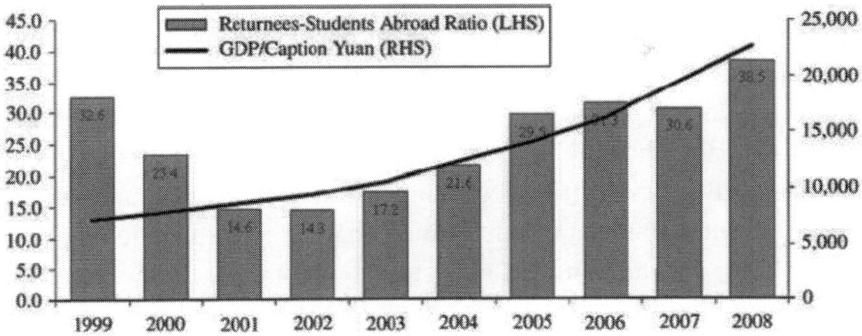

Figure 4: Evolution of GDP per capita and Returnees–Students Going Abroad ratio, 1999–2008.*Sources: China Statistical Yearbook 2009*, pp. 20–28; World Bank (for GDP per capita); own presentation.

The trend of returnees according to their sponsorship status is illustrated in Figure 5. Similar to Figure 1, financial support is provided by the government, by organizations or it is assumed to be provided by the individuals. Overall, from 2003 to 2008 the total number of returnees increased by almost 50,000. The number of self-financed students, in particular, grew by 44,000 within these six years. Figure 5 also shows that the number of students who were financed by the government increased.

Returning students and scholars play a leading role in fostering new high-tech start-ups and upgrading educational institutions.32 The important contributions of these returnees, often called *haiguipai*, are observed in almost all relevant societal domains. Returnees are present in leadership positions at educational institutions, research centers, investment banks, insurance agencies, state and private enterprises, law firms etc., and some are even well-integrated into the Chinese political arena.33 Examining the distribution of the overseas educational attainment of Chinese leaders, Li34 finds that almost 49.2% were visiting scholars, 32.8% Ph.D. graduates, 3.3% post-doctoral fellows, 9.9% M.A./M.S. graduates and 1.6% J.D./M.D., M.B.A. or B.A./B.S. In addition, with regards to their respective fields of responsibility, the author finds that roughly 79% of these returnees were in charge of science and technology, education, industrial development, finance, foreign trade and foreign affairs, 6.6% were in the political scene (organization or political publicity) and 1.6% in charge of rural development. Furthermore, by classifying these returnees according to their (high-ranking leader) length of study time, the author finds that 73.8% spent fewer than three years abroad, and 11.4% stayed for more than six years; however, it should be noted that most of these years were spent in intensive study for a doctorate.

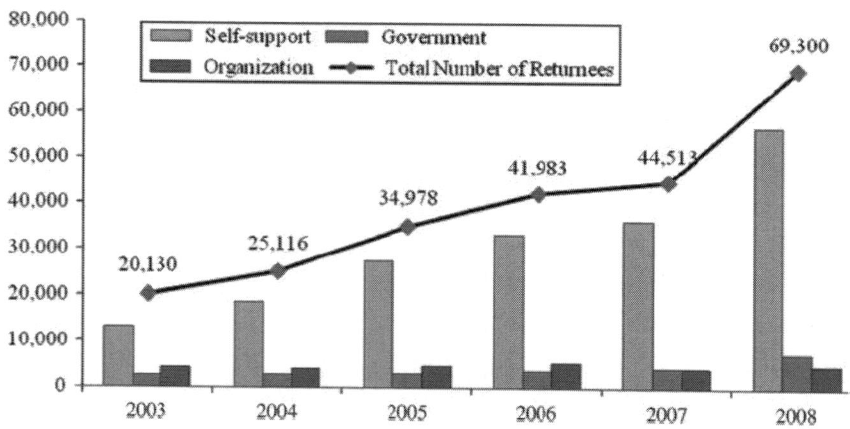

Figure 5: Number of overseas students back to China by sponsorship status: 2003–2008. *Sources*: Ministry of Education of the People's Republic of China; own presentation.

Chinese higher educational institutes have made great efforts to attract returnees as well. Their strategic goal is to be on the list of the world's best universities as soon as possible. For example, Tsinghua University and Peking University, the two most prestigious universities in China, allocated 20% of their annual budget to attract talent, with preference given to those from abroad.35

China's academic presence and influence in the international scene

China's concerted effort to strengthen its international competitiveness was primarily set up in the mid-1990s as 'science, technology and education were put at the forefront of development policy'.36 Statistics on China's educational outcomes as well as its scholarly output, especially in natural sciences and engineering, are impressive. China has followed a steady upward trend of 'first university degrees'37 in natural sciences and engineering. Figure 6 depicts the number of university graduates in natural sciences and engineering in China and other selected developed countries from 1998 to 2006.38 In 1998 already, China had the largest number of university graduates in natural sciences and engineering from the USA, Japan, South Korea and Germany. These numbers remained stagnant throughout this period for all four developed countries. In the USA, in particular, while the numbers of these graduates was higher than Japan, South Korea and Germany, they hardly changed over this period (from 205,000 in 1998 to 237,000 in 2006). Japan, Germany and South Korea had either below or just above 100,000 graduates per annum in natural sciences and engineering over this period. In sharp contrast, the numbers for China kept increasing, going from 239,000 in 1998 to 807,000 in 2006. Since 2002, especially, the number of university graduates in natural sciences and engineering seems to have taken off and keeps rising.39

With regards to Ph.D. graduates in natural sciences and engineering, Figure 7 contains data on those countries (USA, Germany, China, UK, Japan, South Korea and India) that are considered by the National Science Board40 as the leaders in producing doctoral degrees in the field. One finds that China has come a long way since the early 1990s, emerging as a country that is producing a growing number of doctorates at a rapid pace. While the USA still has the sovereignty of and is keeping reins on the production of natural sciences and engineering Ph.D. graduates—staying above all other countries—

China experienced a tenfold increase in its Ph.Ds. While in 1993 the number of awarded doctorates in China was about 1,000, in 2006, it was 21,000. Moreover, since the early 2000s, China's Ph.Ds seem to increase at an increasing rate and they are approaching the USA fast. It is also worth mentioning that other emerging countries, particularly India, have experienced a considerable rise in terms of Ph.D. graduates in natural sciences and engineering as well.41

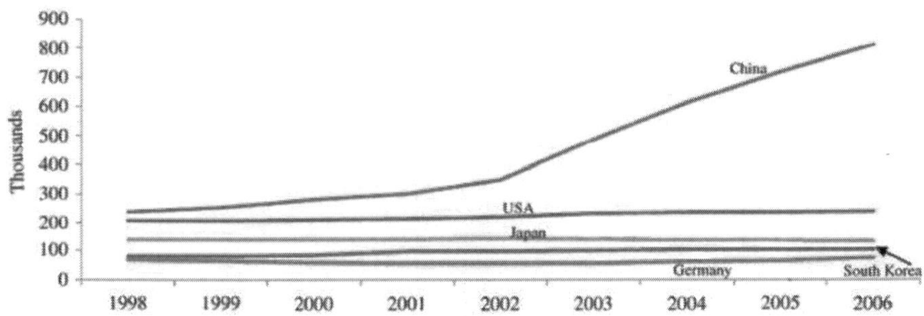

Figure 6: First university degrees in natural sciences and engineering, selected countries: 1998–2006. *Source*: Adopted from National Science Foundation, Science and Engineering Indicators 2010.

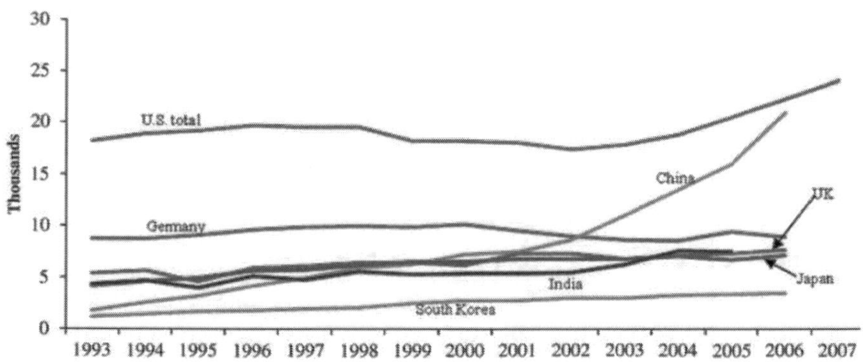

Figure 7: Doctoral degrees in natural sciences and engineering, selected countries: 1993–2007. *Source*: National Science Foundation, Science and Engineering Indicators 2010.

Even more important than the number of Ph.Ds is the scholarly output produced. Looking at the number of refereed journal articles in science and engineering of selected countries42 in 1988 and in 2008, Figure 8 shows that China stands out. In 1988, China produced about 5,000 S&E journal articles, while 20 years later that number had increased more than twelvefold (61,000 in 2008). The later outnumbered the number of S&E journal articles produced by Japan (48,000), and even the Asia-8 (57,000). According to the latest National Science Board report, researchers in the EU and the USA have long dominated the world's journal article production. However, their combined world share of published science and engineering articles steadily decreased from 69% in 1995 to 59% in 2008. On the other hand, both Asia-10 and Asia-8's43 scholarly output in science and engineering articles has been increasing.44

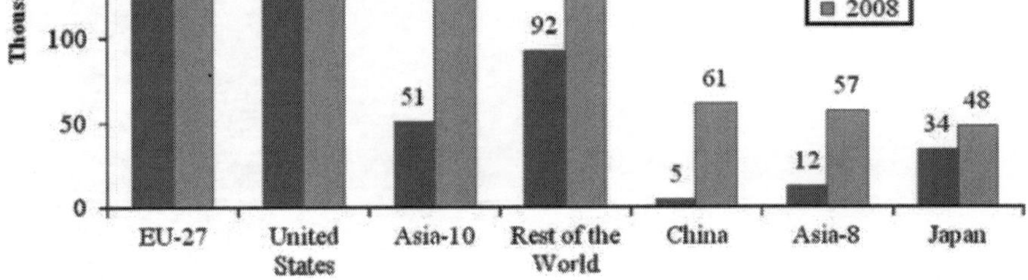

Figure 8: Number of S&E journal articles produced by selected countries: 1988 and 2008. *Notes:* Asia-8: includes India, Indonesia, Malaysia, Philippines, Singapore, South Korea, Taiwan and Thailand. Asia-10: includes China, Japan and the Asia-8. *Sources*: National Science Foundation, Science and Engineering Indicators 2010; own presentation.

Lastly, we examine the distribution of publications by discipline for some selected countries. In a sense this could reflect where a country's research priorities lie; for instance whether they lie in natural sciences, engineering, medical sciences or others. Figure 9 illustrates this distribution in 2007. Compared to other countries in Figure 9, the USA exhibits a more balanced distribution of journal articles among the fields of natural sciences, medical sciences and biological sciences. However, the USA's publications in engineering and the social or behavioral sciences are four times lower. In contrast, China's distribution is completely different. Its scholarly output lies predominantly in the natural sciences with 59% of the scientific papers published by Chinese scholars. China's largest share in natural sciences publication might be justified by the country's need to expand its chemical industry.45 Engineering is the next field with 17% of the publications, followed closely by biological sciences with 15%. Medical sciences claim only 8% of the publications and last are the social and behavioral sciences with only 1%.

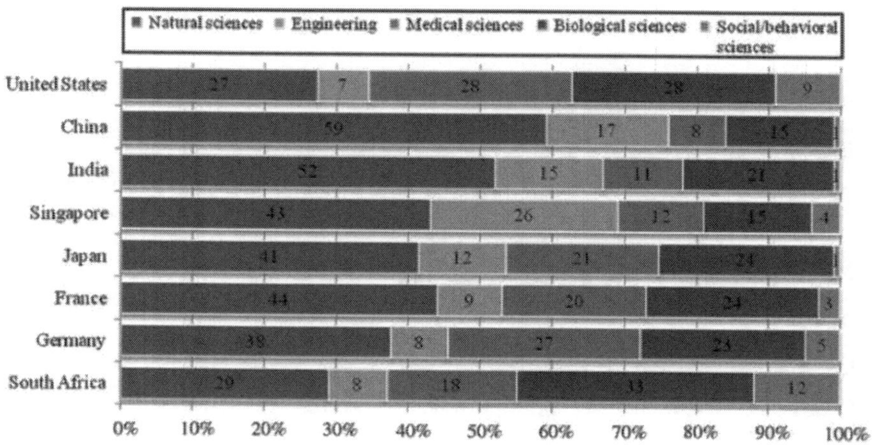

Figure 9: Shares of research articles by field of study for selected countries: 2007. *Source:* Adopted from National Science Foundation, Science and Engineering Indicators 2010.

With the exception of South Africa, all other countries in Figure 9 show that the larger number of publications comes from the natural sciences: India (52%), Singapore (43%), Japan (41%), France (44%) and Germany (38%). Germany's next mostly published fields are medical sciences (27%) and biological sciences (23%). Engineering occupies 8% of the publications and social and behavioral sciences rank last with 5%.

Investments in Research and Development (R&D) go hand in hand with a country's research priorities. Spending in R&D is, undoubtedly, of paramount importance for any country's development and competitiveness. Figure 10 shows R&D expenditures as percentage of GDP in 1996 and 2007 for countries and economic areas selected by the National Science Board (2010). Asian countries, such as South Korea and Japan devoted a large share of their economic output to R&D. China, compared with other economies, spends less on R&D. Nonetheless, China's R&D/GDP ratio more than doubled, from 0.6% in 1996 to 1.5% in 2007. As mentioned by the National Science Board, 'the gap in China's R&D/GDP ratio relative to those of developed economies suggests that China's R&D volume can continue to grow rapidly'.46

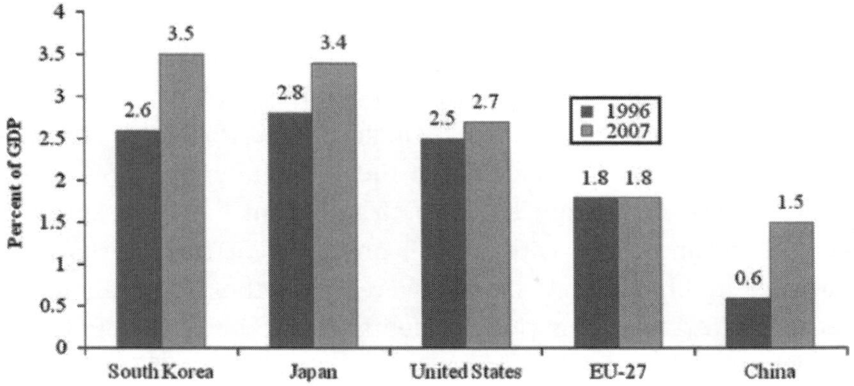

Figure 10: R&D expenditures as share of economic output of selected economies: 1996 and 2007. Sources: National Science

Foundation, Science and Engineering Indicators 2010; own presentation.

'LURING BRAINS IN': CAN CHINA REACH HUMAN CAPITAL SUPREMACY?

At the signing ceremony on scientific and the cultural exchange between the USA and China in 1978, President Jimmy Carter, following Premier Deng Xiaoping's remark, said:

Our aim is to make this kind of exchange between our countries no longer the exception but the norm; no longer a matter of headlines and the historians, but a routine part of the everyday life of both Chinese and American people.47

More than 30 years later, China's booming economy and relatively stable political and social environment have attracted more and more international students to the country.

Official data from the MoE reveal that the overall number of international students in China grew steadily in the last decade, rising from about 50,000 students in 2000 to almost 200,000 in 2007. According to the MoE, 195,503 international students from 188 countries and regions went to study in China; they were distributed among 544 Chinese higher education and research institutes in 2007. The majority of them, 141,689, or 72.5%, were from Asia, especially from South Korea and Japan. European students were in second place with 26,339 or 13.5% of the international students in China; they mostly were from the UK, France and Germany. Next were American students (19,673 or 10.1%), followed by Africans (5,915 or 3%) and people from Oceania (1,887 or 1%).

Figure 11 is produced by plotting these numbers over time (from 2000 to 2007) as well as by country of origin; the year 2000 is used as the reference year. The number of European and African students in China has quadrupled in seven years. We observe a similar pattern for the Asian and American students, albeit their numbers have only tripled; the number of students from Oceania over the same time period doubled. Figure 11 shows that by 2007, there was a serious foreign student presence in China. It is interesting that the SARS pandemic in 2003 decreased the number of students from Europe and the Americas but not those from Oceania and Africa.

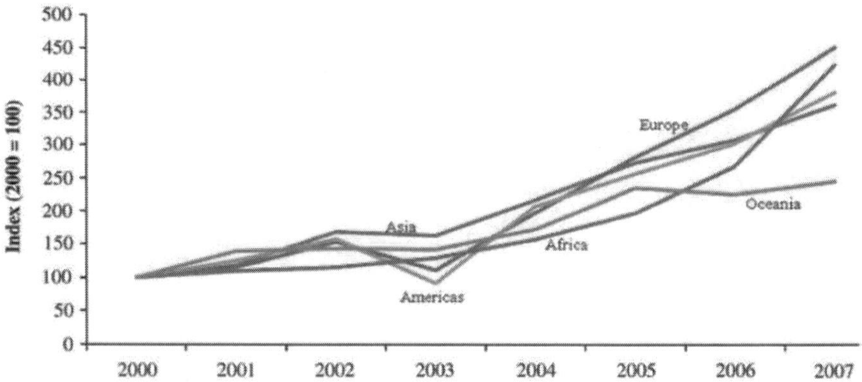

Figure 11 Evolution of international students in China by place of origin: 2000–2007. *Sources*: *China Education Yearbook*, 2001–2008 edns; own calculation.

Another interesting aspect about the international students in China is their sponsorship type. Figure 12 displays the flow of international students into China over the last decade by their financial sponsorship status, with 2000 as the reference year. They are categorized as students who are self-financed and those who are financially supported through a scholarship. Note that self-financed or self-supported status means that these students do not receive support neither from the Chinese government nor from any other Chinese organizations. It includes, however, students who have a scholarship from their home country government or other non-Chinese foundations and organizations.

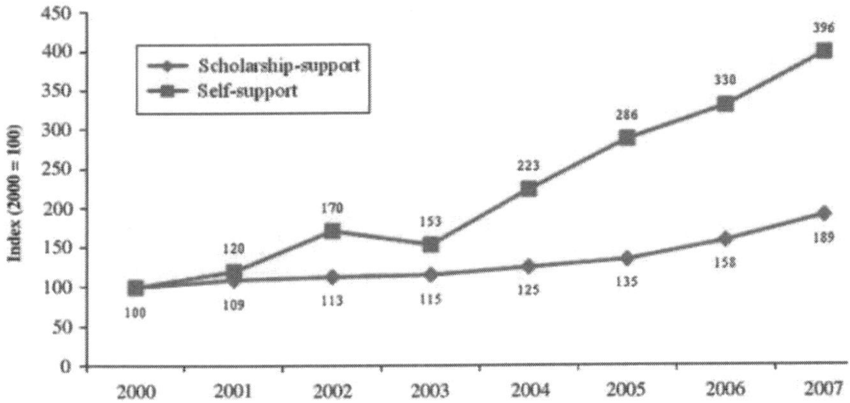

Figure 12: Flows of international students to China by sponsorship status: 2000–2007. *Sources*: *China Education Yearbook*, 2001–2008 edns; own presentation.

Figure 12 clearly shows that the self-financed students have been gradually playing a dominant role. It also expresses a growing demand for Chinese culture, language and know-how by other countries. Aside from the dip in 2003—probably mostly related to the SARS epidemic—the number of self-financed foreign students has increased dramatically over the period of 2000–2007. The scholarship-supported status of foreign students in China indicates students who receive scholarships provided by the Chinese government, such as the Chinese government scholarship, the Great Wall Scholarship, the Excellent Student Scholarship, the HSK Winner Scholarship, the short-term program for foreign teachers of Chinese and the Chinese culture research program.48 Interestingly, the number of scholarship-supported foreign students doubled between 2000 and 2008, indicating a conscious effort to lure and support foreign students wanting to study in China.

Most foreign students in China enroll in non-degree programs, such as studying Chinese language and culture, or in short-term programs of less than six months. In 2007 there were 127,290 such non-degree students, accounting for 65.1% of the entire international student body in China. Undergraduates came second with 29.3% of the entire international student body. Note that the number of Master's (7,628) and Ph.D. (3,218) students was relatively small compared to other student groups, representing 3.9% and 1.6%, respectively. Nonetheless, as shown in Figure 13, the number of international students following academic fields—whether they are at the graduate level (Master's and Ph.D.) or in non-degree programs—has clearly more than tripled over the past eight years (with the year 2000 as the reference year). Undergraduates, in particular, experienced an almost sixfold increase over the same reference period, and their numbers keep increasing. This indicates that the world is expressing a serious interest in China.

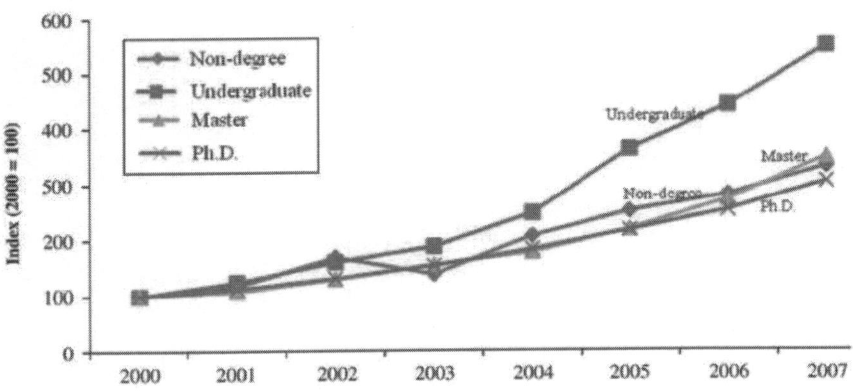

Figure 13: Flows of international students to China by academic level: 2000–2007. *Sources*: *China Education Yearbook*, 2001–2008 eds; own calculation.

Figure 14 illustrates how international students in China were distributed across disciplines in 2007. The vast majority of them go into liberal arts, which includes Chinese language and culture studies. With 135,477 enrolled students, this seems to be the favorite and most popular discipline. The next most attractive discipline is studies in Chinese and Western medicine with 25,573 international students. Economics with 8,804 and engineering with 6,785 international students follow in the enrolment of international students.49[49.] 2008 *China Education Yearbook*.View all notes We conjecture that the relatively high number of international students majoring in medicine in China might be due to the Chinese traditional medicine, i.e. acupuncture practices.

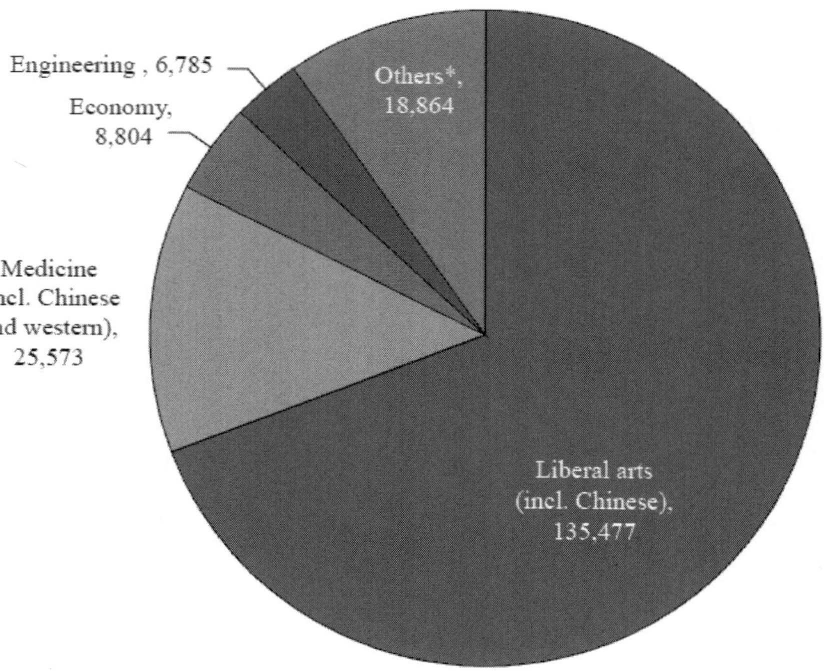

Figure 14: Number of international students by field of study in China: 2007. *Note:* *; Including: Management, Law, Education, Science, History, Agriculture, Philosophy. *Sources*: Ministry of Education of People's Republic of China; own presentation.

One question that concerns policymakers is how to improve the quality of international education in China and attract more international students. In the Action Plan of 2005 the MoE clearly stated that its aim was to 'adopt a strategy of creating "renowned brand names" for selected institutions and academic fields and adhere to the principles of "expanding the scale, raising the level, ensuring the quality, and managing" according to established norms and standards'.50

CONCLUSIONS

In this paper we examined China's lesser known but highly important feature: human capital. Starting with the opening-up reform of 1978—a landmark for the Chinese modern higher education system—we dissected the available statistics with an emphasis on the past decade. China has achieved important milestones in human capital, working painstakingly and following a steady course. In particular, our study shows that: (i) the number of students enrolled in Chinese higher education institutions has increased dramatically; (ii) more and more Chinese students seek higher education abroad (and are encouraged and supported by the government); (iii) China is producing serious scholars and a tremendous amount of scholarly output; and (iv) international students have started to show a steadily growing interest in receiving education in China.

Specifically, we documented an ever-increasing trend of Chinese students going abroad. According to the Ministry of Education statistics, the number of Chinese overseas students reached about 1.4 million in total by 2008. While many students have returned, many more remain abroad after graduating. Some observers think that China may soon face a brain drain problem. Being aware of the issue, astute Chinese officials have been following a steady course to bring their expatriates back to China by creating a welcoming environment and favorable conditions for them to flourish.

Regarding those who choose to stay abroad, China's attitude is to befriend them and keep them happy so that the ethnic network stays alive and can be used in the future.

Today, China aims to provide high-quality education, comparable to international universities in Europe and the USA, and it produces more university degrees in natural sciences and engineering than any other country. If 'science is the ultimate revolution', as Premier Wen said,51 then China is 'revolving' fast: (i) it produces an exorbitant amount of doctoral degrees in science and engineering, reaching the level of the USA; (ii) it has the highest annual growth rate of published refereed papers in science and engineering by far; and (iii) it produces the highest percentage of scholarly output in the natural sciences with 59% of the scientific papers published by Chinese scholars. This is more than double the corresponding percent in the USA (27%), a country that has been long considered the global leader. China is also spending, on average, more on research and development than any other major developed economy in the West. All these facts render China a country that has to be taken seriously in the international academic community.

Lastly, we presented evidence of the Chinese government making great efforts to attract international students from other parts of the world to China for their education, and evidence of the rest of the world expressing a serious interest in China, ranging from learning about the language and culture to Chinese acupuncture or studying other fields. This is manifested by the increasing number of international students studying in China.

The evidence-based analysis presented in this paper suggests that China has already established itself as a global player in the international market for higher education. It has built up internal capacities successfully and seems to attempt to take over the strategy of the USA to internationalize and to attract talent from the world instead of choosing the more inward-looking and hesitant European model. Globalization is at the core of China's human capital strategy. In this way, it is not counterproductive to intensify the outflow of Chinese students to the USA, given the efforts to stabilize the ethnic network to their own diaspora and to encourage return migration. The strong presence of China in the education of students from Asia and the Third World is also in line with its policy to strengthen its access to the natural resources in those countries and to ensure close future economic collaborations. Hence, China will challenge the American role model and may become an educator and employer for the talented of the Third World.

It is said that whoever wins the battle over talents will be the victor of the twenty-first century. All countries advocate the need for skilled immigrants. China has undoubtedly emerged as one of the largest economies in the world and has shown considerable global power, which begs the question of whether China is satisfied with only being the world's cheap manufacturer. If not, can China turn its labor intensive economy into a knowledge-based one and win the global tug-of-war for talents?

NOTES

*Amelie F. Constant is visiting Professor at the Elliott School of International Affairs and the Economics Department at George Washington University, Executive Director of DIWDC, Visiting Fellow and Program Director of Migration at the Institute for the Study of Labor (IZA, Bonn). Bienvenue N. Tien is Research Assistant at DIWDC. Klaus F. Zimmermann is Professor at the University of Bonn and the Director of IZA, Bonn. Jingzhou Meng is in the Country Assistance and Technical Support Team at the International Monetary Fund in Washington, DC. This paper is the revised version of IZA Policy Paper 19, September 2010. We wish to thank Richard Easterlin, Yang Yumei and one anonymous referee for encouragement and helpful suggestions on an earlier draft. The authors can be reached by email at constant@iza.org

1. 1. Wen Jiabao, 'Science and China's modernization', *Science* 322(5902), (2008), p. 649.

2. 2. China recently surpassed Germany and became the largest exporter.

3. 3. Fred C. Bergsten *et al.*, *China's Rise: Challenges and Opportunities* (Washington, DC: Peterson Institute for International Economics and Center for Strategic and International Studies, 2009), p. 9.

4. 4. For an extended historic overview of China's education, see Amelie F. Constant, Bienvenue N. Tien and Jingzhou Meng, 'Can China win the tug-of-war for talents', *DIWDC Synopsis* no. 2, (May–August 2010), pp. 9–17.

5. 5. Uwe Brandenburg and Jiani Zhu, *Higher Education in China in the Light of Massification and Demographic Change: Lessons to be Learned for Germany*, CHE Working Paper No. 97, (October 2007).

6. 6. Kang Ouyang, 'Higher education reform in China today', *Policy Futures in Education*2(1), (2004), pp. 141–149.

7. 7. Junsen Zhang, Pak-Wai Liu and Linda Yung, 'The Cultural Revolution and returns to schooling in China: estimates based on twins', *Journal of Development Economics* 84(2), (2007), pp. 631–639.

8. 8. Xin Meng and Bob Gregory, *Exploring the Impact of Interrupted Education on Earnings: The Educational Cost of the Chinese Cultural Revolution*, IZA Discussion Paper No. 2548, (January 2007).

9. 9. The opening-up policy has been seen as the 'most powerful driving force behind China's rapid transformation'; see Yongnian Zheng, 'Society must be defended: reform,

openness, and social policy in China', *Journal of Contemporary China* 19(67), (2010), pp. 799–818.

10. Richard Mullins, 'Test fever', *China Today*, (2005), available at: http://www.chinatoday.com.cn/English/e2005/e200506/p34.htm (accessed 23 June 2010).

11. Ministry of Education of the People's Republic of China (MoE), *Work Related to Students and Scholars Studying Abroad*, (n.d.), (in Chinese), available at: http://www.moe.edu.cn/english/international_2.htm (accessed 10 June 2010).

12. James J. Heckman, 'China's investment in human capital', *Economic Development and Cultural Change* 51(4), (2003), pp. 795–804.

13. James J. Heckman, 'China's investment in human capital', *Economic Development and Cultural Change* 51(4), (2003), p. 795.

14. James J. Heckman and Xuesong Li, 'Selection bias, comparative advantage and heterogeneous returns to education: evidence from China in 2000', *Pacific Economic Review* 9(3), (2004), pp. 155–171.

15. Shi Li and Chunbing Xing, *China's Higher Education Expansion and its Labor Market Consequences*, IZA Discussion Paper No. 4974, (May 2010).

16. Linqing Yao, 'The Chinese overseas students: an overview of the flows change', paper presented at the *12th Biennial Conference of the Australian Population Association*, Canberra, Australia, 15–17 September 2004.

17. NesoChina, *Chinese Government Scholarship for Outstanding Self-financed Students Studying Abroad*, (2008), available at: http://www.nesochina.org/chinese-

students/information-inenglish/schola rships/governmental-scholarships/chinese-government-scholarship-for-outstanding-self-financed-students-studying-abroad (accessed 10 June 2010).

18. Reported in the *2008 China Education Yearbook*. For more details, see: Ministry of Education of the People's Republic of China (MoE), *2008 China Education Yearbook*(People's Education Press, 2008), (in Chinese), available at: http://www.moe.gov.cn/edoas/website18/top_nianjian.j sp (accessed 10 June 2010).

19. Source: http://www.hanban.org/node_10961.htm (accessed 15 June 2010).

20. National Bureau of Statistics of China, *China Statistical Yearbook 2009* (China Statistics Press, 2009), available at: http://www.stats.gov.cn/tjsj/ndsj/2009/indexeh.htm (ac cessed 15 June 2010).

21. Yao, 'The Chinese overseas students'.

22. Note that we refer to students from mainland China; students from Hong Kong are not included in any of the statistics on education.

23. MoE, *Work Related to Students and Scholars Studying Abroad*.

24. Note that the country comparison choice here and in the sequel is driven by data availability (in the used data source) and by empirical observation regarding which are the most important countries or regions in the analyzed case.

25. Anthony Böhm *et al.*, *Vision 2020: Forecasting International Student Mobility: A UK Perspective* (British Council, 2003), available at: http://www.britishcouncil.org/eumd_-_vision_2020.pdf (accessed 22 June 2010).

26. See http://www.spiegel.de/unispiegel/studium/0,1518,680051,00.html.

27. OPT status allows international students who graduate from American universities to stay in the USA and work for a maximum of 12 months after graduating.

28. Jiabao, 'Science and China's modernization', p. 649.

29. MoE, *Work Related to Students and Scholars Studying Abroad.*

30. Litao Zhao and Jinjing Zhu, 'China attracting global talent: central and local initiatives', *China: An International Journal* 7(2), (2009), pp. 323–335.

31. Litao Zhao and Jinjing Zhu, 'China attracting global talent: central and local initiatives', *China: An International Journal* 7(2), (2009), pp. 323–335

32. Barry Naughton, *The Chinese Economy: Transitions and Growth* (Cambridge, MA: MIT Press, 2007), p. 363.

33. Cheng Li, 'Foreign-educated returnees in the People's Republic of China: increasing political influence with limited official power', *Journal of International Migration and Integration* 7(4), (2006), pp. 493–516.

34. Cheng Li, 'Foreign-educated returnees in the People's Republic of China: increasing political influence with limited official power', *Journal of International Migration and Integration* 7(4), (2006), pp. 493–516

35. Helene Le Bail and Wei Shen, 'The return of the "brains" to China: what are the social, economic, and political impacts?', *Asia Vision* 11, (2008), available at: http://www.ifri.org/downloads/AV11_ENG.pdf (accessed 17 June 2010).

36. Carl J. Dahlman and Jean-Eric Aubert, *China and the Knowledge Economy: Seizing the 21st Century* (Washington, DC: WBI Development Studies, The World Bank, October 2001), p. 18.

37. A first university degree is the equivalent of the American bachelor's degree.

38. The choice of countries is based on the selection made by National Science Board (2010). Data for the first university degree in natural sciences and engineering are not available for other countries in that report. See National Science Board, *Science and Engineering Indicators 2010* (Arlington, VA: National Science Foundation, 2010), 0–7.

39. The choice of countries is based on the selection made by National Science Board (2010). Data for the first university degree in natural sciences and engineering are not available for other countries in that report. See National Science Board, *Science and Engineering Indicators 2010* (Arlington, VA: National Science Foundation, 2010), 0–7.

40. The choice of countries is based on the selection made by National Science Board (2010). Data for the first university degree in natural sciences and engineering are not available for other countries in that report. See National Science Board, *Science and Engineering Indicators 2010* (Arlington, VA: National Science Foundation, 2010), 0–8.

41. The choice of countries is based on the selection made by National Science Board (2010). Data for the first university degree in natural sciences and engineering are not available for other countries in that report. See National Science Board, *Science and Engineering Indicators 2010* (Arlington, VA: National Science Foundation, 2010), 0–8.

42. The geographical distribution of the authors indicates the size of a country's or region's research enterprise and its

ability to produce research results that can pass peer review (The choice of countries is based on the selection made by National Science Board (2010). Data for the first university degree in natural sciences and engineering are not available for other countries in that report. See National Science Board, *Science and Engineering Indicators 2010* (Arlington, VA: National Science Foundation, 2010)., 0–9). The National Science Board (*Ibid.*, 0–10) has 'articles classified by year of publication and assigned to region/country on basis of authors' institutional address(es). For articles with collaborating institutions from multiple countries/economies, each country/economy receives fractional credit on basis of proportion of its participating institutions'.

43. Asia-8 includes India, Indonesia, Malaysia, Philippines, Singapore, South Korea, Taiwan and Thailand. Asia-10 includes China, Japan and the Asia-8 (http://www.nsf.gov/statistics/seind10/c0/c0g.htm).

44. National Science Board, *Science and Engineering Indicators 2010*, 0–9.

45. National Science Board, *Science and Engineering Indicators 2010*, 0–9.

46. National Science Board, *Science and Engineering Indicators 2010*, 0–4.

47. As cited in Cheng Li's comment during a panel discussion *Chinese Foreign-Educated Returnees: Shaping China's Future* (Washington, DC: The Brookings Institution, 2010).

48. MoE, *Work Related to Students and Scholars Studying Abroad.*

49. 2008 *China Education Yearbook.*

50. Ministry of Education Action Plan, *2003–2007 Action Plan for Invigorating Education*(Beijing: Ministry of Education of the People's Republic of China, 2005), p. 29.

51. Jiabao, 'Science and China's modernization'.

5

CHAPTER

Dilemmas and Pathways to Dealing with Flood Problems in Twenty-first Century China

Guoyi Han[1,*] and Roger E. Kasperson[2]

[1] *Stockholm Environment Institute (SEI), 106 91 Stockholm, Sweden*

[2] *Graduate School of Geography, Clark University, MA 01610, USA*

ABSTRACT

With more than 60 percent of China's 1.34 billion population, about 50 percent of its most productive arable land, and the world's second largest and rapidly growing national GDP exposed to flooding of various kinds, China has an intractable flood problem. Envisioning potential impacts of climate change and continued intensification of floodplain development driven by rapid industrialization and urbanization, it is very likely that China will see a continued increase of exposure to floods this century. This overview article outlines and discusses fundamental dilemmas, plausible pathways, and key options for managing future flood risks in China in the context of rapid socioeconomic transition and climate change. Fundamental dilemmas are the embedded difficult trade-off choices, from balancing economic development with flood vulnerability reduction, to coordination and cooperation among increasingly diverse actors and across scales. Among plausible pathways, this article argues that a resilience strategy for managing flood risk is desirable. It would require human adjustment to flood, not by aiming for full protection and control but by adjusting our use of floodplains, integrating and experimenting with a wide range of flood risk management options, so that a dynamic balance is maintained between exposure and coping capacity and flood risk is contained at an acceptable level. Embracing variability and uncertainty lies at the heart of such a flood resilience centered paradigm. Reducing the flood toll cannot be had without trade-offs in economic development, food production, and agricultural productivity.

Keywords: China, flood risk dilemmas, flood management pathways, flood risk management, flood resilience strategy

INTRODUCTION

Globally, recent decades have seen rapid increases in losses due to natural disasters (UNISDR 2009). Despite progress in science and technology and the tremendous amount of atten- tion and investment, vulnerability to flood disasters, in China and the world alike, has increased. There is a range of expla- nations for such a great paradox (White, Kates, and Burton 2001; IPCC 2011). Yet, in the case of flood losses, this also reflects the fundamental dilemma concerning flood risk management—the use and development of floodplains, while increasing the exposure to floods, are also vital for improving the general well-being of the populations and the economy of regions. The problem lies in the imbalance between exposure and coping and adaptive capacity. While coping capacity has also increased as countries have developed and both economic conditions and governance have improved, the pace has not been sufficient to compensate for the increase in exposure and vulnerability, particularly in rapidly emerging economies (UNISDR 2009).

Into the twenty-first century, there has been a worldwide significant shift in the management of risks associated with river and coastal flooding (Harvey, Evans et al. 2009; Harvey, Thorne et al. 2009; Green 2010). The essence of this shift is moving away from control-oriented flood defense to a risk- based, more holistic approach, with an emphasis on system perspective and sustainability. There is now a strong recogni- tion, at least within the flood management community, that sustainable flood mitigation solutions have to be achieved through integrated actions (White 1994; APFM 2003; Cheng 2005; UNDP 2004; UNISDR 2004). This shift can be traced back to the work of geographer Gilbert F. White and others who demonstrated convincingly the inadequacy of relying on engineering solutions alone to address flood problems. It was White who first argued that, instead of trying to control nature, society needs to learn to live more compatibly with the natural occurrence of floods (White 1945; Burton 1962; Burton, Kates, and White 1978).

Embracing variability and uncertainty lies at the heart of the new flood resilience centered paradigm. The fundamental and arguably most difficult change required is therefore for decision makers and society at large to accept that it is neither possible nor necessary to control all floods. A resilience strat- egy for managing flood risk would require human adjustment to flood, not by aiming for full protection and control but by adjusting our use of floodplains, integrating and experiment- ing with a wide range of flood risk management options, so that a dynamic balance is maintained between exposure and coping capacity.

China has an intractable flood problem. Each year, China suffers billions in economic losses and hundreds to thousands of lives are lost. Looking into the future, the country's difficult flood problem is only going to become worse. By the middle of this century, China will be home to about 1.6 billion people and more than 70 percent of them will be living in cities on floodplains (Cheng 2008). If the current trends of socioeconomic development continue, China will become the largest economy in the world and close to 80 per- cent of its productivity will come from floodplains. Per capita GDP will at least quadruple its current value; thus the assets on the floodplains will keep on increasing exponentially. It is likely that climate change will also significantly increase both the intensity and the frequency of extreme weather events, making floods an even more severe threat (Shankman, Davis, and Leeuw 2009; IPCC 2011).

For millennia, China's flood management experience has predominantly centered on controlling floods through engi- neering structural measures, either by blocking or channeling the floodwater. For example, the legislative and institutional apparatus for flood management, such as the Flood Control Law of 1998, focuses primarily on controlling flood hazard and lacks almost completely any component of floodplain management, such as flood risk zoning and land-use regula- tion. To this day, there is little or no regional-scale floodplain planning (Shankman, Davis, and Leeuw 2009). Flood zoning and land-use planning measures in flood management remain at an embryonic stage (Cheng 2008).

As has been concluded by many analysts and observers, the increasing trend of flood losses, particularly during the 1990s, has stimulated a profound reflection and rethinking of flood management strategies in China (Cheng 2006; Harvey, Thorne et al. 2009). In 2003, the Ministry of Water Resources of China proposed to redirect flood prevention from flood control to flood management, which has led to a major institutional shift to enhancing understanding about intercon- nected systemic issues and risk awareness. Flood prevention work has thus shifted from attempts to eliminate floods to building capacity to live with and endure floods (GHD and IWHR 2006; Cheng 2008).

Three main aspects are central to this shift of overall strategy in flood management. First is the shift away from the notion of "full protection" to an acceptance that the flood defense system will have to be balanced with social and economic development on floodplains. Second is the shift from managing flood hazard to emphasizing the importance of floodplain management. Third is the approach to manage floods not only as a risk, but also as an opportunity and resource. This has involved a paradigmatic change from flood control to (ideally) controlled flooding. It is clear that this shift in China is consistent with and a reflection of an overall global rethinking and paradigm shift on humans' relationship with floods and how flood risk can be managed in a changing climate and an increasingly interconnected world. Embracing variability and uncertainty lies at the heart of such a new flood management paradigm.

While the shift in China from preventing flood events to managing flood risks is a fundamental step forward towards a more holistic and comprehensive approach to live with flood risk, it does not guarantee in any sense that the flood problem will be resolved. Fundamental dilemmas are entangled with flood problems in China. To what extent can vulnerability be significantly reduced without interfering with the progress in economic gains and improvements in overall well-being? To what extent are politicians as well as the general public prepared to accept the major investments that will be required for the transition to a more robust resilience strategy? What is an acceptable level of flood risk and how should it be deter- mined? Understanding the fundamental dilemmas is essential for addressing the questions that are critical for devising a strategy that charts a path through complex science-policy- practice interfaces and leads towards balanced, coordinated, and sustainable solutions.

The following two sections outline three fundamental dilemmas and three plausible scenarios of future pathways for managing flood risk in China. The article concludes with some remarks on the importance of embracing uncertainty in developing a resilience strategy.

THREE FUNDAMENTAL DILEMMAS FOR CHINA

A dilemma refers to a situation that requires a choice between options that are or seem equally unfavorable or mutually exclusive (American Heritage Dictionary). In essence, dilemmas are about making choices between alternative courses of action in which, in this case, trade-offs between risks and benefits are central and inescapable. Thus these dilemmas, by definition, defy solutions that appeal to all parties in that trade-offs exist in the course of achieving the resolution of desired societal wants or needs and these trade-offs must be balanced and negotiated.

The contextual environment for flood risks in China is now undergoing rapid change due to global processes (such as globalization and global environmental change) and regional and local processes (such as rapid urbanization, industrialization, and social transformation). Deeply embed- ded in this changing context, China faces a set of fundamental dilemmas for managing its flood risk, where trade-offs are inevitably contentious yet must be made in balancing complex relationships between risk reduction and economic development.

"Space for Water" versus "Space for People"

By definition, floodplains are the land that could and would be flooded periodically. When floodplains are settled and developed, the competition for space between people and water (that is, floods) becomes the basic dilemma. With more than 60 percent of its 1.34 billion population, about 50 percent of its most productive arable land, and close to 80 percent of the world's second largest and rapidly growing national GDP depending on floodplains, China faces intense competition between "space for water" and "space for peo- ple"—a fundamental dilemma between flood risk reduction and economic development on China's floodplains.

Nothing illustrates this dilemma more vividly than the so-called flood detention / retention area dilemma in China. Since the 1950s, an important part of China's flood manage- ment strategy has been to establish designated flood detention and retention zones to accommodate excessive waters. Currently, China has 98 such designated zones, with a total area of 35,000 km2 and a total storage capacity of about 100 billion m3. Yet, through decades of encroachment these zones now contain about 2 million hectares of cropland and more than 17 million people (Cheng 2005; Cheng 2008). Thus, in order for the designated zones to serve the intended flood adjustment function, China will have to find a way to resettle the 17 million people and change the ongoing settlement processes—not an easy dilemma to solve.

Furthermore, this difficult dilemma in all likelihood will only get worse. Within the floodplains, intensification of human activities and a shifting spatial concentration of both people and wealth will significantly increase China's exposure to floods in the coming decades. While China's population growth has slowed considerably due to the strict implementation of the one-child policy, its total population will likely grow to about 1.6 billion around 2030 before declining gradually. China will add the equivalent of the current U.S. population in the next twenty years, and the majority of this population increase will live in cities on floodplains. Even if this population intensification occurs at a slower pace than that experienced historically, the economic intensification on floodplains in the coming decades will still be tremendous and constitute a real challenge in Chinese history. It will shift the nature of the flood problem in China from a predominantly agricultural concern to an urban concern and food security threat.

This fundamental dilemma underlies the general trade-off between flood risk reduction and economic development—it is simply not possible to have both. Choices must be made, ranging from complete retreat from floodplains to bearing the full flood losses for economic gains. Anything in between is caught between irreconcilable goals. So far, the primary approach that China has employed to address this dilemma is to protect development from floods by extensive construction of flood defense infrastructures. Despite major investments, economic losses continue to increase (Cheng, Wu, and Wang 2004). The rising flood damage trend highlights the rapid increase of vulnerability due to intensification of floodplain development and assets accumulation. It also indicates the inherent limitations of the engineering approach.

Increasing flood vulnerability is essentially the result of the rapid development of China's floodplains. Vulnerability reduction thus requires a much broader approach to deal with the trade-offs between economic development and flood risk reduction in the context of multiple stresses and multiple vulnerabilities. Despite rapid development in recent decades, hundreds of millions of people in China are still living in poverty. Environmental deterioration and ecological destruc- tion are widespread and devastating (Liu and Diamond 2005). China faces the dilemma of the need to achieve overall liveli- hood improvement while seeking to build societal resilience against floods. Flood risk reduction therefore will have to be integrated into or balanced against the broader context of poverty reduction, environmental and ecosystem manage- ment, improving overall well-being (longevity, income, education, health, and so forth), and sustainable development. It is a challenge that flood managers would like to avoid.

Cooperation versus Conflict

The second fundamental dilemma in flood risk management that China faces lies in the governance challenges where coordination and cooperation are central for resolving the inevitable conflicting interests among regions and social groups. Cooperation is a key potential resource needed for any viable future flood management approach. At the same time, economic decentralization, market reform and privati- zation, and growing regional and social disparities make cooperation increasingly difficult to achieve.

Reducing vulnerability is a complex task that involves an increasingly diverse range of actors, both public and private, concerning land-use decisions and the built environment (Hall 2008). All measures designed to reduce flood risks will have different spatial and social impacts. They typically involve spatial conflict (upstream and downstream, left and right riverbanks, urban and rural) and social tensions (among social groups, priorities, and so forth), thus demanding an enlarged capacity for balancing, coordination, and coopera- tion among regions and social groups. At the same time, with economic decentralization, the centralized command and control system in China has been weakened in its ability to "force" coordination and cooperation among regions and different stakeholders. The maneuvering space for coordina- tion and cooperation is becoming increasingly small, while the actors and interests are becoming ever more diverse. A combination of balanced government and market instruments has yet to appear on the horizon. China still lacks the required and enabling institutional infrastructure. In the current Chinese flood management system, the roles of the various actors remain opaque and ill-defined and constitute major obstacles for effective coordination and cooperation.

The coordination and cooperation dilemma makes the flood risk management goal-setting process more challeng- ing. What would be an acceptable level of risk reduction against which flood risk management should be measured, monitored, and evaluated? Setting such a goal is critical yet extremely difficult and contentious. An acceptable level of flood risk will always be problematic and uncertain since it rests on a wide range of processes, factors, and conflicting values. Often, as people get richer, their demand for safety correspondingly increases. But the trade-offs between safety and wealth are highly sensitive. Making people safer and less rich may not be politically popular, because the risk reduction gains will be opaque and highly uncertain. Balancing trade- offs between short-term and long-term goals is a difficult dilemma in determining an acceptable level of flood risk.

Related to such goal-setting, a dilemma also exists with corresponding requirements for investment and capacity development. While flood response capacity will undoubt- edly increase as overall development progresses, to keep pace with increasing exposure, an extra pace of capacity develop- ment is needed. Yet who will pay for the extra pace of capac- ity development that will be required to stabilize the risk or even reduce it? What is the right balance between structural and nonstructural measures, and between government and market finances?

Coping with Changing Climate and Uncertainty

The third fundamental dilemma comes with the looming potential climate change impact, and with it, critical uncer- tainties about the patterns of future flood regimes (IPCC 2011). Planning and investment in flood protection infrastruc- tures—such as dams and dykes—depend on predicting future climate variability. But climate change brings inherent unpre- dictability of future flood hazard patterns, adding a profound uncertainty for devising flood prevention and mitigation methods and investments. The climate change dilemma requires long-term planning and resolving a series of perplexing climate change uncertainties.

On a global scale, the Intergovernmental Panel on Climate Change (IPCC) has confirmed that climate change is now altering the predictability, intensity, and geographical distri- bution of many weather-related hazards through increased intensity of the water cycle and glacial melt and sea level rise (UNISDR 2009; IPCC 2011). At a national and regional scale, impacts of climate change on flood hazards are even more uncertain, while global trends seem to be moving towards an increasing frequency and intensity of extreme events (Milly et al. 2002; UNISDR 2009). The average temperature in the Yangtze delta region, for example, is predicted to increase by between 2.3 and 3.3ºC by 2050 (NDRC 2007). This signifi- cant change in temperature is expected to lead to an array of changes in precipitation patterns, sea level rise, and coastal storm surges (Harvey, Evans et al. 2009).

From the perspective of human-environment interactions in coupled social-ecological systems, these dilemmas are all interlinked and characterized by great uncertainties, dynamic feedbacks, threshold effects, and nonlinear changes (Liu et al. 2007). They are fundamentally dilemmas between managing specific resilience (to floods) versus building a greater general resilience (Walker et al. 2004; Folke et al. 2010). These basic dilemmas place flood risk management decisions firmly in the domain of fundamental challenges to the gover- nance of complex adaptive systems and sustainability, where coordination, cooperation, and social relations are essential areas that demand innovation. With these dilemmas in mind, the next section discusses some key factors for future flood risk management, before outlining scenarios of plausible pathways.

KEY FACTORS FOR FUTURE FLOOD RISK MANAGEMENT

The looming climate change impacts and the rapidly chang- ing socioeconomic conditions in China raise serious ques- tions relating to future increases in flood risk. How will flood risk change in the coming decades, what number and level of flood events can we anticipate and prepare for? What policy interventions are available? To what extent will floods be a risk to China's long-term sustainable development? A complex array of factors shape and impact these issues.

Figure 1 is a schematic conceptual model of flood risk in the context of climate change and rapid socioeconomic transi- tion. The key factors involve: (1) the major drivers, as well as the critical uncertainties associated with these drivers and their interactions; (2) the dynamics of vulnerability as determined by the covariance between exposure and response capacity that involves short-term coping and long-term adaptive capacity; and (3) the flood management system with both structural and nonstructural measures.

The interaction of all these factors and processes deter- mines the dynamic pattern and change of flood risks and their impacts on society. Many have illustrated clearly the interac- tive nature of flood events and vulnerability in the context of a coupled human-environment system. Diverse drivers— natural, human, and technical—act as pressure or multiple stresses on the flood risk system, leading to dynamic changes of the control variables that affect and reshape both the pattern of hazard and the system's vulnerability to floods. The dynamics of vulnerability cannot be explained solely either by exposure (for example, population growth and intensification of economic activities) or response capacity (including both short-term coping and long-term adaptive capacities), but are the result of interactive change of both, or the covariance between them (Han 2011).

The key drivers for future flood risks in China are rapid socioeconomic transition, climate change, and the flood defense system itself. While the relative importance of these drivers will vary across river basins, they all are expected to experience major changes in the coming decades. The most challenging drivers for policy and decision makers are those associated with the highest levels of both risk importance and uncertainty, for example, potential climate change.

There is a general linkage between development stage and the pattern of losses from natural disasters. It is often the case that vulnerability tends to rise faster during the phase of transition (Sylves and Kershaw 2004). China today is in the midst of rapid urbanization and industrialization, which will almost certainly continue to increase human exposure to floods. Rapid urbanization, for example, acts as both pathway and receptor in terms of increasing flood risk. As a pathway, urban expansion increases the proportion of the impermeable surfaces and intensifies runoff. The general trend of current urban development decreases storage and drainage capacity for storm water, and heightens the vulnerability of cities to floods and waterlogging (Shi et al. 2005; Harvey, Evans et al. 2009).

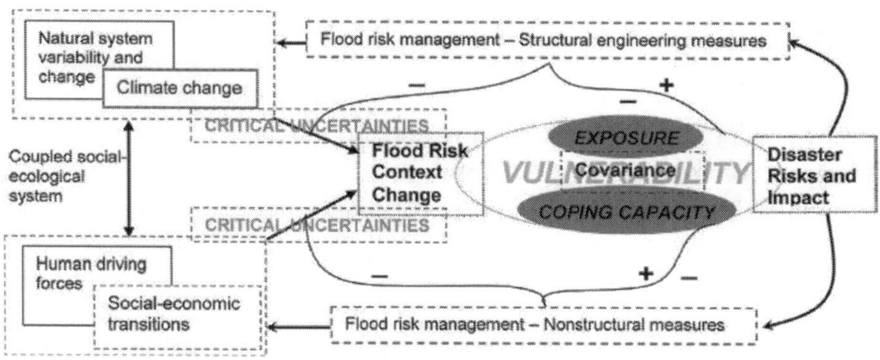

Figure 1. Conceptual model of flood risk in the context of climate change and rapid socioeconomic transition

In relation to the dynamics of vulnerability, the impact surrounding uncertainties arising from the changing socio- economic transitions lies in whether and to what extent the growth of response capacity can match or exceed the increase in exposure (Kundzewicz and Menzel 2003). Examined globally, societal change and economic development are the chief culprits for increasing losses. If the current trends con- tinue, global disaster losses will continue to outpace average economic growth (Bouwer et al. 2007).

In the coming decades, the transformation of the flood management system in China, spurred by ongoing institu- tional shifts, is a critical process that will determine both the direction and pace of flood response capacity change. The critical uncertainties in this respect reside not only with leadership and investment, but also in capacity development at all levels.

China's waterscape has been profoundly human- transformed and the transformation continues with massive water engineering projects such as the Three Gorges Dam and the ongoing South-North Water Transfer. From a system perspective, these transformations will continue to trigger new feedbacks that change the dynamics of the hydrological regimes, which in turn interact with the changing climate and social economic conditions to set the basic parameters for future flood risks in China. Integrating the above system dynamics from the interactions between climate and socio- economic change with uncertainties to form scenarios is a key for robust, flexible, and sustainable risk reduction in the future (Schanze 2009).

PATHWAYS FOR THE FUTURE—SCENARIOS

With growing realization of the limited predictability of com- plex adaptive systems, scenarios are gaining recognition as a useful way for examining future changes. A series of recent scenario-based future risk studies have all confirmed that losses from weather-related disasters are projected to increase, due to a combination of the increasing exposure of people and assets and expected changes in the global climate. In the Netherlands, Bouwer, Bubeck, and Aerts (2010) found that due to socioeconomic change alone, annual expected losses may increase by between 35 and 172 percent by 2040, as compared with a baseline situation in 2000. If no additional measures are taken to reduce flood probabilities or consequences, by 2040 a combination of climate and socioeconomic changes may increase expected losses by between

96 and 719 percent. In the United Kingdom, the Flood Foresight project concluded that expected annual flood damages may increase twentyfold by the 2080s if flood risk management policy were to remain as it is at present (Evans et al. 2004; Hall, Sayers, and Dawson 2005). In Japan, Ikeda, Sato, and Fukuzono (2008) developed various flood risk scenarios in their search for resilient social systems against flood disasters.

In China, similar research is currently under-way in the Taihu (Tai Lake) basini through a China-UK scientific coop- eration project initiated in late 2006, which adopted the UK Foresight Project scenario approach (Harvey, Evans et al. 2009). While uncertainties exist in all the scenarios, given China's current development trend, there is little doubt that China's future flood losses will increase. This is not, however, to say that China's vulnerability to flood must also increase. The future state of flood risks in China will not only be influ- enced by critical uncertainties within the key drivers (for example, the speed and scale of climate and socioeconomic changes) (see Figure 1), but also by human choices that China makes today and along the way. Those choices will largely determine the pathway through which China's flood risk management system will evolve.

To highlight the different pathways, three plausible future flood risk management scenarios are outlined below. The underlying logic for constructing the scenarios is the priority- setting on dealing with the trade-offs between flood risk reduction and economic development. In the first scenario, China maximizes economic development while continuing to deal with floods largely through engineering approaches. In the second scenario, China prioritizes flood vulnerability reduction by developing and enforcing strict floodplain land- use regulations to limit and control floodplain development. The third scenario outlines a pathway of "living with floods" in which building resilience is achieved through embracing and internalizing, rather than controlling, variability and uncertainty in balancing flood risk reduction and economic development.

Controlling Floods—Continuation of the Engineering Approach

This is the more or less "business as usual" scenario in which China maximizes economic development while it continues its massive investment in structural measures to control floods. In the short term, economic gains and a technocratic bias will very likely make this pathway irresistible. But in the long term, the result of this pathway will lead China to be increasingly locked into a highly rigid system vulnerable to catastrophic floods, a likely "building up for disaster" scenario.

Over a span of more than half a century since 1949, China has constructed a massive flood control structure system, including more than 85,000 reservoirs of various sizes,ii a total of 286,900 km of dykes/levees of various standards,iii and close to 100 designated flood detention and retention (storage) zones with a total area of 35,000 km2 and a total volume of 103 billion m3. Together, these measures form an extensive and effective flood defense system that has played a crucial role in flood control in China, reducing the annual inundation area by about 70 percent (as compared with that of 1949) and reducing loss of life dramatically. In the 1950s, the average annual casualties due to floods in China were 8976; this number was reduced to 1507 in the first decade of the twenty-first century (Cheng 2008).

While engineering protection has reduced the total area and frequency of inundation, the economic losses have grown enormously. Flood-related damage (yuan per hectare) has increased from 2190 in the 1960s to 12,120 in the 1980s and more than 20,000 in the 1990s on a national average. In rapidly developed areas such as the Tai Lake basin in the Yangtze delta, it has increased from 5565 in the 1960s to more than 30,000 in the 1980s (Shi and Pan 1997).

While structural approaches to flood control are essential to reduce flood losses, they have now reached a point where further expansion has become largely unsustainable. First, the "dyke syndrome" or the "dyke effect" (that is, dyke protec- tion induces further development of floodplains that result in further demand for higher dykes) has been increasingly recognized as a driver for the erosion of long-term flood resilience of flood-prone human-environment systems. This has resulted in a continuously worsening discharge and flood level relationship.

Second, the cost-effectiveness of raising dykes/levees has been limited by economic, technological, and environmental constraints. Table 1 shows the investment feasibility calcu- lated by the Institute of Water and Hydropower Research under the Ministry of Water Resources of China. It is extremely difficult to achieve the cost-effectiveness that is required (Xiang 2003).

Third, the existing flood control structures require tremen- dous investment in quality assurance and maintenance. More than one-third of the 85,000 reservoirs in China now require serious repairs.iv The levee systems along the major rivers are the result of centuries of construction, with extremely mixed quality and serious defects. Since 1998, more than 30 billion yuan have been invested in the levees in the middle and lower Yangtze River alone. Most of the investment has been in repair and infrastructure strengthening (Xiang 2003; Cheng 2006).

Lastly, China is running out of places to construct major water infrastructures. With the completion of the Three Gorges Dam on the Yangtze River, the Xiaolangdi Dam on the Yellow River, the Feilaixia Dam on the Pearl River, and the Nierji Dam on the Nen River in the Northeast, China has now basically run out of possible sites for major water control engineering constructions. In addition, many other factors (such as resettlement and migration and ecological impacts) are now raising heightened concerns about new dam construction.

If China cannot break away from the current heavy reliance on its water engineering approach to flood control, one plausible future state of its flood risk system is an increasingly rigid system in which major investment is locked into the vicious circle of increasing and maintaining the protection standard of the dyke/levee system. At the same time, the natural flood carrying capacity of the rivers as well as the riverine ecosystems will remain in continuous decline, and waterlogging in cities will become intractable.

Table 1. Feasibility of flood loss reduction by raising levee protection standards

Current annual average river flood losses (billion yuan)	Loss reduction (%)	Loss reduction benefit (billion yuan)	Investment required for feasible engineering construction (billion yuan)
25	10	2.5	<30
	30	7.5	<90
	50	12.5	<150

Source: Xiang 2003.

While it sounds highly undesirable, this scenario is not only plausible but highly likely. This is the least-resisted path- way in the existing system because it simply requires doing business more or less as usual. In addition, compared to many developed countries, the standard of the flood control struc- tures in China still has much catching up to do. For example, while Japan and China share a very similar percentage in population and assets on the floodplains, most cities in Japan are protected for 500- to 1000-year floods whereas most of the cities in China currently are only protected for 20- to 50-year floods. Furthermore, controlling floods is politically and socially much more straightforward than dealing with vulnerability reduction. Last but not least, many nested inter-ests or "systemic institutional inertia" resist transformative changes (Ostrom 2004, 2007).

Reducing Vulnerability—Strict Regulation of the Floodplains

This is a scenario in which China prioritizes flood risk reduc- tion and attempts to reverse the trend of increasing economic losses to floods by interfering and shaping developments on its floodplains. While a range of floodplain management options is available and need to be explored in China to strengthen the virtually nonexistent nonstructural measures for flood risk reduction, the biggest challenge for this path- way is how far it can go without interfering with economic development. Given China's extremely high dependence on its floodplains, a pathway that prioritizes flood risk reduction by limiting economic development will almost certainly encounter tremendous difficulties.

Floodplain management for flood risk reduction is a particularly weak component in flood management in China. There are still many win-win solutions where integrative floodplain management can achieve both economic develop- ment and flood vulnerability reduction. Table 2 shows some initial results of the future flood risk scenario study in the Tai Lake basin, with a focus on the scope of risk reduction by careful land-use planning (Wang, Cheng, and Yu 2010). In all of the three scenarios they have analyzed—socioeconomic change only; climate change only; and combined impacts of socioeconomic and climate change—there is significant scope of potential flood loss reduction through careful risk mitigation-oriented land-use planning, which is nonexistent at present. Yet, in all three scenarios, even with careful land-use planning, expected annual flood losses will continue to increase, ranging from 3.64 to 8.01 billion yuan per year by 2050.[v]

The positive results of this pathway would push China towards a more balanced approach between structural and nonstructural measures for flood risk management. But reversing the trend of increasing economic losses to floods in the future without major interference with the current trend of development intensification in the floodplains, both urbanization and industrialization, is highly unlikely.

Building Resilience—Living with Floods

The third potential pathway incorporates components from the two previous scenarios and rests on a series of changes that embrace variability and uncertainties, thus moving towards a strategy of building resilience and living with floods. Many regional flood studies have identified the need to break the feedback loops that have resulted in increasingly fragile and rigid systems with continuously declining capacity in coping with flood and waterlogging. Resilience strategies, such as the "space for water" program to regain the system's natural flood adjustment capacity, are essential for achieving the sustainability of flood risk management in the future.

In this scenario, the current flood management institutional shift in China takes strong root in the coming years. China moves to adopt a resilience flood risk management strategy that seeks to restore the feedbacks required for a resilient and adaptable flood risk system in the future. A series of principal changes are critical for this scenario. First, the objective in flood risk management is not solely to reduce flood losses but to ensure the good functioning of human-environment systems on the floodplains in terms of the overall benefits from human use and ecosystem services and functions, taking into account risks and uncertainties associated with flooding (Green 2010). Risk management focuses not only on flood losses, but on anticipating the "threshold" or "boundary" losses that could fundamentally undermine the sustainability of the system. In this perspective, the absolute number of direct flood economic losses may not be as important as the ratio of such losses to GDP, since the latter can serve as a boundary or threshold variable that must be managed. Figure 2 shows the direct economic losses and their corresponding ratio to GDP in China from 1991 to 2004. It is clear that while the two are certainly correlated, their trends can be different depending on economic (GDP) development. For instance, while the direct economic losses in 1991 were roughly the same as in 2002, the loss to GDP ratio was significantly lower in 2002. The losses in 2002 were much less of a disturbance to the system than those in 1991.

Table 2. Expected future flood risks in the Tai Lake basin and benefit of land-use planning

	Scenarios	2050– Socioeconomic change only	2050– Climate change only	2050– Socioeconomic and climate change
Expected annual damage (billion yuan)	Without land-use planning	6.69	7.14	13.23
	With land-use planning	3.95	3.64	8.01
Benefits of land-use planning (billion yuan/year)		2.75	3.50	5.23

Source: Wang, Cheng, and Yu 2010.

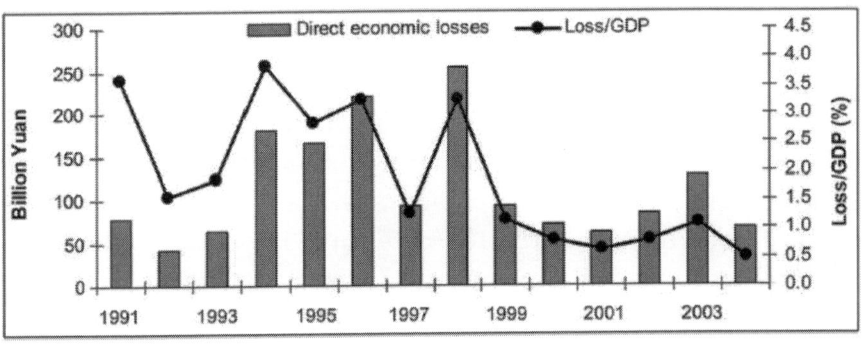

Figure 2. Direct economic losses due to floods and their ratio to GDP in China: 1991–2004

In the near future, China could focus on two specific goals in this respect. One is to aim for a continued reduction in the loss of life due to floods. With continued socioeconomic development and improvement of general well-being, exces- sive loss of life due to floods will be increasingly unaccept- able, socially and politically.vi The other goal should be to lower the ratio of flood economic loss to GDP, which on average stands around 1 percent in the early twenty-first century in China, considerably higher than that in most flood- prone developed countries such as the United States (average ratio 0.03 percent) or Japan (0.2 percent) (Xiang 2003).

Second, effective flood management strategies are based on experimenting and learning to live with floods; land-use adaptation is essential (Klijn, van Buuren, and van Rooij 2004). A full range of floodplain management tools can and should be used to address the flooding problems in China, but the combination and integrated application of those tools will vary among places and communities. Their effectiveness will have to be assessed locally (White 1945, 1974, 1994). Since 1998, the implementation of the "space for water" program in China has encountered tremendous difficulties, partly due to the strict and inflexible top-down scheme that overlooks local dynamics and regional variations.

Third, "controlled flooding" can be applied innovatively as a central strategy to deal with and embrace natural vari- ability and uncertainty. It seeks to manage floods not only as hazards but also as a resource. Controlled flooding seeks to allow places to be flooded when there is excessive water but is flooding by design in terms of locations and sequences. It is a way to accommodate and retain the natural river dynamics and, at the same time, to minimize flood losses and maximize the benefit of natural floods. In the coming decade, major investment can be made to modify and readjust the existing massive flood defense structures so they are adapted from flood control to controlled flooding. The designated flood detention and retention areas (with a total area of about 5 percent of the flood-prone areas) would be the prior- ity areas to initiate such experiments. One critical enabling condition to make the controlled flooding approach plausible is the rapid technological advancement in recent decades in flood forecasting, real-time monitoring, and transformative changes in communication technology (White 1998).

While a resilience flood risk management approach is possible, implementation of such a strategy often is beset with major socioeconomic dilemmas, such as balancing and accepting major investment in the short term while seeing benefits only in the long term. Shifting the short-term, small- scale rationality to the long-term and large-scale rationality that a resilience strategy requires is not only a challenge for Chinese society, but globally a major obstacle for the pursuit of sustainability (Klijn, van Buuren, and van Rooij 2004; Turner 2010). As illustrated by the Dongting Lake case (Han 2011), or the Poyang Lake case (Shankman, Davis, and Leeuw 2009) and Tai Lake (Taihu) case (Harvey, Thorne et al. 2009), a resilience strategy requires many trade-offs, each of which embodies a range of difficult social, economic, and political issues including investment, compensation, social justice and social stability, poverty reduction, ecosystem services, and biodiversity.

Looking into future flood risks in China, a broader approach is needed, which integrates comprehensively the vulnerability components and aims for building resilience. Until that is done, the "dyke syndrome" will remain and the vicious circle of "higher dyke—more development—even higher dyke" will continue. Ultimately, it is a hard choice to make between less return and more resilient and more short-term gains and less resilient in the long run. So far, few modern societies have chosen the resilience path. To do so requires nothing less than a paradigm shift to embrace rather than control and eliminate variability and uncertainty. That requires fundamental change in the way we perceive the world, what we believe, and the ways we act (Holling 1996, 2001).

CONCLUSIONS

By outlining three fundamental dilemmas and three plausible pathways for managing future flood risk in China, this article concludes:

As the development on floodplains in China continues and intensifies in the coming decades, climate change will very likely increase both the intensity and the frequency of extreme weather events. Accordingly, China will need to learn to live with an increasing vulnerability to flood risk in the foreseeable future. To reduce human vulnerability to floods, multiple pathways exist but all involve difficult trade-offs. Hard choices are inevitable and inescapable.

China needs a new flood management strategy—one that incorporates vulnerability reduction and resilience building. Compared with the traditional engineering approach, a resil- ience approach requires not only changing the focus from modifying flood hazard events to reducing vulnerability. But it is also essential to embrace and internalize variability and uncertainty in decision making. The latter is essential for changing the management bias from community prepared- ness achieving full protection or zero flood risk. While vulnerability reduction must be integrated into overall devel- opment planning, society will always be vulnerable as long as people live in and develop floodplains.

A resilience strategy for managing flood risk thus requires human adjustment to flood, but not an approach aiming for full protection and control but for adapting human uses of floodplains, integrating, and experimenting with a wide range of flood risk management options. In this way, a reasonably dynamic balance, while not perfect, can be achieved between exposure and response capacity, and flood risk can be contained at a level judged to be socially and economically acceptable.

While a resilience strategy embodies a wide range of opportunities for long-term sustainable flood risk prevention and mitigation, it also raises major challenges. China faces major dilemmas in managing its future flood risks. Trade-offs between economic development and flood vulnerability reduction and between cooperation and tensions across diverse actors and scales cannot be escaped.

Floods are part of Chinese culture, and for many in the floodplains a way of life. Moving from flood control to controlled flooding is a strategic choice towards living with floods in its true meaning. It requires a broad flood risk management approach that is centered on vulnerability reduction and resilience building of the social-ecological system within which the overall goal of sustainability is considered paramount and overall well-being is pursued.

An effective flood risk strategy will only emerge as a result of social learning and innovation and through human interac- tions with the flood risk system. Embracing variability and uncertainty will be the departure point. Given the past thirty years of transformative changes in the country, China may be a place where such a policy experiment and innovation are not only timely but also embraced.

ACKNOWLEDGMENT

This work was partly supported by the Risk and Hazard Science Base (111 Project) at the State Key Laboratory of Earth Surface Processes and Resource Ecology, Beijing Normal University, China.

NOTES

i. Taihu (Tai Lake) is the third largest fresh water body in China, with an area of over 2000 km2. The drainage basin of the Tai Lake covers 36,985 km2, including some of the most economically developed areas in the delta region of the Yangtze River.

ii. In 1949, China had only six large reservoirs. The 42,000 km levees were in poor condition.

iii. In comparison, this number in the United States is about 40,000 km. In Japan it is less than 10,000 km, in the Netherlands it is about 4800 km, and in India 20,000 km.

iv. According to the Ministry of Water Resources, there were 30,413 (36 percent of the total) "sick and dangerous" reservoirs in China in 2009: of these 143 were large reservoirs, and 1118 were medium- sized reservoirs. These reservoirs now present a severe source of flooding risks threatening hundreds of millions of people and huge areas of cropland.

v. Current annual average flood economic losses amount to less than 2 billion yuan in the Taihu basin; in the 1990s the annual average flood economic losses were around 70 billion yuan nationwide (Xiang 2003).

vi. The annual average loss of life due to floods in China is still above 2000 people.

REFERENCES

1. APFM (Associated Programme on Flood Management). 2003. *Integrated Flood Management: Concept Paper*. Technical Document No.1. Geneva: The Associated Programme on Flood Management.

2. Bouwer, L., P. Bubeck, and J. Aerts. 2010. Changes in Future Flood Risk due to Climate and Development on a Dutch Polder Area. *Global Environmental Change* 20(3): 463–471.

3. Bouwer, L. M., R. P. Crompton, E. Faust, and P. Höppe. 2007. Confronting Disaster Losses. *Science* 318(5851): 753.

4. Burton, I. 1962. *Types of Agricultural Occupance of Flood Plains in the United States*. Research Paper No. 75. Chicago: Department of Geography, University of Chicago.

5. Burton, I., R. W. Kates, and G. F. White. 1978. *The Environment as Hazard*. New York: Oxford University Press.

6. Cheng, X. T. 2005. Changes of Flood Control Situations and Adjustments of Flood Management Strategies in China. *Water International* 30(1): 108–113.

7. —. 2006. Recent Progress in Flood Management in China. *Irrigation and Drainage* 55(s1): 75–82.

8. —. 2008. Recent Progress in Flood and Drought Management Research. *Journal of the Institute of Water Resources and Hydropowe r Research of China* 6(3): 191–198 (in Chinese).

9. Cheng, X. T., Y. C. Wu, and Y. Y. Wang. 2004. On the New Concepts of Flood Management and Flood Security Systems. Beijing: China WaterPower Press (in Chinese).

10. Evans, E. P., R. Ashley, J. W. Hall, E. Penning-Rowsell, P. B. Sayers, C. R Thorne, and A. Watkinson. 2004. *Foresight. Future Flooding. Scientific Summary: Volume I—Future Risks and their Drivers*. London: Office of Science and Technology.

11. Folke, C., S. R. Carpenter, B. Walker, M. Scheffer, T. Chapin, and J. Rockström. 2010. Resilience Thinking: Integrating Resilience, Adaptability and Transformability. *Ecology and Society* 15(4). Article 20. http://www.ecologyandsociety.org/vol15/iss4/art20/.

12. GHD and IWHR (Institute of Water Resources and Hydropower Research). 2006. *National Flood Management Strategy Study*. Zhengzhou: Yellow River Water Press (in Chinese).

13. Green, C. 2010. Towards Sustainable Flood Risk Management. *International Journal of Disaster Risk Science* 1(1): 33–43.

14. Hall, J. 2008. Editorial. *Journal of Flood Risk Management* 1(3): 131–132.

15. Hall, J. W., P. B. Sayers, and R. J. Dawson. 2005. National Scale Flood Risk Assessment of Current and Future Flood Risk in England and Wales. *Natural Hazards* 36(1–2): 147–164.

16. Han, G. Y. 2011. *Understanding Regional Dynamics of Vulnerability: A Historical Approach to the Flood Problem in China*. Ph.D. Dissertation. Graduate School of Geography, Clark University, Worcester, MA, USA.

17. Harvey, G. L., E. P. Evans, C. R. Thorne, and X. T. Cheng. 2009. *Scenario Analysis Technology for River Basin Flood Risk Management in the Taihu Basin: A China-UK Scientific Cooperation Project*. Discussion Paper 44. Nottingham: China Policy Institute, University of Nottingham.

18. Harvey, G. L., C. R. Thorne, X. T. Cheng, E. P. Evans, S. Han, J. D. Simm, and Y. Wang. 2009. Qualitative Analysis of Future Flood Risk in the Taihu Basin, China. *Journal of Flood Risk Management* 2(2): 85–100.

19. Holling, C. S. 1996. Surprise for Science, Resilience for Ecosystems, and Incentives for People. *Ecological Applications* 6(3): 733–735.

20. —. 2001. Understanding the Complexity of Economic, Social and Ecological Systems. *Ecosystems* 4(5): 390–405.

21. Ikeda, S., T. Sato, and T. Fukuzono. 2008. Towards an Integrated Management Framework for Emerging Disaster Risks in Japan. *Natural Hazards* 44(2): 267–280.

22. IPCC (Intergovernmental Panel on Climate Change). 2011. Summary for Policymakers. In *Intergovernmental Panel on Climate Change Special Report on Managing the Risks of*

Extreme Events and Disasters to Advance Climate Change Adaptation, edited by C. B. Field, V. Barros, T. F. Stocker, D. Qin, D. Dokken, K. L. Ebi, M. D. Mastrandrea, K. J. Mach, G.-K. Plattner, S. Allen, M. Tignor, and P. M. Midgley. Cambridge and New York: Cambridge University Press.

23. Klijn, F., M. van Buuren, and S. van Rooij. 2004. Flood-Risk Management Strategies for an Uncertain Future: Living with Rhine River Floods in the Netherlands? *Ambio* 33(3): 141–147.

24. Kundzewicz, Z., and L. Menzel. 2003. Flood Risk and Vulnerability in the Changing World. Paper presented at the International Conference: Towards Natural Flood Reduction Strategies, 6–13 September, Warsaw, Poland.

25. Liu, J. G., and J. Diamond. 2005. China's Environment in a Globalizing World. *Nature* 435(7046): 1179–1186

26. Liu, J. G., T. Dietz, S. Carpenter, M. Alberti, C. Folke, E. Moran, A. N. Pell, P. Deadman, et al. 2007. Complexity of Coupled Human and Natural Systems. *Science* 317(5844): 1513-1516.

27. Milly, P. C. D., R. T. Wetherald, K. A. Dunne, and T. L. Delworth. 2002. Increasing Risk of Great Floods in Changing Climate. *Nature* 415(6871): 514–517.

28. NDRC (National Development and Reform Commission). 2007. *China's National Climate Change Programme*. Beijing: National Development and Reform Commission, People's Republic of China.

29. Ostrom, E. 2004. Book Review of *Panarchy: Understanding Transformations in Human and Natural Systems*: Lance H. Gunderson and C. S. Holling (Eds.), Island Press, Washington, DC, 2002, ISBN: 1559638575, 450 pp. *Ecological Economics* 49 (4): 488–91.

30. —. 2007. A Diagnostic Approach for Going beyond Panaceas. *PNAS* 104(39): 15181–151887.

31. Schanze, J. 2009. Editorial. *Journal of Flood Risk Management* 2(3):149–150.

32. Shankman, D., L. Davis, and J. de Leeuw. 2009. River Management, Landuse Change, and Future Flood Risk in China's Poyang Lake Region. *International Journal of River Basin Management* 7(4): 423–431.

33. Shi, P. J., Y. Ge, Y. Yuan, and W. P. Guo. 2005. Integrated Risk Management of Flood Disasters in Metropolitan Areas of China. *Internationa l Journal of Water Resources Development* 21(4): 613–627.

34. Shi, P. J., and Y. Z. Pan. 1997. Flood, Typhoon and Storm Surge Disaster in China. Paper presented at the Seminar on Natural Perils and Insurance/Reinsurance Techniques. September 1997, Beijing, China.

35. Sylves, R., and P. J. Kershaw. 2004. *Reducing Future Flood Losses: The Role of Human Actions* (Summary of the Disasters Roundtable, March 2, 2004). Washington, DC: National Research Council and National Academies Press.

36. Turner, B. L., II. 2010. Vulnerability and Resilience: Coalescing or Paralleling Approaches for Sustainability Science? *Global Environmental Change* 20(4): 570–576.

37. UNDP (United Nations Development Programme). 2004. *A Global Report: Reducing Disaster Risk—A Challenge for Development.* New York: United Nations Development Programme.

38. UNISDR (United Nations International Strategy for Disaster Reduction). 2004. *Guidelines for Reducing Flood Losses*. Geneva: United Nations International Strategy for Disaster Reduction.

39. —. 2009. *Global Assessment Report on Disaster Risk Reduction: Risk and Poverty in a Changing Climate*. Geneva: United Nations International Strategy for Disaster Reduction.

40. Walker, B., C. S. Holling, S. R. Carpenter, and A. Kinzig. 2004. Resilience, Adaptability and Transformability in Social-Ecological Systems. *Ecology and Society* 9(2). Article 5. http://www.ecologyandsociety.org/vol9/iss2/art5/.

41. Wang, Y. Y., X. T. Cheng, and C. Q. Yu. 2010. The Benefit of Land Use Planning of Taihu Basin. Workshop Presentation at the International Policy-Oriented Discussions—International Flood Risk Management Approaches: From Theory to Practice, November 30–December 1, 2010, Washington, DC. http://www.nfrmp.us/ifrma/docs/pre/summary/YanyanPaper.pdf.

42. White, G. F. 1945. *Human Adjustment to Floods: A Geographical Approach to the Flood Problem in the United States*. Research Paper No. 29. Chicago: Department of Geography, University of Chicago.

43. —, ed. 1974. *Natural Hazards: Local, National, Global*. New York: Oxford University Press.

44. —. 1994. Testimony and Prepared Statement for the "Midwest Floods of 1993: Flood Control and Floodplain Policy and Proposal: Hearing before the Subcommittee on Water Resources and Environment," October 27, 1993, 103d Congress, 1st Session, House Committee on Public Works and Transportation. Washington, DC: US Government Printing Office.

45. —. 1998. Looking toward the Horizon: Prospects for Floodplain Managers. Paper Read at Floodplain Management in a Multifaced World—Proceedings of the 21st Annual Conference, April 28–May 2, 1998, Little Rock, Arkansas.

46. White, G. F., R. W. Kates, and I. Burton. 2001. Knowing Better and Losing Even More: The Use of Knowledge in Hazards Management. *Environmental Hazards* 3(3–4): 81–92.

47. Xiang, L. Y. 2003. Comparative Study of Flood Management Strategies between China and Selected Countries. *Water Resources Development Research* 3(5): 12–18 (in Chinese).

48. Yang, K. 2005. Flood Emergency Management in China. Paper presente d at the ICID 21st European Regional Conference 2005, May 15–19, Frankfurt (Oder) and Slubice, Germany and Poland.

6

CHAPTER

Cultural Consciousness of Chinese Ethnic Minority under the Economic Globalization

Hongyu Xie[1,2]*, Jidong Yi[2], Jianhou Gan[2]

[1]*College of Travelism and Geography Sciences, Yunnan Normal University, Kunming, China*

[2]*Key Laboratory of Educational Informalization for Nationalities, Ministry of Education, Yunnan Normal University, Kunming, China*

ABSTRACT

Culture is the soul of a nation, and national culture is the sign which distinguishes other ethnics. National culture is the direct reflection of cultural consciousness in real life, and cultural consciousness is the basic of national culture. The ethnical culture is easy to be impacted by the foreign culture under the rapid development of information globalization in China. As study subjects, 291 people of Shilin Autonomous in Yunnan province answered the questionnaire and investigator also made a random interview among the 291 people. Through the questionnaires and statistical analysis of the EXCEL 2003 and DELPHL method, the conclusion is the following: the ethnic cultural consciousness of Yi people in Shilin Autonomous County is rather weak today in China, the most obvious aspects showed on the ethnical language, folk dancing and costumes, festive culture and so on. At last, this paper suggested that people should protect their own culture under the strong urbanization and economic development. How to protect and develop the culture of the ethnic minority is an urgent matter in China.

Keywords: Yunnan; Ethnical Culture; Globalization; Urbanization

1. INTRODUCTION

Cultural consciousness of nationalities has long been paid close attention to by many experts and studiers throughout the world. So is there any problem about the cultural consciousness of nationalities among the ethnical people? The answer seems to be positive since the rapid development of information globalization in the last few decades. In the Chinese modern and contemporary history, both the conservatives and liberalists share a cultural anxiety in terms of the problems in modernity and nationalism. How to deal with this cultural anxiety is an important theoretic problem as well as a political, economic and cultural problem [1] . Numerous studies had been published in recent years regarding that there exists many problems on the heritage of traditional culture. In the wave of globalization today, the traditional culture among ethnic minorities is in the status of fracture and reconstruction, which those demise on the traditional culture universal in China [2] . It is an inevitable trend that the economic globalization will lead to the cultural globalization, economic power derived from cultural power [3] . Globalization may also be a cultural trap, which "smooth" the diversity of human cultural differences through the economic expansion and political coercion, so that let the human civilization and culture loses its natural, and at last it will become tedious.

Shilin Autonomous County is mainly dominated in the ethnic Yi who account for about 97% of the total population. There are ethnics of Sani, black Yi, white Yi, Yi pro, a fine, Ah Yi son. Ethnic Yi has a long history and ancient culture in Chinese ethnic minorities, and the total population is no less than ethnics of Zhuang, Manchu, Hui, and Uygur which ranked the fifth of the ethnics in China. The amazing scenery and vast fertile land nurtured Yi people generation by generation, but also gave birth to the Yi people rich history and colorful ethnical cultures [4] .

Ethnic Yi has its own language, there are six kinds of tongues; and they also have their own calendar; music and dancing. The traditional arts and crafts like embroidery, silver, sculpture, painting are all rich in national characteristics. In the ethnic Yi Autonomous, the most solemn festival is the Torch, Torch Festival usually hold in Lunar June 25th, people point the torch, dance and sing around the blazing burning fire in the night. In 2006, Shilin County declared "Ashima" which was selected the first batch of national intangible cultural heritage, and the serial number is 28.

The ethnical culture is easy to be impacted by the foreign culture under the rapid development of information globalization, marketing economy and urbanization [5] [6] . The rise of industrialization and tourism in Shilin Autonomous has its advantages and disadvantages, it not only bring the opportunities of innovating and developing their own culture, but also affect the lives of ethnic Yi people, and the culture is changing constantly.

2. METHOD OF EVALUATING NATIONAL CULTURAL CONSCIOUSNESSES

The purpose of evaluating of national cultural consciousnesses is that it will provide a scientific basis for cultural heritage and development.

2.1. Participants

The participants are the ethnic Yi people from seven major towns of Shilin County in Yunnan province; they are Lufu Town, Shilin Town, Banqiao Town, Changhu Town, Gui Town, Xi Jiekou Town and Dahe Country. 300 people were surveyed randomly who were from those seven towns with different levels and different ages. At last, there were 291 valid questionnaires, so the effective rate of recovery is 97.00% (see Table 1). Meanwhile, some ethnic Yi people were interviewed during the investigation.

2.2. Questionnaire

2.2.1. Definitions of 7 Kinds of Cultural Consciousness

There are 7 kinds of cultural consciousness in this paper, they are cognitive consciousness of national culture (NCC1), concerning consciousness of national culture (NCC2), participating consciousness of national culture (NCP1), behavior consciousness of national culture (NCB), protecting consciousness of national culture (NCP2), inheriting consciousness of national culture (NCI1), innovating consciousness of national culture (NCI2), the following are the definitions of them.

NCC1—It is a consciousness of getting the national cultural knowledge through people's mental activity, such as the formation of the concept, perception, judgment or imagined.

NCC2—It is a consciousness of treating national culture with people's eyes or the practical action.

NCP1—It is a consciousness of integrating cultural things by the identity of the second or the third party.

Table 1. Basic situations of investigated residents.

Items	Categories	Numbers	Percentage (%)
Sex	Male	191	65.6
	Female	100	34.3
Sites	Lufu Town	40	13.7
	Shilin Town	41	13.8
	Banqiao Town	40	13.7
	Changhu Town	39	13.6
	Guishan Town	32	10.9
	Xi Jiekou Town	29	9.9
	Dahe Town	70	24.4
Age	7 - 18	6	2.1
	19 - 35	68	23.4
	36 - 45	51	17.5
	45 - 60	99	34.0
	60 - 83	67	23.0
Educational level	Primary	97	33.0
	Junior	102	35.3
	Senior	46	15.8
	Undergraduate	30	10.3
	Graduate	16	6.6
Profession	Student	61	21.0
	Worker	14	4.8
	Teacher	17	5.8
	Farmer	155	53.3
	Doctor	8	2.7
	Driver	1	0.3
	Other	35	12.0

NCB—It is a consciousness of doing something about the culture through the usual activity.
NCP2—It is a consciousness of caring of so that the culture can not be encountered from injury, damage or harmful influence.
NCI1—It is a consciousness of accepting the culture from ancestors.
NCI2—It is a consciousness of innovating culture with the new thinking, new inventions and new features.

2.2.2. Questionnaire Designing

There are 2 parts in the questionnaire designing; the first part is basic situations of investigated residents, including the site where the participants belong to, gender, age, educational level and occupational range. The second part is the survey of cultural consciousness for nationalities, including cognitive consciousness of national culture (NCC1), concerning consciousness of national culture (NCC2), participating consciousness of national culture

(NCP1), behavior consciousness of national culture (NCB), protecting consciousness of national culture (NCP2), inheriting consciousness of national culture (NCI1), innovating consciousness of national culture (NCI2).

2.2.3. Questionnaire Distribution

The survey mainly used questionnaires and interviews; the investigation time was in November 2012-November 2013. And the survey in the seven towns sites were focused on the following: 1) school survey: the subjects were students and teachers, investigators hand out the questionnaires to the people with the issuance of school, and made a interview to some subjects; 2) community survey: the questionnaire were distributed randomly in the community, investigators let the participants fill the questionnaire face to face, if the subjects were uneducated, the investigators would quiz and fill the questionnaires.

2.3. Process of Evaluating National Cultural Consciousnesses

There are two main tools of statistics, one is the EXCEL 2003, and the other is the VISUL FOXPRO 6.0, so that the results are summarized by them.

2.3.1. Establishment of Indicators

The establishment of evaluating index system is the result which consulted with the research experts who are from the Key Laboratory of Educational Information for Nationalities, Ministry of Education, China (Yunnan Normal University). The level of national culture consciousnesses is characterized by a comprehensive evaluation, including seven first level indicators, namely cognitive consciousness of national culture (NCC1), concerning consciousness of national culture (NCC2), participating consciousness of national culture (NCP1), behavior consciousness of national culture (NCB), protecting consciousness of national culture (NCP2), inheriting consciousness of national culture (NCI1), innovating consciousness of national culture (NCI2) (See Table 2). And every first index is associated with the secondary level index, as well as the second level index was characterized by the third level index, and the third level index is the specific topics which have concrete scores.

2.3.2. Determination of Weight Coefficient

The DELPHL method was adopted by this paper which determined the weights coefficient. There were 25 relevant experts who were from Yunnan Normal University and Yunnan University, they gave the scores to every first level index, secondary level index and every specific topic, and the average score were finally statistic by the investigators. And the first level weights, the secondary level weights were all reached at last, (see Table 2), the third weights was dialed with according to the average score.

2.3.3. Specific Method of Calculating Evaluation

The method of calculating evaluation is based on every specific topic in the third indicators, which give four different scores of 0, 5, 10, and 15.

Comprehensive indicator scores, first level indicator, secondary level indicator were obtained by the following formula:

$$S = \frac{1}{m}\sum_{i=1}^{n} A_i \cdot W_i$$

In the above equation, S is the average score of every level indicator, n is the number of next level, A_i is the value of every level index, W_i is the value of every level weight, m is the valid number of the questionnaire. For example, S_{NCI1} includes two secondary level indexes and six third level indicators, so the specific practices are as follows:

$$S_{NCI1} = 1/m\left[(S1+S2+S3)\times 0.3749+(S4+S5+S6)\times 0.6251\right]\times 0.1312$$

In this equation, S_{NCI1} is the total scores of inheriting consciousness of national culture in some one town of the Shilin County, m is the total number of valid samples, S is the score of the third level index, and (S1 + S2 + S3) × 0.3749 is the calculation process on the education of inheriting NC in the second indicators; (S4 + S5 + S6) × 0.6251 is the calculating process on the ability of inheriting NC in the secondary indicator.

The seven first level indicators were calculated through the above equation; therefore, the total score of S_{NCC} can be got through the following formula:

$$S = \left(\frac{1}{m} \sum_{i=1}^{n} A_i \cdot W_i \right) \cdot W_i$$

that is: $S_{NCC} = S_{NCC1} \times 0.1541 + S_{NCC2} \times 0.1334 + S_{NCP1} \times 0.1982 + S_{NCB} \times 0.2691 + S_{NCP2} \times 0.1132 + S_{NCI1} \times 0.1312 + S_{NCI2} \times 0.1008$

Based on the above analysis, the total score of every level index will be reached, specifically shown in Table 3, of which the theoretical value refers to the average score which the 25 experts given to the questions of the questionnaire, and the actual score refers to a specific value which were calculated by the DELPHL method.

2.4. Statistical Analysis and Discussion

It can be seen that the national cultural consciousness of Yi people is not high in Shilin Autonomous County after the statistical analysis, in the Figure 1; all the actual values are lower than the theoretical weight values in the survey. The detail is the following figure:

Table 2. Indicators and weights of NCC in Shilin Yi autonomous.

Comprehensive index	First level index and weights		Second level index and weights	
	Indexes	Weights	Indexes	Weights
Comprehensive national cultural consciousness	NCC1	0.1541	1) Common sense of understanding NC	0.5541
			2) Degree of mastering NC	0.4459
	NCC2	0.1334	1) Development of concerning NC	0.5238
			2) Education of concerning NC	0.4762
	NCP1	0.1982	1) Activity of participating NC	0.5012
			2) Propaganda of participating NC	0.4998
	NCB	0.2691	1) Habit of NC	0.4678
			2) Behavior of NC	0.5322
	NCP2	0.1132	1) Common sense of protecting NC	0.4190
			2) Policy of protecting NC	0.5810
	NCI1	0.1312	1) Education of inheriting NC	0.3749
			2) Ability of inheriting NC	0.6251
	NCI2	0.1008	1) Concept of innovating NC	0.6137
			2) Ability of innovating NC	0.3863

NC = National Culture.

Table 3. Total scores of the first and secondary level.

Comprehensive index	First level index			Secondary level index		
	Index	T'score	A'score	Index	T'score	A'score
Comprehensive national cultural consciousness	NCC1	0.1541	0.0836	1) Common sense of understanding NC	0.5541	0.4231
				2) Degree of mastering NC	0.4459	0.2691
	NCC2	0.1334	0.1069	1) Development of concerning NC	0.5328	0.3719
				2) Education of concerning NC	0.4762	0.3927
	NCP1	0.1982	0.1098	1) Activity of participating NC	0.5012	0.4194
				2) Propaganda of participating NC	0.4998	0.4479
	NCB	0.2691	0.1285	1) Habit of NC	0.4678	0.3741
				2) Behavior of NC	0.5322	0.3701
	NCP2	0.1132	0.1117	1) Common sense of protecting NC	0.4190	0.4610
				2) Policy of protecting NC	0.5810	0.3379
	NCI1	0.1312	0.1148	1) Education of inheriting NC	0.3749	0.2690
				2) Ability of inheriting NC	0.6251	0.4183
	NCI2	0.1008	0.0941	1) Concept of innovating NC	0.6137	0.5709
				2) Ability of innovating NC	0.3863	0.2180

T = theoretical; A = actual.

Through the statistics, this paper will analysis cultural consciousness from 3 obvious aspects: 1) language use 2) folk dancing and costumes 3) cultural festival.

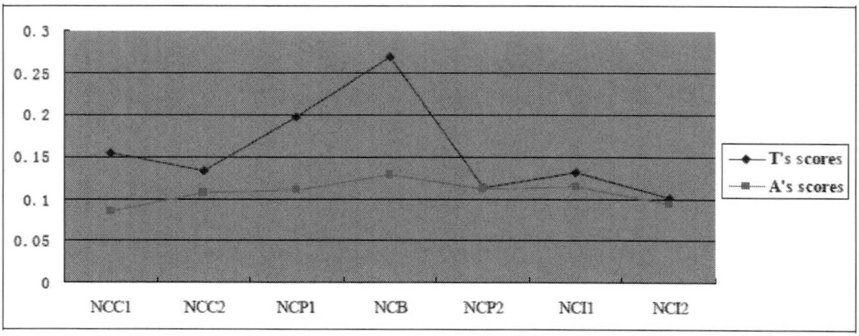

Figure 1. Comparison between the theoretical score and actual score of 7 cultural consciousnesses.

1) Language use

As we all known, language has the dual functions as a tool of communication and the identity of ethnic culture. In a multi-ethnic society or country, its common language bears more the function of social communication while the languages of minority groups bear more the function of cultural identity [7] . As cultural carrier, one of manifestations of national culture and the result of national spirit created. National language is of extremely important meaning for culture study [8] . The assimilation and use of loanwords is a natural phenomenon in the evolutionary process of a national language [9] . In Table 3 and Figure 1, it can be seen that the score is relative large between theoretical value and the actual value in the NCC2 and NCB, in which the theoretical scores is less 0.1406 than the actual weight value of NCB. The most obvious was embodied in the language use.

Through the random interview, most respondents are no longer speak the mother tongue in the 7 major towns, of which over the age of 60 Yi people speak mother tongue accounted for 59.6%, the group between 50-year-old and 30-year-old age are mainly speak Chinese which account for 30.2%, and the young people of 25 years old speak Yi language in "Chinese", the frequency only account for 11.2%, so it can be said that the younger the people are, the mother tongue they speak less. The phenomenon of "Chinese" is a precursor to shake the foundation of the Yi culture which explains that the Yi language and culture has been endangered.

2) Folk dancing and costume

Yi people are good at singing and dancing in Shilin Yi Autonomous County, the Yi folk song and dancing are the essence of Yi culture, which convey the daily living conditions of them vividly. The dancing costumes are not only the simple clothes and ornaments, but also the substantial factor of the dancing art [10] . With the rapid development of Chinese economy, Chinese society is facing from a traditional agricultural society to a modern industrial society in transition, resulting in China's traditional agricultural society folk dance costumes, and modern social life, the aesthetic needs of the masses of people there not meet with the uncoordinated, national traditional Dance Costumes and function of culture is also increasingly diluted, or even lost, distorted, alienated. However, national traditions passed down since ancient times, dance costumes, after all, has its own unique ethnic cultural values and meaning, of which the content implied in some traditional and cultural implication of the ceremony along with the disappearance of national traditions and customs gradually forgotten by people [11] .

As for the master of songs and dancing, the statistics showed that it has a higher proportion of 62.19% among the elderly people over the age of 55, which singing and dancing have become a "patent" for the older age groups; the youth group who see the dancing and singing as the "antique" now. According to the statistics, people can singing and dancing among the age 20 to 55 years old which only account for18.27%; the reason why it happened like this is that these young men went out to work or study, and they have a close contact with the foreign world, so the way of life and the environment around them have changed, so that the ability of singing and dancing gradually disappears.

In Table 3 and Figure 1, It can be seen that Yi people has some improvement in the innovation of national culture while it has somewhat distorted because of the differences between the theoretical value and the actual value weights in the NCB and NCI2. the obvious aspects embodied in the traditional costumes of the Yi people, Yi traditional clothing has been kept the history for thousands of years, but people enter the complete openness of the living environment from the late 1980s and early 1990s, each ethnical people began to communicate with outside world gradually. The clothing exchange along with the external contact occurs, which resulted in the absorption of outside culture, Yi people began to change clothes quickly, most of the them have generally accepted Han Chinese clothing styles of Han, especially men's clothing, suits and the modern equipment mainly occupied men's daily life which accounted for 87.2% among the young men, Yi people in the age of 25 thought it needs to wear traditional costumes only accounted for 10.2%, 11.9% people thought it does not matter, most people thought that festival clothing should wear in the festival which account for 77.9%. The survey found that the declining of the ethnic costumes and cultural has two main reasons, one is the aesthetic ideas of people has changed, and machinery clothing have come into modern life, on the other hand, it needs a lot of manpower, material resources to make traditional folk costumes which is not keep up with the times.

3) Cultural festivals

It can be concluded that the traditional festival of Yi people is also undergoing a gradual alienation from the third indexes of NCB and NCC2 in Shilin County. For example, there are a few specific topics in third level indicators asked: "Do you think the traditional cultural festivals should cut off some taboos or procedure?" the answers were that it should be accounted for 69.8% and the people thought it should not be accounted for 21.7%, and "it does not matter" was account for 8.5%. Cultural globalization offers new historical opportunities for the modernization of national festival culture [12] . The phenomenon of contemporary variation of national festival culture is very general, it is mainly shown as the adjustment, changing, developing and innovation of all forms, content respects of traditional festival culture, at the same time, it is also shown as the appertaining a large amount of new festival [13] . There are many taboos and procedures in the traditional festival activities, along with the foreign exchange, Yi people began to change ideas, and a lot of taboos and cumbersome procedures have been streamlined, followed by the loss of festive cultural connotation and the alienation of honest folk.

3. CONCLUSION

Because of the development of history and the condition of natural history, traditional culture of Yi people presented different characteristics in the process of development. It reflected in different culture of Yi customs, religion, ethics and aesthetics. In recent years, Yi people especially the government began to attach importance to the ethnic cultural development along with the rapid development of the national culture tourism, but it is not optimistic for ethnic cultural consciousness of Yi people, which showed a gradual decay trend. So how to protect the traditional culture and development has become an urgent question, it has an important significance to raise the cultural consciousness of the Yi people in Shilin Autonomous County of Yunnan in China.

ACKNOWLEDGEMENTS

This work was supported by Soft Science Program of China (2013GXS4D149), Ministry of Education, Humanities and Social Sciences Project (12YJCZH053), Minority Native Culture of Quality Engineering Projects in Yunnan.

REFERENCES

1. Liu, S.W. (2004) Reflections on the Cross Culture in the Ethnic Cultural Awareness and Resources. Journal of Chuxiong Normal University, 4, 63-66. [Citation Time(s):1]

2. Yang, F.Q. (1998) The Protection of Minority Cultures under the Modernization Process in China. Ideological Front, 5, 30-35. [Citation Time(s):1]

3. Liao, J.F. (2005) Globalization and Ethnic Cultural Diversity. The People Publishing, Beijing, 225-227. [Citation Time(s):1]

4. Huang, G.C. (2007) Yunnan Ethnic Culture Aspect Probe. Sciences Press, Beijing. [Citation Time(s):1]

5. Li, Y.M. (2007) Native Cultural Transformation of Rapid Urbanization Process. Shanghai People's Publishing House, Beijing. [Citation Time(s):1]

6. Miriam, M. (2007) Development of Western Ethnic and Cultural Resource to Market. Ethnic Publishing House, Shanghai. [Citation Time(s):1]

7. Xing, H. (2012) National Language Identity and Ethnic Language Identity. Journal of Yunnan Normal University, 3, 36-44. [Citation Time(s):1]

8. Tao, Y.G. (2001) A Preliminary Research on the Culture Studies' Meaning of the National Language. Nationalities Research in Qinghai, 2, 18-22. [Citation Time(s):1]

9. Ma, X.M. (2006) Study on the Assimilation and Use of Loanwords and Protection of National Languages. Journal of Harbin Institute of Vocational Technology, 1, 71-73. [Citation Time(s):1]

10. Yan, Y. (2004) The Cultural Connaotation Refracted by the Art Character of the National Dancing Costumes. Journal of Wuhan University of Science and Engineering, 3, 27-29. [Citation Time(s):1]

11. Yan, W.H. (2011) Traditional National Dance Apparel Research. Suzhou University, 1, 2-3. [Citation Time(s):1]

12. Yi, J. (2004) Discussing the Modernization of National Festival Culture. Journal of Heir Longjiang Social Science, 3, 58-62. [Citation Time(s):1]

13. Yang, S.Y. (2003) Contemporary Variation of National Festival Culture. Journal of Guizhou Normal University (Social Science), 6, 66-69. [Citation Time(s):1]

7

CHAPTER

Nature–Culture Relations: Early Globalization, Climate Changes, and System Crisis

Sing C. Chew[1,*] and Daniel Sarabia[2]

[1] Department of Urban and Environmental Sociology, Helmholtz Centre for Environmental Research—UFZ, Leipzig 04105 Germany

[2] Department of Sociology, Roanoke College, 221 College Lane, Salem, VA 24153, USA

ABSTRACT

Globalization has been on everyone's lips in light of the contemporary conditions. It has been viewed mostly as a stage reached as a result of long-term societal changes over the course of world history. For us, globalization has been an ongoing process for at least the last 5000 years. Little attention has been paid to the socioeconomic and natural processes that led to the current transformation. With the exception of historical sociologists, there is less interest in examining the long-term past as it is often assumed that the past has nothing to teach us, and it is the future that we have to turn our intellectual gaze. This paper will argue the opposite. We believe a long-term tracing of the socioeconomic and political processes of the making of the modern world will allow us to have a more incisive understanding of the current trajectory of world development and transformations. To plead our case, we outline the emergence of the ***first*** Eurasian World Economy linking seven regions (Europe, the Arabian Peninsula, East Africa, the Persian Gulf, Central Asia, South Asia, Ceylon, Southeast Asia, and China) of the world, with the exception of the Americas, starting as early as 200 BC, and the sequence of structural crises and transformations (trading networks and commodities) that has circumscribed the structures and trends of the current global system. Such consideration in our view is limited if we do not also include the relations between social systems and Nature, and the rhythms of the climate. For the latter, an awareness of the natural rhythms of the climate as well as human induced changes or climate forcing have triggered system-wide level collapses during certain early historical periods.

Keywords: social system crisis, social change, globalization

1. INTRODUCTION

Materialistically, world history has always been a history of the relationship between Culture and Nature. For at least the last five thousand years, this relationship has been an enduring one, whereby human communities from the least transformed in terms of complexity to the most advanced postmodern social systems have required Nature to meet their basic needs of survival and reproduction. If such is the case, then for the discipline of sociology this, therefore, should be *the overall dimension* that sociology should expend its overall efforts in understanding and explaining the processes and structures that reproduces this relationship. A relationship described by Marx [1] in his early writings as "the humanization of nature" and "the naturalization of man". Unfortunately, the history of sociological scholarship does not reflect this interest nor accept it as *the* dimension that should be its focus. With the global concern now focusing on global warming with environmental changes affecting social, political and economic processes, notwithstanding the "fashionability" of studying environmental changes these days, sociologists have over the last decade or so come around to addressing this dimensional relationship with much fervor. Rather than using a broad brush to paint the absence and neglect of sociological scholarship in examining Nature and Culture relations, we wish to note of the early scholarship of Catton and Dunlap [2], O'Connor [3,4] and Schnaiberg [5] that did try to explore this Nature–culture dimension in depth, and especially Catton and Dunlap's call for an end to the human exemptionalist paradigm that has been underlining sociological scholarship. The outcome of this early intervention did not result in sociological scholarship focusing on biophysical factors as causal and dependent/independent variables and dealing with Nature as the phenomenon all to be examined *holistically and in a dialectical fashion*; instead what resulted was to treat such calls as *a* dimension of study (environmental sociology) in sociology like the various dimensions that sociologists were already focused on (sociology of the military, economic sociology, political sociology, *etc.*).

Our endeavor in this exercise is not to revisit every direction that sociological scholarship has taken in the area of the environment since the call of Catton and Dunlap [2], but rather to review only briefly the sociological scholarship focusing on political economy and system crisis that is the focus of our paper dealing with Nature–culture relations. The latter scholarship we are referring to are those theoretical analyses that utilize political economy models (for example, see Foster [6,7] and Moore [8] that have their anchors dropped in Karl Marx's ocean in their attempts to account for the social, political and economic processes in the reproduction of "capitalist mode of production" systems of the last 500 years. In doing this, we suggest that these Marxian political economy studies have not gone far enough in their frameworks ontologically and theoretically, for they have refrained from putting Nature front and center in their analytical calculations. Instead, these analyses treat Nature as a benign substrate as the base by which capital and its various modalities of modes of production utilize and desecrates in telling their versions of Marxist inspired history. We believe, they continue to treat Nature still within the human exemptionalist paradigm, and in certain cases Nature is viewed as a social construction, or in our view anthropocentrically, instead of seeing Nature and other natural processes as having independent and causal dimensions that have impacted on the reproduction of human societies over world history, thus, generating system crisis that these political economy analyses have endeavored to explain.

Our response to the aforementioned paragraph, without relying on theoretical or ontological rationalizations, will be through a historical materialistic exercise, propose our *ecocentric* framework through our articulation of world history whereby we combine "theoretically informed history and historically informed theory" to explain system crisis over *la longue durée*. Our *la longue durée* is not the 500-year time span starting from supposedly capitalist Western Europe that some like Foster [7] and Moore [8] present, but one that stretches over 5000 years of world history. Historically, in this context, we like to focus specifically on globalization as a phenomenon that has also gained wide currency and popularity these days, and specify the evolution of this global process in relation to the occurrence of natural phenomenon such as climate changes resulting in social system crisis over world history. We assert that Nature can be both an independent and dependent variable in determining the evolution of human societies. We suggest that Nature can be the "agent" in long-term social change (see for example, [9,10,11,12]). In this context, perhaps it is not "capitalist" socioeconomic relation that is the determinant in the last instance that shapes the trends and tendencies of world history over *la longue durée* like the Marxian political economists have asserted [13] (p. 9).

2. THE ATTEMPT TO GREEN MARX

Among the Neo-Marxists, James O'Connor's [3,4] contribution was the first major reinterpretation of Marx's political economy with his insertion of Nature into the overall equation of understanding the contradiction of the process of capital accumulation in late industrial social formations. With the first contradiction of capital between labor and the owners of production ultimately leading to system crisis, O'Connor's insisted that there was a second contradiction of capital as well that has to be added and considered. This being the expansionism of capital tends to cause environmental problems that will ultimately lead to crisis in the reproduction of capital. The significance of O'Connor's writings is his infusion and highlighting of Nature as the substrate for the reproduction of capital accumulation and that there is the tendency to cause social system crises with the exploitative use of Nature as a consequence of capital's inherent expansionism and incessant drive for increasing accumulation. Unlike other Neo-Marxists who at that time (1970s–1980s) were still preoccupied towards addressing system crisis via the process of accumulation and the social relations of production along with the role of the Capitalist state in this process, the insertion of Nature by O'Connor's stress on the second contradiction of capital shifted attention to the conditions of the times then. For that his intervention has to be applauded.

We can see that O'Connor's work influenced numerous Neo-Marxists leading to the development of a number of Neo-Marxist frameworks today. Instead of commenting on these developed frameworks *in toto* which will take up too much space, we propose to examine one that has garnered Neo-Marxist support in terms of publication and citations in sociology that we feel is pertinent to our article's proposals and objective. Here we are referring to the Metabolic Rift framework of Foster's [6,7] and extended by Moore [8,14].

In this model, Foster [6,7,15] proceeded by mining the seams of Marx's mother lode, especially *Das Kapital*, even to the level of footnotes to support Foster's attribution that Marx had always paid attention to Nature in his writings. In response to numerous critics of Marx who have stated that Marx did not in any systematic, exhaustive way address issues such as "the exploitation of Nature, Nature's role in the creation of value, the existence of distinct natural limits, Nature's changing character and the impact of this on human society, the role of technology in environmental degradation, and the inability of mere economic abundance to solve environmental problems" [7] (p. 168); Foster [7] argued that the ecological blinders are not present in Marx's thought, and that each of the aforementioned criticisms was addressed in his theory of metabolic rift. Delivering in his analyses coverage of environmental issues of salience during his time period, Marx addressed the problem of agriculture under capitalism and in particular made observations regarding the soil, while also turning his attention to deforestation, pollution in urban centers, and overpopulation [13] (p. 168). Through this particular lens, Marx came to understand sustainability and the tensions brought about by a rural urban divide, a nexus of relations some analysts conclude Marx captured in his model of social ecological metabolism [8].

Foster shows that in Marx's *Das Kapital* there is a critique of capitalist arrangements linked to the depletion of soil [13]. Marx, according to Foster [13], presented an explanation of "how large scale-industry and large-scale agriculture combined to impoverish the soil and the worker" (pp. 174–175). Foster [13] contends that both Marx's retort of Darwinian evolutionary theory and his formulation of social and ecological metabolism significantly explains the dialectic of capital accumulation and the exploitation of Nature and its various consequences while at the same time considering the relations of production.

In more recent publications, Foster [13] in keeping with the times updated his diagnosis and prognosis of late capitalist systems by alerting us to the supra level that we should be concerned with of the dangers that have now evolved to the level of the world system and the *planetary rift* that we are experiencing, and will face in the future. Foster [13] (pp. 213, 229) however true to his Marxian roots, continues to maintain that we should focus on the relations of production that is undermining ecological sustainability, and that "long-term prospects demand truly revolutionary change, especially a rupture with the accumulation/growth imperative of capitalism". Clearly one can see that Foster's metabolic rift is still placing its emphasis on the paramount status of Culture, with Nature being the substrate that provides value formation for capitalist social relations that are extended to other social structures such as urban and rural areas spanning geo-spatial boundaries on a planetary scale. By Culture's actions (capitalist social relations) Nature is impacted and degraded. This model just follows O'Connor's second contradiction of Capitalism type of argument nothing more nothing less theoretically. Anthropocentric in orientation, it is simply following the basic Marxian argument of the theory of value and crisis dressed up with specific references to natural elements and environmental sustainability.

Moore [8,16,17,18,19,20,21,22,23,24] satisfied with the Neo-Marxian ecological foundations that Foster had carefully constructed and legitimated via the publication of Foster's seminal piece in the *American Journal of Sociology* in 1999, proceeded to utilize this theoretical model to fashion a defense of Wallerstein's world system perspective accused of being neglectful of Nature [25,26,27,28]. Keeping within the dogmas of leftist understanding of the emergence Capitalism in Western Europe over a certain time period from either the 16th century to the late 18th century, Moore [16] undertook an exercise to "naturalize" the work of Wallerstein's analysis. By then, Wallerstein [29,30] himself had started to include Nature as a factor in his continuing analysis of the evolution of the modern world-system.

In trying to extend a Marxian analysis of Nature–culture relations, Moore's [8,17] recent attempt is to criticize the metabolic rift theory of Foster's by suggesting that Foster's model is dualistic, based on a Cartesian binary that puts "biophysical (nature) crises in one box and accumulation (culture/socioeconomic) crises in another" [8] (p. 2). For Moore, this leads to the conclusion that biophysical problems are outcomes of capitalist accumulation "but not constitutive of capitalism as a historical system" as he puts it [8] (p. 2). What this means is that Capitalism "develops through nature-society relations" and does not act on Nature. By fiat, Moore [8] (p. 2) declares capitalism is an "ecological regime"! Our reply to this is so is everything else! By such a theoretical move, Moore has flattened and collapsed society and nature into one with no distinguishing features, and not as young Marx [1] and Habermas [31] had distinguished of the different objectifications: that of the natural world and that of social/individual worlds, and in praxis, nature is socialized and the human is naturalized. This attribution of Moore's that Capitalism as World Ecology advances Capitalism—which is a theoretical concept—into a concretized entity having nature-like properties and rhythms. Therefore, Nature to Moore is a *social construction* devoid of its natural properties, and instead Capitalism is the living, breathing organism oozing the sweat of labor. Again, instead of giving *equal* weight to the dimension of Nature and the dimension of Culture, and acknowledging the distinct characteristics of Nature as subject/object, Moore's model remains within the framework of awarding paramount status to Culture, in this case for Moore, Capitalism; and hence anthropocentric. To further this notion of Capitalism as an ecological regime, the theory of value of Marx was imported by Moore to furnish the scaffolding for his model of Capitalism as World Ecology. Distinguishing distinctions in Marx's theory of value under conditions of overproduction and underproduction, Moore proceeds to sketch out the different historical periods that can be explained according to the different types of the logics of capital accumulation in order not to flatten the historical epochs nor generalize the logic of capital accumulation. Such a theoretical stance is then used to turn the different logics of capital accumulation to account for the history of capitalism or historical capitalism.

We have several reservations concerning Moore's model: Firstly, inspite of Moore's persistent reference to *the dialectic*, we do not see any dialectical process in Moore's model. With his constant resort to *the dialectic* to explain the logic of the model he is proposing, one wonders *what is the interplay between the "particular" and "universal" or of the "moment" and totality for him?* By in the "moment", we mean a phase or aspect of a cumulative dialectical process; and not just a period in time. Moore for wanting to be dialectical chose in referring to the logic of capital accumulation process from *Das Kapital* as his methodological reference point instead of Marx's *Grundrisse. We are confused as to what is the particular in relation to the totality for Moore.* For him, we think, Capitalism is his totality and everything else gets subsumed. It is rather difficult for us to accept ontologically that Capital is considered the totality and everything else are particulars. But if one wants to employ the dialectical process, the universal or totality and the particular proceed through history in a constant interplay resulting in a transcendence (*Aufhebung*) with no end (no complete identity). For Moore the culture/nature relation is Historical Capitalism, therefore the totality and particular are one, or as he [8] (p. 34) puts it: "Capitalism does not have an ecological regime; it is an ecological regime." Collapsing the "universal" and the "particular" is by no means dialectical nor transcending, it annihilates the course of history (*Auflösung*); hence no freedom and no history! We are puzzled that Moore would subscribe to this philosophy of history for he is undertaking a Marxist dialectical analysis or at least that is his intention.

Secondly, Moore [8] (p. 17) suggests that his project moves "from the analysis of what *makes* capital to what capital makes, from the logic of capital to the history of capitalism". This means a rigorous inspection of historical events of accumulation on a world ecological basis. Despite Moore's enthusiasm [8,16,17,18,19,20,21,22,23,24] for the work of Marx and the Neo-Marxists and their analyses of Capitalism, Moore seems to be unaware of the vigorous debate on the nature of "capitalism", its time emergence and its duration that have taken place in world-systems analyses. Moore's fervent attempt to theorize Capitalism as historical capitalism with its long cycles never grapples with the numerous works that have been produced over the last two decades under the umbrella term of world system history whereby there are concentrated discussions on what is "capitalism", the duration of the world system, and the various dynamics underlining such a system from hegemonic rivalry, core-periphery relations, the global accumulation process and long waves (see for example, [9,10,32,33,34,35,36,37,38,39,40,41]). Following Wallerstein [42] for Moore, the emergence of capitalism and the capitalist mode of production, its duration and nature all began in the 15th century in Western Europe. World history for Moore starts then, and there was no history before then. Moore's historical capitalism began then and evolved, anything else before this watershed moment were ignored or considered unnecessary to our understanding of culture/nature relations over world history. Moore's historical analysis therefore is limited and this reservation on our part can also be applied to Foster's work [7]. The adherence to the 15th century for the rise of the "capitalist" mode of production in Western Europe, Moore's model suffers from the same accusation of being Eurocentric that the late Frank [36] had leveled at the world-system history of Wallerstein [42].

3. HISTORICAL GLOBALIZATION AND SYSTEM CRISIS

For the Left, in trying to explain globalization there are basically two narratives. The first argues that globalization is the *stage* reached with the process of accumulation starting at the nation-state level followed with the export of capital in the form of imperialism, and over time the accumulation of capital covers the globe. The other states that globalization is a process that has occurred through world history, and that it is not a stage reached but one that started at different time periods. For Wallerstein [42], it was the 15th century, whereas for Frank [36] and others [9,10,37,40,41] the process started at least 5000 years ago.

If it is not a stage reached but an evolving process, we can make the assumption of the evolution of a structure that we can categorize as a world economy/system. We use the term world economy instead of world-economy as the latter has been utilized by world-systems specialists for a historical structure that has a certain set of socioeconomic and political attributes and trends "capitalistic" in nature that do not necessarily cover a wide geographic space. To world-system specialists, this historical structure of a world-economy is a world in itself, hence the hyphenation between world and economy [43]. In our case, a world economy is not distinguished necessarily by a mode of production but that it covers a *global geographic* space with multiple cores/regions linked at a minimum by a trading system. *It is an evolving global economy "of the world"*. Depending on the temporal sequence, an economy of the world encompassing different chiefdoms, kingdoms, civilizations, empires, and states in a global division of labor, technology, and knowledge circumscribed by different cultural patterns.

Regardless of time or geographic space, this historical globalization process is punctuated with system crisis that impacts on the regions of the world. The spread of such crisis conditions and what it covers is determined by the systemic connections of this world economic structure that continues to evolve and transform to overcome these systemic crisis phases. These systemic crisis phases termed as Dark Ages are not only distinguished by downturns in socioeconomic conditions and political rivalry but are also characterized by climate changes and natural environmental degradations [9,10,11]. These crisis phases—occurring in the past and more to come in the future—were by no means continuously exhibiting increasing ecological degradation. These periods also led to lesser ecological degradative practices because of the socioeconomic decline [10]. Climate changes should also be considered as a major factor in the precipitation of system crisis [11].

If we examine world history in terms of trade connections, we can trace the contours of a "regional" world economy encompassing the Eurasian region of Mesopotamia, the Arabian Peninsula, Levant, Anatolia, Iran, the Indus Valley, and Egypt by 3000 BC [9,10]. Beaujard [44,45,46] has identified three possible regional world systems from 1000 BC onwards. For him, there was the Western world system, the Eastern world system, and the Indian world system during the Iron Age with growing interactions between these systems from 350 BC onwards. Regardless of whether it is a single world system that started in the Fertile Crescent and over time encompassing other regions of the world as postulated by Frank and Gills [33] or Beaujard's [46] three regional world systems coalescing into one world system, what is clear is that by *the turn of the first century of the current era* we find a world system encompassing Europe, East Africa, and Asia (South, Southeast and East) [9,10,46]. In world history, we can conceive of it as the *first Eurasian* world economy as the only major region that has not been connected at this point in world history is the Americas.

Conceptually, the factors and processes that trigger system crises or Dark Ages over the last five thousand years of recorded human history have not been fully understood. Their identifications have relied on analyses of the political economy of the world system in the 1970s and 1980s, and on the whole, based on Marxian crisis theory. The outcome of this is that several interrelated and intrinsic factors have been distinguished providing conditions for the generation of barriers to system reproduction:

overproduction/under consumption, crisis of state authority and competition, social exploitation and polarization leading to antisystemic social movements, and crisis of sustainability. Clearly, the first three factors relate to the dynamics occurring at the social (world) system level with the fourth focusing on the interaction between the social (world) system and the natural system. With the first three factors being anthropogenic in origin, system crisis and transformations are considered to have socioeconomic and political roots.

Notwithstanding such a declaration of economy as being determinant in "the last instance" in terms of system reproduction, others for example, such as O'Connor [3,4], Chew [25,26], and Roberts and Grimes [27] have declared the need to treat Nature as part of the equation towards understanding system dynamics. As we have identified in the previous section, O'Connor [3] has stated that besides the widely accepted capital/labor relation contradiction, there is also a second basic contradiction of capitalism: the capitalist system's insatiable consumption of natural resources leading to crisis conditions. If the latter is the case, on several occasions, one of us (see for example Chew [9,25]) has suggested that based on a materialist conception of history we should reintroduce Nature back into social analysis, and perhaps it is "ecology in command" in *the last instance* that induces system crisis conditions. The rationale for this is based simply on the material fact that the social system requires the natural system to reproduce itself. Along this vein, some historians have also recently raised the issue of Nature's historical agency in conditioning the transformation of human societies [12,47]. Besides Nature's agency, we would like to assert that in the long run, perhaps climate is an important driver of social system structural crisis. This we will attempt to show in this paper.

Besides the above considerations, it is also clear the duration of these world system crisis phases have not been worked out clearly. Different duration for each crisis phase has been proposed according to the different views of world system development [9,33,36,38,41,42,48]. Time-wise, the duration stretches from 50 years to a thousand year in length. Such differences are based on a number of factors and conditions such as the span of historical epochs, empirical verification of economic stagnation, sociopolitical trends, and natural system indicators such as the rate of deforestation.

What the Marxists and other world-system theorists have suggested to date for the past system crises have been recurring and contingent factors of an anthropogenic nature that condition system crises. What about those of ecological and natural origins? Ecologically stressed conditions (deforestation, soil erosion, desiccation, *etc.*), climate changes, and tectonic shifts/volcanicity have been proposed as factors that can precipitate system crises [9,25,26]. How can we be more precise in demarcating these ecological factors? We believe our precision can be enhanced by materialistically identifying system crises with recurring Dark Ages that have occurred in human world history. For it is during these Dark Ages that system transformations occur. Not only do we witness socioeconomic and political declines, but also, ecological degradation, climatological shifts, and natural disturbances. Climatological changes and natural disturbances (tectonic shifts) recalibrate our understanding of the evolution of the world system by adding natural system factors to the already declared anthropogenic ones for our understanding of system transformation.

Given the above parameters, we can abstract historically the several processes and factors that depict a Dark Age period in order to have a clearer understanding of the various factors that precipitate a system crisis and transformation. Such an abstraction starts by delineating the connections between the natural system and social system in the reproduction of the world (social) system.

Barriers to the reproduction of the world system are formed when humans induced changes to the ecology and climate. The degradative aspects of human activity are conditioned by social organizational factors (urbanization, accumulation, wars, technological innovations, and population) that impact on system reproduction. Natural disturbances such as earthquakes and volcanic eruptions also condition the reproduction and evolution of the world system, and thus work independently. Climate as well can affect precipitate and affect the crisis independently and also dependently. For the latter, human actions can cause climate changes, for example, global warming, and thus causing the crisis. We need, therefore, to consider the degree of weight these factors have in precipitating a system crisis.

Through the course of human history, system crises have appeared in the "concrete" in the form of Dark Ages. Over world history, these historical phases are rare. Between 3000 BC and AD 1000, there have been indications of only two such identified phases (2200 BC, 1700 BC and 1200 BC–700 BC (considered as one phase in terms of the crisis of the Bronze Age) and AD 400–AD 800/900) occurring in the world system from Northwestern India, West Asia, the Mediterranean, and Europe. Several scholars such as Desborough [49], Snodgrass [50,51,52], and Braudel [53,54,55,56,57,58] have discussed the conditions of life during past Dark Ages highlighting the economic, political and social disorder with population losses, deurbanization, *etc.* Furthermore, historical records and archaeological evidence indicate a flattening of the social hierarchy, and devolution away from a complex form of sociopolitical organization and lifestyles that existed prior to the onset of Dark Ages. The trends and patterns of Dark Ages therefore show developmental reversals: fall in population levels, decline or loss in certain material skills, deurbanization and migration, decay in cultural aspects of life, fall in living standards and thus wealth and trading contacts.

If Dark Ages are prolonged ecological crisis periods, crisis provides opportunities. In other words, crisis conditions provide the opportunities for the resolution of contradictions that have developed to such a state that inhibits the reproduction of the world system. It leads to pathways and processes that would mean system reorganization and transition. If reorganization does not occur, system collapse usually follows. This has been seen historically (see for example [9,25,26,59,60,61]). If this is the case, ecological limits become also the limits of the socioeconomic processes of the world system, and the interplay between ecological limits and the dynamics of the social system define the historical tendencies of the human enterprise [9,11,60].

To this extent, Dark Ages or system crises also offer opportunities for Nature. Dark Ages should be appreciated as periods for the restoration of the ecological balance that has been disrupted by centuries of intensive human exploitation of the natural system. The downscaling of socioeconomic processes during Dark Ages provides the opportunity for Nature to recover.

4. THE BRONZE AGE CRISIS

The Ancient World System

The ancient world of the Near East and Northwestern Indian subcontinent during the third millennium was characterized by a system of overlapping core regions (for example, Egypt, Mesopotamia, and Harappan Civilization of Northwestern India) (see for example [9,33,62]). Within such a political economic matrix, each core interacted with its immediate hinterland and with each other leading to certain core regions attempting to manipulate its adjacent hinterland, and at times trying to control it [9]. Given such political incursions and trading initiatives, systemic connections were established, and during moments of systemic crisis, crisis-like conditions reverberated throughout the system providing opportunities and constraints depending on the circumstances.

In the Far East, there were no systemic connections with the Near East at this point in time. It was to come later around 200 BC. System-wise, we have two subsystems in place at the start of the Bronze Age crisis. In the Near East we have a subsystem encompassing Southern Mesopotamia, Northwestern India, the Eastern Mediterranean including Egypt, and Central Europe. In the Far East, there was a subsystem with geographic coverage enclosing China and other parts of East Asia.

The accumulation of surplus, urbanization, and population growth are the prime drivers of the processes of the social (world) system, which in turn, define the social (world) system's interactions with the natural system [9]. The interacting relationships among urbanization, population and production/trade mean that resources from the natural system are utilized for the reproduction of the social systems. Thus social collapse and/or crisis of the natural world can be attributed to the excessiveness of the dynamics—accumulation of surplus, urbanization and population growth—of the social world. This is just one side of the equation. We contend that the other side of the equation that encompasses Nature–culture relations (leading to natural resource scarcities and landscape degradation) and *climate* are also key factors affecting socioeconomic and political collapse.

By the late third millennium, sailors from the Aegean were able to sail to the Syro-Palestinian coast thus linking the Aegean and Central Europe by sea with the Near East. Such types of connections foster the beginnings of a "global" division of labor from Northwestern India to the Eastern Mediterranean, and of long-distance trade articulated within a single interacting whole: the Bronze Age World System. We thus have the beginnings of a globalization process, and the emergence of the world system that started five thousand years ago.

Viewed from the perspective of Nature, such world historical processes (urbanization and accumulation) induced a continuous and degradative transformation of the landscape. Trees were removed for agriculture, and to meet the energy and material needs of urbanizing communities. The valleys were excavated for canals to provide irrigation for crops, and for the transportation of people and goods. Other lands were dug up for their natural resources and building materials. Such wide-scale human activities such as deforestation led to soil erosion in the mountains and hills, and the continuous impact of human activities further heightened the process. Rivers were dammed. In all, socioeconomic activities along with wars were transforming the landscape with scars revealing the scale of such acts.

In *World Ecological Degradation*, the level and scale of resource use by the core centers from near and afar in the third millennium BC was traced [9]. This history started on an intense trajectory from the fourth millennium onwards, and by the third millennium BC, after one millennium of drawdown of the natural capital, the natural system and social system was exhibiting signs of crisis type conditions. They emerged stretching over very long duration. Accompanying these long phases of ecological crisis were climate shifts and eruptions of natural processes that impacted on the social, political, and economic landscapes. Economic downturns followed with social-political unrest. The combination of all these conditions induces a *systemic* crisis of the world system. One such *systemic* crisis or Dark Age began around 2200 BC impacting initially Northwestern India, the Gulf, Mesopotamia, Egypt, and West Asia and had repercussions for the urbanized core areas such as Mesopotamia, Indus, and Egypt [9,63,64,65,66]. Following this phase of the crisis ending around 1700 BC, new power centers emerged in the Near East, Northern Mesopotamia, and the Eastern Mediterranean. This systemic crisis reemerged around 1200 BC at the social system level and continued until 700 BC, impacting the main areas of West Asia, Egypt, Eastern Mediterranean, and central Europe (from 800 BC onwards).

5. THE EARLY PHASE OF THE NEAR EAST SYSTEM CRISIS (2200 BC–1700 BC)

Natural System Changes

If as we have argued in the previous pages that world system crisis is also an ecological crisis accompanied with climate changes and natural disturbances (tectonic shifts, *etc.*), we should be able to find trends that reflect the ecological injuries that Nature suffered as a consequence of social (world) system dynamics of accumulation, urbanization, and population increases. The level of deforestation is a good proxy to indicate the state of the natural environment and we do find indicators of severe deforestation during the Bronze Age crisis period starting from 2200 BC onwards.

Over world history from at least 3000 BC onwards, the available forests have been intensively exploited to meet the needs of an evolving world system, starting from the core centers such as Egypt, Mesopotamia, and Harappa [9,67,68]. In the Mesopotamian case, high quality timber were sought for either through military expeditions or trade in the Zagros and Taurus mountains, the Caspian Sea area, the Eastern Mediterranean, and in Punjab [69,70]. In the Harappan case, NorthEastern Punjab (on the Siwaliks and the foothills), and the Western Ghats were the immediate areas of deforestation. Teak came from the Gir forests or from the Panch Mahals, Surat and the Dangs [71]. Timber was also sought as far as the Himalayas. The Egyptians sought their wood in neighboring areas of Lebanon and parts of the Syrian coast. For Northwestern Europe, from as early as the third millennium BC, there was extreme deforestation caused by extensive land use and animal husbandry [60] (pp. 281–292).

From an empirical analysis of the trend lines of arboreal pollen covering four geographic regions of the world: Western Europe,

Central and Eastern Europe including Russia, Northern Europe and the Mediterranean, we note of severe deforestation phases [10].

The first phase of deforestation started from 3854 BC–2400 BC, and there were three/four subsequent phases of deforestation followed by reforestation that occurred towards the latter period of the course of a Dark Age. Deforestation periods are the most pertinent time points for our discussion of the ecological degradation of the early Bronze Age crisis. With one deforestation period starting around approximately 2400 BC, this dating also corresponds with Barbara Bell's [65] identification of the first Dark Age of the Ancient World. In Western Europe, arboreal pollen from areas in Belgium, Germany, and France exhibit the deforestation period starting around 2200 BC–2000 BC. In Central and Eastern Europe, trend lines of arboreal pollen show deforestation levels in areas of Hungary and Ukraine. In Northern Europe, the trend line of arboreal pollen in an area in Finland also supports this deforestation pattern. Finally, in the Mediterranean, we find areas of Greece, Spain, and Turkey exhibiting such trends. The latter area of Turkey is most pertinent for present discussion for it is where the Southern Mesopotamians sought their natural resources.

Agriculture and other anthropogenic induced changes naturally lead to forest fragmentation and deforestation, and the rise in the pollen record of indicator plants and ground weeds such as *Plantago lanceolata* [72] (p. 224); [68] (pp. 12–25). Time phases of the *rise* in the number of *Plantago* pollen when there was a *decline* in the number of arboreal pollen, supports the thesis of anthropogenic induced deforestation over five thousand years of world history.

Climate-wise, there is evidence of temperature changes (higher temperatures) and increasing drought-like conditions persisting in the Eastern Mediterranean, Egypt, West Asia, Mesopotamia, Northwestern India, Central Asia, Africa and parts of the New

World starting from 2200 BC onwards during the onset of the Dark Age of the third millennium [9,73,74,75,76,77,78].

According to Fagan [77] who has argued on the impact of climate change on civilizations, this start of a warming trend again was a global event. Affected areas covered Egypt, Northern Africa, Greece, Indus, the Fertile Crescent, Crete, Russia, West Asia, and Palestine [9,65,74,77,78]. Between 2710 BC and 2345 BC, Anatolia and the Northern Crescent had arid conditions, however the Nile floodings continue to be high [79]. However, by 2205 BC, the starting time point initializing the start of the Bronze Age crisis, the Nile floods had weakened. From 2205 BC–650 BC, a period that covered the Bronze Age crisis, there was widespread aridity in Anatolia and the Northern part of the Fertile Crescent including Northern Africa [79].

For social systems with agricultural practices that are reliant on irrigation waters or from annual floods, this loss of moisture would place tremendous stress on the agricultural systems and hence, the economy and social-political stability [73]. Such was the case for the core centers of Mesopotamia, Egypt, and the Harappan civilization. Each responded differently to such stressed conditions depending on what they were facing.

The climate changes were also accompanied with the occurrences of tectonic shifts that added further strain to the social system. Tectonic shifts by themselves would not immediately impact on the reproduction of the social system unless they are in the immediate proximity of human communities or they reshape the contours of the landscape by shifting river courses. The latter is what happened in the second millennium BC By diverting watercourses, the diversions transformed some rivers into dry waterbeds that further exacerbated the already existing aridity, thus impacting on social system.

For this time period, in Northwestern India, Agrawal and Sood [80] noted of tectonic shifts that diverted the course of the Satluz and the easterly rivers away from the Ghaggar, which over time transformed into a lake-like depression during this period. The Ghaggar or Sarasvati which feeds into the Indus River was alive until the late Harappan Period (1800 BC) but was dead by the time of the Painted Grey Ware period (1000 BC). Possehl [81,82] has also confirmed this drying up of the Sarasvati and its implications for the Harappan urban complexes located on its riverbank.

Beyond the above core centers of Mesopotamia, Egypt, and the Harappan Civilization of Northwestern India, temperature changes also impacted on other ecological landscapes. In Western Asia, the introduction of Zebu cattle, which can withstand aridity, occurred during the two arid periods (2200 BC and 1200 BC) of the Bronze Age [83,84]. In central Eurasia, preliminary data also confirmed marked changes in vegetation, beginning around 2200 BC and lasting until 1700 BC [85,86]. Pollen cores indicate a sharp decrease in arboreal pollen and an increase in steppe pollen. From 2200 BC to 2000 BC, there was a severe drop in forest cover and an increase in steppification, leading to an expansion in steppe landscape from 1800 BC to 1700 BC. The pollen profiles for the region discussed in the previous section also confirmed the deforestation process. Arid conditions also affected arable land, which caused severe pressure on animal husbandry of the steppe population. The lush feather grass steppe growing on the landscape near Kalmykia for example, from 2500 BC–2200 BC gave way to dry scrubby vegetation—wormwood steppe—and even desertification by 2200 BC–1700 BC. This changed ecological landscape led to outmigration of the sedentary population from river valleys with time, and exploitation of the steppes for animal feed.

6. SOCIOECONOMIC AND POLITICAL TRANSFORMATIONS 2200 BC–1700 BC

Socioeconomic and political trends during Dark Ages are reversals of what occur during periods of expansionary growth.

6.1. Deurbanization and Migration

Tracking the reversals in socioeconomic trends during Dark Ages or over the very long-term requires considerable effort, especially when the quantitative data are sparse. Some recent attempts such as that of Modelski [37] and Thompson [40] on urbanization and economic expansion have provided us with some broad contours on these processes. In terms of urbanization, by 3500 BC for the "heartland of cities" such as Southern Mesopotamia, urban growth had progressed to such an extent that it had three cities with population at or over 10,000 [37].

By 2500 BC, during the period of Early Dynastic III, the rise of Sumer exhibited the largest urban conglomeration at 60,000 persons. Uruk by this time had been reduced to a population of 40,000 in comparison to 80,000 in 2800 BC [37] (p. 28). However, the total urban population of Mesopotamia at 2500 BC had reached 290,000 [40]. Outside of the "heartland of cities", we find Ebla located in Northern Syria with a population of about 40,000 and Mari in Northern Mesopotamia with a similar population size. Elsewhere, we have Memphis in Egypt at 30,000 persons, Mohenjo-daro and Harappa in Northwestern India at 20,000 and 15,000, respectively.

By 2200 BC, the Akkadian period and the start of the Dark Age Phase 2, the total urban population of Mesopotamia had been reduced to 210,000. This shift is also reflected in the proportion of declining urban settlement sizes. During the Early Dynastic Period II/III (2800 BC–2300 BC) the percentage of urban settlements with more than 40 hectares was about 78.4%, by the Akkadian

Period (2200 BC) it had been reduced to 63.5%. Further deurbanization continued that in the Ur III and Isin-Larsa periods (2100 BC–1900 BC), and the percentage dropped further to 55.1%. This slippage continued to the Old Babylonian period, reducing further to 50.2% (1600 BC). Conversely, non-urban settlement sizes (10 hectares or less) increased. During the early Dynastic II/III period, it was about 10%, almost doubling by the Akkadian period. With the arrival of the Ur III and Isin-Larsa periods, the percentage had risen to 25%, and almost tripled to about 29.6% by the Old Babylonian period in comparison to the Early Dynastic period. This deurbanization process and migration to rural communities are also supported by the population decreases in Mesopotamian cities. From 210,000 during the Akkadian period (2200 BC), the population in Mesopotamian cities was reduced to 190,000 by the Isin-Larsa period (1900 BC). This was a loss of 10%. The population level was reduced further to 70,000 by the Old Babylonian Period (1600 BC). Overall therefore, between the start of Dark Age Phase 2 (Akkadian Period) and its end around 1700 BC (Isin-Larsa and Old Babylonian periods) we see a loss of over 66% of the urban population in Mesopotamia.

Deurbanization and population losses were also repeated in Northwestern India. According to Possehl [81,82], by the late third millennium BC there was evidence of abandonment of important buildings in the highly urbanized setting such as Mohenjo-daro where we find the Great Bath and the Granary devoid of human use. Concurrently, the Sindh region and the Baluchi Highlands also witnessed depletion and deterioration. By the early second millennium BC, Baluchistan was uninhabited. Cholistan, in Northwestern India, experienced a drop in size in terms of settled areas from an average of 6.5 hectares in 3800 BC–3200 BC to 5.1 hectares by 1900 BC–1700 BC, and finally to almost 50% less (2.6 hectares) by 1000 BC [81]. In the Sarasvati region, the shifting and drying up of the river system saw the abandonment of settlements in the inland delta of Fort Derawar. The latter area was the breadbasket of the Mature Harappan civilization.

Elsewhere for the time period of 2200 BC, similar signs of deteriorating conditions were also encounters in Anatolia, with abandonment of urban centers such as Troy II to Troy III–IV [48,87] (p. 139–152). Consequently, depopulation also resulted. Sedentary population settlements on the Anatolian plateau were also abandoned. To the west of Anatolia, Palestine also suffered such crisis conditions [88]. Walled towns were replaced by unwalled villages. There were signs of cave occupation and migratory movements. In some areas, settlements completely disappeared, and remaining settlement sites were reduced by more than half of what existed before 2200 BC [89] (pp. 1–38). Across the Mediterranean from Palestine, the Aegean experienced distress, though to a lesser extent. Between 2300 BC and 1900 BC there was a loss of sedentary population. Such losses were experienced both on mainland Greece and even Crete [90,91].

For central Eurasia similar stress conditions also prevailed. The changed ecological landscape led to out outmigration of the sedentary population from river valleys over time, and exploitation of the steppes for animal feed. Denucleation occurred with the establishment of smaller communities near oases. This spread occurred in Central Asia at Korezm (south of the Aral Sea) and Margiana (Murghab Delta) in Turkmenistan, Bactria, and Western China. This process prompted by ecological degradation and environmental changes, also occurred in Syria and Jordan. Migration out of urban centers located on the coast to the interior, and the establishment of smaller village type-settlements resulted [92] (pp. 267–273).

6.2. Political and Social Changes

If we examine the Dark Age of 2200 BC–1700 BC, political instability is one feature that highlights the political economic events. Climate changes as identified above led to famines that in turn generated political upheavals and the dissipation of central authority in Egypt. Drought conditions and lowered Nile flooding impacted on the farmers' ability to pay taxes because of lower harvest yields. This resulted in local administrators and governors, who collected taxes, having to delay their transfers to the Royal House. In turn, the King's revenues plummeted, and thus impaired his ability to pay for an army or to deal effectively with drought and famine. As a result, the stability of the political regime was affected. The sum effects of this in terms of political stability, as Bell [65] has concluded, were short reigns.

Besides political instability in Egypt during the third millennium Dark Age of 2200 BC, other reversals also occurred such as artistic degeneration and the downsizing of monumental buildings as a result of diminishing resources. The size and elaborateness of the pharaonic tombs were reduced; by this time, the tombs of kings were one-chambered affairs with less ambitious layouts [93] (pp. 316–319). Boundaries of provinces were also closed to prevent mass migration out of famine stricken areas. All these initiatives proved fruitless at times as riots broke out along with the ransacking of granaries.

In other parts of the system such as Southern Mesopotamia and Northwestern India, structural political, economic and social reversals were also occurring. These transformations were extremely impactful in view of the trading relations of the region among Southern Mesopotamia, the Gulf, and Northwestern India, and led to the demise of social systems in place with repercussions system-wide. By the third millennium BC, Southern Mesopotamia, the Gulf region and Northwestern India were linked in a trading network of commodity exchanges. Therefore, a crisis in one part of the system would also mean a translation of this stress to other parts of the system. Therefore, an ecological stress in Southern Mesopotamia would mean a lowering of agricultural output or production, and hence a drop in imports and demand. Reductions of demand in Southern Mesopotamia would impact on other regions such as Dilmun in the Gulf and the Harappan civilization through a diminished demand for their material and goods. What this type of dynamics further suggests is that supply and demand might not necessarily be a consequence of the state of the economy or based on consumer tastes and needs. But rather, supply demand dynamics are inextricably linked to the connections between the natural system and social system. Thus, anthropocentric explanations provided for systems demise have ecological roots.

Southern Mesopotamia by 2200 BC was experiencing salinization problems leading to lowered agricultural productivity and this became acute by 1700 BC. It never recovered from the disastrous decline in agricultural yields that accompanied the salinity issue. Deurbanization was the order of the day as we have indicated previously. Urban life and culture continued on a declining scale with the population concentrating only in major towns [94]. The Harappan civilization not only had to face ecological stress, climate changes with temperature increases and arid conditions like Southern Mesopotamia, it also had to undergo tectonic shifts. As the urbanized communities of the Harappan civilization were linked to the overarching Gulf trade and beyond, its infrastructure and surrounding hinterlands had therefore developed and specialized in the manufacture of products and natural resources for export. Thus, when its exports to the Gulf and beyond disappeared, it could no longer reproduce the accumulation process that had sustained its urban growth. This led to migration to the rural areas of the North and south.

7. THE FINAL PHASE OF THE NEAR EAST BRONZE AGE CRISIS (1200 BC–700 BC)

The demise of Southern Mesopotamia and Northwestern India coupled with the socioeconomic and political upheavals in Egypt and their associated hinterlands from 2200 BC to 1700 BC initiated a significant system crisis of the Bronze Age. With the socioeconomic collapse of Southern Mesopotamia and Northwestern India, the demise of these economies meant also the breakdown of the Gulf trade. After 1700 BC, at the social system level, despite the fact that ecological stress (at the natural system level) continued as reflected in the arboreal profiles listed in [10] (p. 49–53), economic recovery resumed. With recovery, other parts of the Bronze Age system such as the Eastern Mediterranean littoral (centered around Crete and mainland Greece) along with central Europe and Anatolia increasingly began to take advantage of the vacuum generated by the collapse of the Southern portion (the Gulf Trade) of the Bronze Age system. Egypt, Syria-Levant (such as Ugarit, Mari, Byblos, Ras Shamra), Crete, Cyprus and mainland Greece expanded their trading volumes utilizing the peripheral areas such as Central and Eastern Europe, and Nubia for their resource needs [9,95]. With the loss of trading dominance of Southern Mesopotamia, Mesopotamian trade shifted Northwards, thus making Anatolia an important Eastern node of this Bronze Age trading network [9]. In sum, the Eastern Mediterranean littoral became the prime axis where economic activity of the Bronze Age system concentrated during this period.

The social system adaptation and resolution of the crisis of the Bronze Age that started at 2200 BC and ending around 1700 BC was only *temporary*, for over *la longue durée*, because of the continued ecological stress and degradation including climate changes, social (world) system crisis would only appear again in 1200 BC The system crisis of 1200 BC repeated what occurred in

2200 BC except that when it finally dissipated we have system transformation with the arrival of the Iron Age.

The collapse of the Southern portion of the Bronze Age world system led to the reconfiguration of the trading networks. Shifting away from the Gulf region, the trading networks range from Crete, the Cyclades, and the Greek mainland on one side of the Aegean Sea with Troy, Cyprus, and Anatolia located across from it. Included in this configuration were the communities of Syria and Palestine, and the kingdom of Egypt. This network of socioeconomic exchanges of the Eastern Mediterranean region was also linked to communities of Western, central, and Eastern Europe, and Central Asia [61]. It was a globalized system of trade and sociopolitical exchanges.

Within this trading network, intermediary centers such as Crete increasingly played a part in the Eastern Mediterranean. The Minoan command-palace economy was involved not only in the export of surplus agricultural produce such as grains and oil, but also in the export of textiles, metal works, pottery, wood work, *etc.* [9,61]. Initially, such a diversified economic structure provided it with a competitive advantage over other regions of the Bronze Age system such as mainland Greece, the Cyclades, and Europe to the North.

Later in the millennium, the rise of Mycenaean Greece in this era increasingly eclipsed the role Crete played in the Easternmost region of the Bronze Age world economy [9]. On this trading backbone, Mycenaean Greece began to establish its economic dominance within the Aegean. Similar to the Cretan economy, Mycenaean Greece exported wine, olive oil, grains and manufactured products to Eastern and Northern Europe, and the Eastern part of the Mediterranean, and in turn, received needed natural resources such as copper, tin, and horses. To the East of this globalized Bronze Age trading system was the kingdom of Hatti with metallic resources such gold and silver whereby these precious metals were exchanged for textiles, lapis lazuli, olive oil, grain, horses, tin, *etc.* Trade contacts were established with Babylon, Mittani, Assyria, Syro-Palestine, Egypt, and Crete.

The globalizing trajectory was extended starting as early as 2000 BC onwards when these cores in the Near East as Kristiansen and Larsson [61] (p. 99) put it "turned their interest towards the barbarian peripheries in Central and Western Europe" for their natural resources and livestock such as horses. In the Caucasus, the mines supplied the copper, and there was the development of a Circum-Pontic metallurgical province that included Anatolia [61,96,97,98]. With such development, the central and Western European metallurgical centers were "increasingly drawn into trade relations with the palace cultures and city states of the Eastern Mediterranean and Anatolia, which reached a new flourishing after 2000 BC when the Minoan palaces were built" [61] (p. 104).

It should not be assumed that these trading networks were stable structures over time. It was a globalized system of interconnected regions and polities—a world system. Their vitality and concentration changed over time, and were conditioned by the pulsations of ecological and climate changes, notwithstanding political and economic ones. Thus, when the Dark Age returned in 1200 BC, the collapse was system-wide due to the level of connectivity.

7.1. The End of the Bronze Age in The Near East

If 2200 BC was the start of system crisis at both the natural and social systems levels, and with the natural system in continuous crisis throughout the late Bronze Age, 1200 BC signaled the beginning of social system transformation leading to the end of the Bronze Age. Starting from about 1200 BC, socioeconomic and political collapses during this period ranged from Mycenae through Egypt, the Levant, and Northern Mesopotamia to Anatolia.

With the exception of parts of the periphery, the core centers of the Bronze Age system at this point in time were in crisis.

The collapse of the Bronze Age world has been explained rooted on a variety of factors. On the whole, they have been rationalized and based on anthropocentric ones such as barbarian invasions, unceasing consumption and cultural decadence, power rivalries and state competition, vagaries of development, overcentralization of authority, military and weapon innovations, and famines and diseases (see for example, [52,63,99,100]). Without a doubt, these factors at the social system level are ones to consider. However, what is lacking is a consideration of the *linkage* between the social system and the natural system, and how a disruption of this connection would ultimately induce crisis conditions, for the former (the social system) depends on the latter (natural system) for its continued reproduction. It is to underscore again the viewpoint that in the last instance it is perhaps Nature that has the final say!

For Crete, the intensive exploitation of resources for economic transactions impacted on the landscape. Deforestation generated soil erosion and flash flooding; the latter impacted on the manufacturing processes of Crete. Wood scarcity forced changes in production locations or resulted in the closure of facilities. It has even been suggested that such land deterioration contributed to the demise of Minoan Crete [101] (p. 68). These ecologically devastating trends were also repeated throughout the Bronze Age system. Mainland Greece—which provided the wood supplies to Crete when Crete's supply ran out—and other areas in Europe and Central Asia showed such scars as well. Intensification of land use and animal husbandry led to severe alteration of the landscape. Population increases along with the adoption of the ox-drawn plow further exacerbated the intensity of land utilization. Pollen record from Osmanaga Lagoon in southwest Greece in Messinia shows extreme forest removal by 2000 BC [102] (p. 5). Between 1600 BC and 1400 BC, the pine forests in Messinia were totally wiped out due to agriculture and overgrazing. Soil erosion was endemic and was controlled by terracing and the building of terrace walls. As a consequence agricultural production was affected. In the Argolid, production of cereals and olive oil generated deforestation of oak trees on the hillsides. It resulted in large amounts of earth and water draining from the slopes onto the plain of Argos and filling up stream beds leading to extensive flooding [103].

Besides terrace walls to deal with soil erosion, other technological solutions were also tried, such as the building of dams to divert water courses and dikes to facilitate drainage [104]. However, by the late second millennium BC such efforts began to fail. Erosion became uncontrollable during the Dark Age crisis of 1200 BC when socio-political life was at a standstill and population density had dropped precipitously [105].

With scarcity of wood for fuel, metallurgical and pottery works were affected which resulted in further population decline. Population migration followed the closure of these manufacturing centers, and the abandonment of Phylakopi coincided with the deforestation of Melos, where the town was located. Towns and settlements disappeared. In southwest Peloponnese, the number dropped from 150 to 14. Other regions experienced similar declines; Laconias, Argolid, Corinthia, Attica, Boeotia, Phocis, and Locris all registered losses [9,67].

In Southern Europe, there were also degradative impacts on soil formation from Urnfield settlements [59]. Kristiansen and Larsson [61] have also documented widespread ecological degradation in the Caucasus as a result of mining for metals to supply the Eastern Mediterranean and the Near East. It was also repeated for the mining area of Kargaly in the Urals that supplied metals to the whole steppe region where deforestation was the consequence according to Kristiansen and Larsson [61]. Time-series of arboreal pollen profiles of Central and Eastern Europe including Russia parallels the deforestation trajectories.

Collapse came for the Eastern Mediterranean when circumstances started to change. Ecological stress coupled with climate changes and natural disturbances impacted on Crete, Greece and the Near East. For Crete, such arid conditions impacted on agricultural production. This development was serious, as it was an important part of Cretan exports needed to offset its import of wood and other natural resources. Furthermore, geological conditions also provide grounds for the arguments made first by Marinatos [106] and followed by Chadwick [107] and Warren [108] on their impacts on Crete. The volcanic eruption on Thera following the earthquakes killed vegetation and destroyed the Minoan naval fleet. The loss of this fleet undermined Crete's power to exercise its dominant position in this region of the world system. In addition, these natural system conditions should also be considered with the political changes impacting on Crete. From 1500 BC onwards, the increasing competitive roles played by the Hittites and Kassites through their expansion and dominance of Anatolia and Mesopotamia corralled Crete's dominance. Blended into this political mixture, the ascendancy of Mycenaean Greece eclipsed the economic position that Crete enjoyed. Furthermore experiencing the loss of their sources for natural resources located on the Greek mainland that by this point in time were increasingly under Mycenaean control; Crete's reproductive capacity was stretched. Faced with these desperate conditions in the spheres of the social system and the natural system, Minoan civilization slid downhill.

What occurred in Crete was repeated in Mycenaean Greece except it was much later starting around 1200 BC By this time the natural environment was severely stretched. Rhys Carpenter's [109] thesis of climate change leading to the demise of Mycenaean Greece needs to be considered. Basically, Carpenter's proposal is that with the shift in the tracks of the cyclonic storms, which normally bring rain to Mycenaean Greece, arid conditions resulted during the 13th to the 12th centuries. As a consequence, the socioeconomic structure was impacted. Chadwick [107] and Drews [110] have challenged this thesis with Lamb [111], Braudel [58], Bryson *et al.* [112], and Bryson and Padoch [113] supporting Carpenter's position.

Along with these desperate conditions due to climate changes and natural disturbances, invading forces of Dorians and Sea Peoples made the circumstances even more dire. Such invading forces most likely have also been displaced from their habitation due to changing climate conditions and natural disasters. Climate changes and disruptions in trade routes also played a part in the overall reproductive capacity of the Hittites and the Egyptians in the other parts of this system. Lowered Nile flows affected Egyptian agriculture leading to famines. The Hittite Empire's grain shortage led to growing imports from other parts of the world system through Ugarit, and from the Syro-Palestine area. In all, the crisis was system-wide affecting the Aegean, Central and Western Europe, Egypt, Anatolia, Palestine, and Babylonia.

7.2. Socioeconomic and Political Transformations

Greece encountered a decline in socioeconomic life from 1200 BC till 700 BC, such as decline or loss of certain material skills, decay in cultural aspects of life, a fall in living standard and thus wealth, deurbanization, population losses, and loss of trading contacts within and without Greece (see for example [9,49,50,51,63,114,115,116,117,118]). The archaeological evidence unearthed suggests socioeconomic patterns that are distinctively different from the style and level of socio-cultural life prevailing prior to the onset of the Dark Age.

Population decreases occurred between 1250 BC and 1100 BC Morris [114,115,116] has estimated losses of about 75% followed with emigration from the core areas of the Mycenaean civilization, this trend continued for central Greece as well by 1100 BC According to Snodgrass [50] between the 12th and the 11th centuries, there was a reduction of over three quarters of the population.

Pottery and other objects recovered from excavated sites along with the architecture and design of dwellings reflect ecological stress and scarcity of natural resources. Architectural standards were lowered and there were very few signs of good stone-built construction. Small stone construction was prevalent, and we also increasingly see signs of mud-brick construction. Mud-brick structures predominated in the building structures between the 11th and 10th centuries. The emergence of a class of handmade burnished pottery, "Barbarian Ware", had few obvious links to Mycenaean styles. The appearance of this style has been attributed as an economic response to the collapse of centralized production with the demise of the palace economies, and a regression to simpler technology [119]. Furthermore, pottery styles of the period in Greece became austere, unlike the decadent style of the previous era.

Starting with the Submycenaean style of pottery (*ca.* 1125 BC–1100 BC), the austerity of the design can be seen. As Desborough [49] has put it, the standards deteriorated sharply not only to the making of the pottery but also to the painting and decoration. The design was of the simplest kind and "was a virtual bankruptcy... and often carelessly applied" [49] (p. 41). The variety of styles in terms of vase shapes of this type of pottery was also reduced. Rutter [120] has also suggested that luxury vases and other pottery items were quickly abandoned as necessary frills when hard times hit. There was less variety of material goods, the artifactual correlate of a less complex social order. The emergence of the Protogeometric style (*ca.* 900 BC) continued to reflect the austerity of the period [50]. Snodgrass [51] has also alerted us to the appearance of hand-made pottery during the Dark Ages. The reversion to hand-made pottery when the pottery wheel had been adopted previously suggests to us the decay of manufacturing production or even perhaps the loss of manufacturing skills. It could also mean that with social decay and collapse, there was a revival in the utilization of indigenous material in view of the disruption in trade routes.

In terms of decorations and finishing, the bulk of the pot or vase was usually left plain in the natural color of the clay and the decorations covered a third of the surface area at most [49]. The lack of intense firing also suggests to us dwindling energy supplies. The compass and the multiple brush were used for decorating the pottery. As recovery proceeds and the balance of Nature is restored, we find the plain, rectilinear or curvilinear patterns in pottery designs giving way to images depicting animals and humans. In the later Protogeometric style period, we already saw the introduction of silhouette figures of a horse or a human on the design. If we consider the decay of cultural life and the loss of the art of writing, and view pottery design as a way the potter as artist could depict sociocultural life then, the motifs that we find in these pottery designs would summarize life in Dark Age Greece. By the late Geometric style period, we find scenes of organized groups of men in uniforms, the portrayal of warfare and chariots depicting social life when the Dark Age was receding, and the return of biodiversity with animals and sea creatures being depicted.

Beyond pottery styles, other objects recovered indicate a scarcity of natural resources, especially metals, or that the supply sources had dried up. The use of obsidian, stone, and bones for blades and weapons underscores such scarcity, and also suggests that trading routes and centers for sourcing the metals might have disappeared or disrupted. Other primitive materials reappear as apparent substitutes such as bone spacer-beads for amber in jewelry, and stones were used to replace lead in sling bullets. Objects buried with the deceased increasingly were made out of iron such as iron pins and fibulae and even weapons, which all in the past were bronze, and bronze wares only returned towards the end of the Dark Age period [51]. Where bronze was used, it was found on the bulb of pins thus revealing the scarcity of bronze [49,50].

Ecological scarcity required a downscaling of material and cultural lifestyles. Such changes are reflected in burial practices that exhibited a reorganization of life along modest lines. The design of clothing and shoes was of the plainest kind [50]. A one-piece woolen garment without requiring cutting or sewing gained popularity among the female population in Submycenaean Athens and became the predominant dress design in the Protogeometric Period. Pins for dresses were scarcely used. The downscaling process is exhibited further in the formation of decentralized communities and associated population losses. The collapse of the palace driven economies with centralized monarchies were replaced by smaller political organizations dominated by an aristocrat and his family.

Whether this life-style is one that was actively sought as a consequence of ecological scarcity or occurred as an outcome of the depressive conditions of the Dark Age is difficult to gauge. It is clear however, that there was a shift from the Mycenaean way of reproducing life for they longer provided practical models. The loss of sophistication is clearly seen and as Morris [116] (p. 207) has stated, "in their funerals people seem more concerned with showing what they were *not* than with what they were". What we are sure of is that as recovery proceeded—we begin to witness this by the mid-half of the 10th century BC—trading networks were re-established and communities revived. Such an upswing was characterized by exuberance, materialistic consumption, and accumulation. As the social system recovered, we see the rise of the Bronze industry, increasing quantity of pottery buried in the tombs, the quantity of gold deposited in the burials, and signs of social cultural recovery. During the Dark Age, materialistic consumption declined, and most of the trading networks disappeared or were restricted only to the area of the Aegean Sea.

What the Dark Age of this period represented for the Mediterranean region is one where extreme degradation of the ecological landscape precipitated socioeconomic and organizational changes to meet the scarcity of resources so as to reproduce some semblance of cultural and economic life of prior times. As a consequence, systemic reorganization occurred at various levels, from the way commodities were produced to clothing fashions and designs. Hierarchical social structures disappeared during the Dark Age, as evident by burial practices, and were restored when recovery proceeded [117]. To Whitley [117] (p. 20) burial practices "may be seen as an expression both of social relations and ideology..." During the Dark Ages, there was a shift from multiple tombs burial to single burials which reflected the change from an emphasis on heredity signifying a stratified order with ruling classes to one which reflect no expectations of descendants and little regard for extravagance [51]. The single tombs lack monumental significance and architectural quality. From the graves excavated of the Protogeometric Period (*ca.* 900 BC) there are no indications of disparities in wealth and social distinction, as exemplified in the Athenian graves. Distinction was based on age and sex rather than other social dimensions [117] (p. 115). This was to change by the Early Geometric Period (*ca.* 860 BC–840 BC) where there is an amplification of status of the person buried. Social and sexual identities of the person interred became more evident. Thus, we find the return of a hierarchical pattern and a departure from the more egalitarian structure of the Protogeometric Period. Such hierarchization continued in the Middle to Late Geometric Periods (*ca.* 770 BC–700 BC). By this period however, there was also a breakdown of the aristocratic order with the arrival of early state formation, though social hierarchical differentiation remained in place.

With the Dark Age, not only was there a loss of population, but deurbanization was also underway. The latter process continued giving rise to small communities with lower population levels

[90,91]. Seen from an ecological point of view, this downscaling provided the necessary timing for Nature to restore its balance, and for socioeconomic life to start afresh when recovery returned. The collapse of the palace economies enabled the ecological landscape to restore itself that in the past were intensively exploited by the palace driven economics. In the Argolid and Messenia, according to Deger-Jalkotzy [121] (pp. 123–124), the land recovered and the tree population increased. Furthermore, with the loss of centralized control from the various palaces, not only deurbanization occurred but also decentralization. Each region thus had the opportunity to search for new mechanisms and ways to administer and reproduce socioeconomic life in general. New trends emerge following the collapse of the palaces as a consequence of the unexpected liberty that resulted from the collapse, and each region/community began to make contacts with others outside Greece towards the end of the Dark Age.

From these small communities, in the case of Greece, the preconditions for the rise of the Greek polis (cluster of villages) were put into play, and what followed was a flourishing of political and economic life as soon as the social system recovered [51]. Muhly [122] (p. 20) has put this in a succinct fashion: "the importance of the Dark Age, then, must be that it created the conditions that made possible the growth of this distinctly Greek political organization". To this extent, the stressed ecological conditions that engendered deurbanization and the formation of small isolated communities precipitated the rise of the polis and the Greek city-states. We need to realize, therefore, that perhaps scarcity of resources can also have productive outcomes which otherwise under bountiful conditions might not have occurred. Stanislawski [123] (p. 18) has suggested that instead of seeing the Greek Dark Ages as a period of darkness it should be seen as one of enlightenment with contributions such as: the first use of stone-walled agricultural terraces, the use of chicken eggs in domestic diet, the beginning of the spread of alphabetic writing, the spread of iron, the general use of olive as food, and the first use of waterproof plaster.

Systemic reorganization occurred, and the lengthy duration of the Dark Age is one that we need to note. The fact that it is of such a long duration underscores the length of time required for ecological recovery to take place, and the immensity of the degradation that occurred. What followed in the recovery phase, however, was a Dark Age-conditioned social-cultural and political lifestyle that formed the basis of Western civilization as we know it today.

Given that Dark Ages in world history are significant moments signaling system crisis and system reorganization; the final phase of the Bronze Age crisis led to ecological recovery, certain political-economic realignments and reorganization, and the transition to a new working metal: iron. The Dark Age crisis was *system transformative* for it led to fundamental social system changes evolving to a set of new patterns [25,26,96].

The adoption of iron brought to an end centuries of bronze use that was in the control of palace economies and elites. Gordon Childe [63] has suggested that cheap iron with its wide availability provided the opportunities for agriculture, industry, and even warfare with the adoption of iron as the base metal. With trade route disruption and copper scarcity, the adoption of iron use spread further, especially among the communities in Greece that was isolated as a consequent of Dark Age conditions, for iron was available locally. It led to the development of local iron producing industries [51]. The low cost of iron because it was available locally facilitated its widespread use in agriculture and industry [63,124]. Cultivation was made easier with iron plowshares in heavy clay soils. This enabled the rural communities to participate further in the economy beyond subsistence, and in maintaining a class of miners, smelters, and metal smiths fabricating the iron implements to reproduce material life. Such an explanation is also supported by Heichelheim [125] and Polanyi [126], who have suggested that the widespread adoption iron was the result of the opportunity for rural communities in south Russia, Italy, North Africa, Spain, Gaul, Germany, and Eurasia to work the heavy soils with iron implements, thus increasing their production levels. Production increases can be seen by the fluctuations in grain prices according to Heichelheim [125]. The consequence of such transformation is that the urban elites in the Near East who in the past controlled the grain and other commodities trade suffered losses as a consequent of changing prices, and the falling demand for copper, tin and bronze, which they also controlled.

As a result of the above, the social structures were transformed with the formation of different regional centers in the periphery and in the Mediterranean. The opportunity for the farmers to farm in heavy clay soils utilizing cheap iron implements also provided the conditions for economic and system expansion following the end of the Dark Age where in the past these areas were not as productive. It enabled economic expansion, and the move into newer areas for agriculture as by this time some of the older settled areas were ecologically degraded and overworked.

In addition, at the social system level, the Dark Age crisis thus usher forth the dissociation of high value commodities away from the control of the palace/state, for by the end of the Dark Age, the command palace economies were in the Eastern Mediterranean were dissolved. What emerged was the continued differentiation of commercial/economic structures from the political structures [126]. Instead of bureaucratic palace centered trade, we see the development of mercantile city-states where merchant enterprise replaced the palace-controlled exchange. With this transformation, new forms of political powers and structures emerged. We have the emergence of a new political structure, the city-state (polis) in the Aegean, and the continuation of empire type political structures where the rule was via direct political and military control.

The new political structure, the polis, as a social organization and political concept emerged in 8th century Greece [114,115]. It was, as Morris [115] (p. 752) has stated, unique among ancient states for "its citizen body was actually the state". The rise of such a state form was a consequence of the collapse of the aristocratic society during the Greek Dark Ages. Other factors also precipitated its formation. Deurbanization and the loss of population in the urban areas resulting in the development of isolated communities during the Dark Age engendered the structural conditions for the development of the polis. In addition, with the scarcity of resources and the abundance of poverty leading to less hierarchical social structures, the groundwork for the development of the polis was also put into place. The polis thus was one where all authority was divested to the community unlike previous political forms in Mycenaean Greece. Force, therefore was located in the citizen body as a whole, and thus there was little need for a standing military. Individual natural rights were not sanctioned by a higher power and the highest authority was the polis, *i.e.*, the community. Such a political structure found expression in the Aegean. However, in other parts of the Near East, divine kingship was maintained with some minor modifications. According to Childe [63], Assyria, Babylonia, and Egypt continued as Bronze Age states.

Recovery returned around 700 BC with social systems expanding and growing in complexity again. Expansion came first in the form of colonization by the Greeks in two phases. Between 775 and 675 BC such expansion was for agricultural purposes, where the soils and lands of Greece which were degraded after centuries of erosion and intensive cultivation could no longer produce to meet the needs of the population. The excessive population mostly comprised of poor peasants who were turned into tenant farmers (*hectemores*) with debts that were increasing, and thus forced to swell the cities. With the state of the degraded environment in Greece, with the exception of Boetia, Attica, and Sparta where internal colonization was still possible with some fertile agricultural land left, expansion of the system came with migration to other arenas such as Italy, Sicily, Southern France, and West Asia. Growth in this case comes from a colonization process that was extensive in nature, and a consequence of the ecological crisis of the Dark Age that has just ended. Following the success of the agricultural colonization strategies with surplus generation, a second round of colonization from 675 BC to 600 BC followed, mainly focusing on commercial activities. With this phase of colonization, trade routes were further fixed and strengthened. Wealth for the colonial cities was derived from agricultural exports, trade and production. Other growth poles of the system then were Egypt, Persia and Phoenicia, and as Braudel [58] (p. 225) puts it, the Mediterranean never became a "Greek Lake." With these different centers, no polity ever gained control of the Mediterranean. It was only the arrival of Rome that the Mediterranean became a Roman sea. The growing rise of Rome and the demise of Greece did not interrupt the continuous degradation of the environment [9]. Forests were removed in Northern Africa and almost everywhere Roman rule was established. Mines were dug in Spain, with cities, roads, and production facilities established within the Roman Empire. Crisis emerged again 700 years later, around AD 400 with similar trends and tendencies in terms of ecological and socioeconomic variables like that of the Dark Ages that occurred during the Bronze Age. This time the collapses were not Mesopotamia, Harappa, Mycenaean Greece, Crete or the Hittite Empire, but it was the Western portion of the Roman Empire and the system of the Iron Age.

8. SYSTEM CRISIS IN BRONZE AGE EAST ASIA

The archaeological record reveals the presence of human communities from the Korean peninsula throughout Manchuria, the Gulf of Bohai in East Asia, the Yangtze river, and the islands of Japan as early as the Paleolithic period in 3000 BC [127]. Beyond indication of the dispersal of human communities across East Asia, there is evidence to substantiate the claim that contacts between these communities predate Dark Age periods [127,128]. In particular, one can surmise that due to geographic proximity the peoples of present-day China and Korea have an early history of economic and cultural exchanges. Early in the prehistory of East Asia, one observes contacts among Yemaek, Mongol, Manchu, Han, and other Northern tribes in the Korean Peninsula [129]. In addition, Chinese records indicate the habitation of local tribes such as the Puyo, the Okcho, the Yemaek and the I-Lou in Korea [129]. Furthermore, during China's Shang Dynasty (1600 BC–1046 BC), the Chinese settled at Lolang near modern day Pyongyang. In fact, around 1200 BC, in Northwest Korea, a state was founded under Chinese rule. The Chinese presence was further solidified on the Korean peninsula in 109 BC with an invasion that established four commandeered centers of Chinese administration at Nangnang [130].

8.1. Socioeconomic and Political Connections

Archeological research of the region reveals, five major trade routes in East Asia well in use prior to the 6th century BC: (1) the North route from Siberia; (2) the Korean route via its peninsula and across the Tsushima or Korean Strait; (3) the Jiangsu and Zhejiang route across the East China Sea to Kyushu; (4) the Taiwan and Fujian route via Ryukyu Islands to Kyushu; and (5) and the south sea route from the South Pacific via South China Sea islands to Manchuria [127,131,132,133]. These major trade routes physically illustrate the ability of human communities early in East Asian pre-history to engage in cultural and economic exchanges. Moreover, the presence of minor routes, or sub routes, through the Korean peninsula also further provided the linkages that connected the Asian mainland to the Japanese islands [127].

Although different explanations have surfaced regarding the flow of goods and people in East Asia, from an archeological perspective the South China Sea was a major route for cultural and economic exchanges [128]. This interaction is observed in the similarities exhibited in jade jewelry, lacquerware, agricultural cultivation, construction, and crops along the East China Sea route [128]. The cultural and economic linkages between China and Japan become evident in the presence of *ge*-shaped large earthenware pots, *yinwen* pottery, circularly-arranged tribal houses and mound-shaped graves in Japan [128]. Scholars note the similarity between items found in Japan and those in the lower Yangtze basin. Further back in history to the New Stone Age, some 7000 years ago, excavation at the Hemudu site in Eastern China revealed the presence of wooden oars and clay boat models [128]. During the same period, similar sites in the Zhoushan Islands off the coast of Zhejiang Province also reveal the ability of ancient communities to travel via waterways [134]. The route from the lower Yangtze basin via the East China Sea to Korea and Japan, was the preferred course of travel in the Late Shengwen period, during the tenth century BC, and became more popular during Japan's late Jomon and Yayoi periods (1500 BC–AD 500) [128]. Agricultural exchanges were not solely confined to seed or crops, but archeologists argue that the origins of the Japanese stone ax, ploughshares, hoes, and crescent-shaped harvesting knives can be traced to the Yangtze basin [128]. Physical evidence suggests that interactions between human communities in East Asia continued and intensified throughout the Bronze Age, and into the Iron Age.

Early iron use in China can be traced back to the Shang period (1766 BC–1122 BC) in a comparable sense to the utilization of iron in the West. Specifically, meteoritic iron was utilized, and was occasionally used in later periods [135,136,137,138,139]. The diffusion of iron throughout East Asia can be tied to the smelting of ore in China's Southern provinces. In this regard, Huang Zhanyue [140,141] provides evidence, along with persuasive arguments, that the smelting of iron in China began in the south and spreads to the Korean peninsula and Japan. Wagner [142,143,144] reviews Huang Zhanyue's [140] evidence and, coupled with other archeological data, has suggested that iron artifacts can be dated to as early as the Zhou Dynasty, and specific pieces may yet prove that the use of iron can be traced to earlier periods [145].

Chinese involvement on the Korean peninsula from the Shang to the early Han Dynastic period (1600 BC–AD 9) undoubtedly came to affect the political, cultural, and economic life of its inhabitants. China's influence was intensified as successive Chinese kingdoms emerged and sought to expand their political control. For example, during the early Han dynasty Chinese commandeering centers were established within the present-day geographical territory of Korea. Of these commandeering centers Lolang formed the core of Chinese colonial administration during the Han period [142,143,144,145,146]. Lolang not only served an important political role, but also proved to be an important economic point whereby Chinese goods could be distributed to points across Korea and Japan. As the Chinese administration center on the peninsula, Lolang "was in essence a Chinese city where the governor, officials, merchants, and Chinese colonists lived. Their way of life in general can be surmised from the investigation of remains unearthed at T'osong-ni, the site of Lolang administrative center near modern Pyongyang. The variety of burial objects found in their wooden and brickwork tombs attest to the lavish life style of these Chinese officials, merchants, and colonial overlords in Lolang's capital" [146] (p. 14).

Political administration by China of portions of the Korean peninsula influenced not only those populations under direct Chinese rule, but communities further South and East who were exposed and drawn to Chinese culture. The commandeering centers on the Korean peninsula brought China closer and "ultimately (created) a new China-oriented elite class" [146] (p. 14). Within areas outside of Chinese control the absorption of Chinese culture by local populations led to increased economic and cultural exchanges. As the most economically and culturally advanced society in East Asia, China attracted "neighboring states, which coveted the highly advanced Chinese culture" [146] (p. 14).

Although portions of the Korean peninsula were not under direct Chinese political control, the Chinese influence "is apparent from the fact that for the most part the leaders of the...states in the Southern half of the peninsula willingly accepted the grants of office and rank, official seals, and ceremonial attire that constituted...tokens of their submission to Lolang's (and China's) authority" [146] (p. 14). The availability of natural and human resources on the Korean peninsula made the area economically attractive to the Chinese who "were able to command the labor services of the native population they governed, for (enterprises such as) the large-scale cutting of timber. It is known, too, that iron ore deposits in the Southeast corner of the peninsula were supplied to Lolang" [146] (p. 14).

Although Japan is geographically disconnected from the Asian mainland by the sea, its islands were once connected extensions of the mainland when Ice Age sea levels fell [127]. Historically, land bridges at one point served to link the Chinese mainland to Japan. Early in East Asia's prehistory, initial habitation, cultural growth, and production were closely tied to the Asian mainland. Once the land bridge disappeared, the sea not only separated them, but also provided a method of transportation. According to Wagner [142] (p. 35), the sea makes "it logical that Japan was continuously influenced by mainland cultures since (East Asian prehistory)." Beyond analyses of early maritime trade, archeologists have unearthed ancient East Asian trading links following the discovery of meteorological tools [127]. Further substantiating the connections between human communities, Sima Qian, in the *Records of the Gran Historian*, writes about the use of horse-drawn war chariots introduced from the West and spread through Central Asia during the Shang Dynasty (1600 BC–1046 BC).

8.2. East Asia During the Final Phase of the Bronze Age Crisis

While the early Chinese Shang Dynasty (1600 BC–1046 BC) experienced a political and territorial expansion, the late period is characterized by fragmentation. Entering the Zhou period (770 BC–256 BC) warring factions in China sought to consolidate their power. In the "Annals of Zhou", written by Sima Qian (*ca.* 100 BC), the struggle between Shang and Zhou is well documented. East Asia has undergone periods where political, social, and economic life is disrupted. Although the duration and the precipitating agent of these disruptions requires some specificity, several general points, as related to trade, can be made about a Dark Age period in East Asia. First, previously established trade networks were disrupted. The disruption of trade networks leads to a decrease in economic and cultural contacts between human communities in the region. Secondly, the decrease in trade linkages creates a climate were local products are looked to as substitutes for previously imported foreign objects. However, the imprint of previous exchanges still manifests itself physically in the products that are manufactured, but they increasingly take on a local character. Third, as a result of linkages being disrupted cultural exchanges are also impacted and facilitate the re-emergence of local practices. During the Dark Age period in East Asia, this leads to indigenous or local practices being re-embraced. The archeological record, coupled with the reading of historical documents, indicates that in East Asia the disruption of cultural exchanges leads to a re-emergence of indigenous or local practices. Although we observe the presence of indigenous practices, and locally produced goods, during the pre-Dark Age period, Chinese objects and practices are predominant. As early as the Shang Dynastic period, there is a strong Chinese influence in Korea and Japan as evident in tools and objects traceable to the Yangtze basin. After a successful period of economic and cultural growth in East Asia, problems in the Chinese mainland lead to a decrease in trade exchanges. Internal crisis in China comes to impact the Korean peninsula and Japan.

Additionally, political fragmentation is an important aspect of Dark Ages. The chaos, disorder, and disruptions that characterize these periods in human history are in many respects the result of political strife and struggles over power. During the breakup of Shang rule around the 11th century BC, political power in China was transferred to local warlords. These local warlords were not content to share the Shang Empire. This resulted in the political disunity of China that carried into the Zhou period (770 BC–256 BC). The perpetual military incursions by competing warlords in China extended into the Korean peninsula. Although historically the peninsula has always had a Chinese presence, the move toward greater Korean autonomy from China can be traced to the disorder and wars that engulfed the Asian mainland during subsequent periods. The goal of expansion brought the Chinese Empire to Korea, but it also resulted in disastrous wars and ineffective expeditions.

In addition to the political fragmentation and wars, population loss and dispersal also characterizes Dark Age periods. There is evidence that a cooling period during Japan's late Jomon period (2000 BC–1000 BC) led to a significant depopulation and a downsizing of large settlement areas [147]. Additionally, one can surmise that the constant fighting not only resulted in population losses from combat, but war was also responsible for food shortages and emigration. In particular, border areas suffered mass departures as people attempted to flee war torn areas.

The human imprint in East Asia is clear in the earth because of the industrious husbandry of hundreds of generations, in the degradation of forests, in the eroded and impoverished lands, and in the barren unproductiveness of formerly fertile and populous terrain, all of which attest to prolonged human abuse. Environmental degradation, climate change, and social upheavals all serve as precipitating agents that led to a contraction of the social system and created an opportunity for a restructuring. In subsequent years, that extend into the Chinese Zhou Dynastic period (770 BC–200 BC), core-periphery relations are transformed, political boundaries are reconfigured, trade relations are intensified, and cultural practices are impacted.

8.3. Climate Fluctuations in Bronze Age East Asia

Preceding the rise of China's first dynastic period (2100 BC–1600 BC), prehistory reveals the formation of settlements during the Neolithic Age. Advances in agriculture led to settled communities and the beginnings of city-states. Prehistoric culture in East Asia is characterized by the development of systems of social stratification and the accompanying cultural objects typical of agricultural societies. Communities in East Asia succumb to the first phase of the Bronze Age crisis (2200 BC–1700 BC) during this Neolithic period as fluctuations in climate led to floods, drought and a disruption of settled agriculture. The collapse of Yueshi Culture in East Asia exemplifies the dependent character of social development [148]. Human communities do not develop separately from the limitations, setbacks, or good disposition of nature.

From the Neolithic Age onward, climate fluctuations in East Asia have been documented [149,150,151]. Historically, these have led to the collapse and flourishing of cultures, population growth and decline, and have halted and supported social development. Related to climate fluctuations, desertification cycles, and decreasing biological diversity over the last 5000 years in the region have been cited as a reason for the emergence and downfall of past empires [152]. Militaristic incursions by outsiders and internal socio-political conditions have long been explanations for the settlement patterns observe in East Asian history. However, it is important to incorporate the observations made in recent paleoclimactic studies that document changes in the physical environment of the Bronze Age world [153].

In the midst of the final phase of the Bronze Age crisis (1200 BC–700 BC), the archaeological record reveals a relocation of human communities [154]. The Western Zhou period (1046 BC–771 BC) in China is characterized by forays into neighboring communities, infighting amongst royals, and peasant uprisings. Although socio-economic issues partly explain the dissatisfaction amongst groups in Zhou society, and the impetus for migration, climate aridity around 1150 BC also pushed people out of former political and economic centers [155]. Written records of the time also corroborate the relocation of peoples. During the Bronze Age crisis, the change in climate led to excessive flooding. From the 16th century BC till 771 BC, several floods struck the Asian mainland that led to migration [156]. Historically, cultural adaptation is observed as a response to challenging social and environmental conditions. However, as demonstrated in East Asia, peoples also sought resource rich areas to recreate lifestyles no longer supported by the current physical environment.

Suggestive of the ebb and flow of history and the cyclical nature of climate, in subsequent periods, human communities are again equipped with the necessary physical conditions to support a sedentary lifestyle. Moving pass the final phase of the Bronze Age crisis and into the Zhou Dynastic period (1046 BC–256 BC), the climate begins to stabilize in the later periods of the Chou Dynasty [154]. Ultimately, an improved environment contributed to the bourgeoning of Bronze Age culture in East Asia and the prosperity observed during the Han Dynasty (202 BC–AD 220). Although climate and other exogenous factors impact social development, it is understood that human activities also contribute to the trajectory of communities.

8.4. Climate and System Crisis

It is clear from our theoretically informed historical narrative that the drivers that caused system crisis have their origins in Culture's relations with the natural environment. Included in this equation are the changes in climate. The late Bronze Age system crisis that impacted both West and East—even though at this point in time, from 1200 BC to 700 BC, there were no systemic connections in terms of trade, cultural exchanges, and socioeconomic relations between the two regions—suggest to us that climate is an important driver that impacted on the social formations in both regions consequently leading to changing socioeconomic and political demise and transitions.

Is climate the factor that is "determinate in the last instance", to borrow a phrase from structural Marxism, for our understanding and explanation of system crisis and transformation? We suggest it is certainly a factor, amongst others, that deserves attention. For the discipline of the social sciences, this might be quite unsettling as the discipline's *raison d'être* is to discover the socioeconomic and political factors that determine the social evolution of human social formations. Our historically informed theoretical framework has demarcated the factors that engender system transformations and crisis. By considering social system evolution over the *long historical time and geographic space*, we have been able to discriminate the relative impacts the various socioeconomic and political factors along with other natural environmental and climatic factors that determine the trajectory of system evolution. The fact that the late Bronze Age crisis showed parallel outcomes between the East and West when systemic trade, cultural and political connections were not in existence (or minimal at best) at this time period in world history, it has enabled us to pinpoint that climate should be considered and further research may reveal it is a principal driver that caused the cacophony of socioeconomic and political change that followed.

8.5. Concluding Remarks

While acknowledging that systemic crisis and transformation feature anthropogenic causal agents, our research makes clear that a more comprehensive study of system transformations must include Nature and the climate. Study of past system crises can inform our understanding of contemporary trends and the potential adjustments that await modern society. To the latter, despite the negative imagery the adjective "Dark" connotes, Dark Ages provide an opportunity for human creativity and ingenuity to surface in response to changing social and physical conditions. The creativity has a lasting impact that, even when conditions do change, endures and comes to alter and influence the character of subsequent exchanges between peoples.

This study also demonstrates that human history can be broadened beyond an anthropocentric discussion of peoples' circumstances, to include an examination of the impact human activities have on the Earth. Tangible remnants of the past remain, such as historical texts and artifacts, which provide vivid evidence of humankind's reach and the ability of human communities to interact directly and indirectly through large expanses as part of a Eurasian global economy. Climate changes and environmental degradation in the ancient world ominously shadows the present and speaks to the humanocentric conduct evident in ecological relations to this day.

Historically, a pattern is observed where periods characterized by prosperity, growth, consumption and materialism, are then followed by a "Dark" epoch that ushers in wars, disease, political instability, economic decline, and a curbing of previous consumptive habits. The social and physical circumstances necessary for unimpeded growth are disrupted allowing for the opportunity for Nature to recoup its losses [9]. This research illustrates that human populations, in interacting with each other and their environments, attempt to accommodate social, political, economic, and cultural activities to very specific environmental conditions. As a result, *the climate* and the ecological landscape are not only central to our analysis, that they should be recognized as the factors that inform the structure of economic and cultural practices that, in turn, conduce the trajectory of social systems.

ACKNOWLEDGMENTS

The authors wish to thank Megan Pullin and Dasha Mikhailova who helped along the way.

AUTHOR CONTRIBUTIONS

The research is the outcome of a collaboration between the authors that involved discussions on design, an extensive review of the literature, analysis, and several drafts of the paper. All authors have read and approved the final manuscript.

CONFLICTS OF INTEREST

The authors declare no conflict of interest.

REFERENCES

1. Marx, K. *Early Writings*; Vintage Books: New York, NY, USA, 1963.
2. Catton, W.; Dunlap, R. Environmental Sociology: A New Paradigm. *Am. Sociol.* **1978**, *13*, 41–49.
3. O'Connor, J. Capitalism, Nature, Socialism: A Theoretical Introduction. *Capital. Nat. Social.* **1988**, *1*, 11–38.

4. O'Connor, J. The Conditions of Production and the Production of Conditions. In *Natural Causes: Essays in Ecological Marxism*; Guilford: New York, NY, USA, 1998; pp. 135–178.

5. Schnaiberg, A. *The Environment from Surplus to Scarcity*; Oxford University Press: New York, NY, USA, 1980.

6. Foster, J.B. Marx's Theory of Metabolic Rift: Classical Foundations for Environmental Sociology. *Am. J. Sociol.* **1999**, *105*, 366–405.

7. Foster, J.B. *The Ecological Revolution: Making Peace with the Planet*; Monthly Review Press: New York, NY, USA, 2009.

8. Foster, J.B. *The Vulnerable Planet: A Short Economic History of the Environment*; Monthly Review Press: New York, NY, USA, 1999.

9. Chew, S. *World Ecological Degradation: Accumulation, Urbanization, and Deforestation*; AltaMira Press/Rowman and Littlefield Publishers: Lanham, MD, USA, 2001.

10. Chew, S. *The Recurring Dark Ages: Ecological Stress, Climate Changes and System Transformation*; AltaMira Press/Rowman and Littlefield Publishers: Lanham, MD, USA, 2007.

11. Chew, S. *Ecological Futures: What History Can Teach Us*; AltaMira Press/Rowman and Littlefield Publishers: Lanham, MD, USA, 2008.

12. Flotz, R.C. Does Nature Have Historical Agency? World History and Environmental History and How Histories Can Help to Save the Planet. *Hist. Teach.* **2003**, *37*, 9–28.

13. Foster, J.B. Transcending the Metabolic Rift: A Theory of Crises in the Capitalist World Ecology. *J. Peasant Stud.* **2011**, *38*, 1–46.

14. Moore, J.W. Environmental Crises and the Metabolic Rift in World-Historical Perspective. *Organ. Environ.* **2000**, *13*, 123–157.

15. Foster, J.B. *Marx's Ecology: Materialism and Nature*; Monthly Review Press: New York, NY, USA, 2000.

16. Foster, J. The Modern World-System as Environmental History? Ecology and the Rise of Capitalism. *Theory Soc.* **2003**, *32*, 307–377.

17. Foster, J. Madeira, Sugar, & the Conquest of Nature in the First Sixteenth Century, Part I: From Island of Timber to Sugar Revolution, 1420–1506. *Rev. J. Fernand Braudel Center* **2009**, *32*, 345–390.

18. Foster, J. Amsterdam is Standing on Norway, Part I: The Alchemy of Capital, Empire, and Nature in the Diaspora of Silver, 1545–1648. *J. Agrar. Chang.* **2010**, *10*, 35–71.

19. Foster, J. Amsterdam is Standing on Norway, Part II: The Global North Atlantic in the Ecological Revolution of the Seventeenth Century. *J. Agrar. Chang.* **2010**, *10*, 188–227.

20. Moore, J. The End of the Road? Agricultural Revolutions in the Capitalist World-Ecology, 1450–2010. *J. Agrar. Chang.***2010**, *10*, 389–413.

21. Moore, J. Madeira, Sugar, & the Conquest of Nature in the First Sixteenth Century, Part II: From Regional Crisis to Commodity Frontier, 1506–1530. *Rev. J. Fernand Braudel Center* **2010**, *33*.

22. Moore, J. This Lofty Mountain of Silver Could Conquer the Whole World: Potosí and the Political Ecology of

Underdevelopment, 1545–1800. *J. Philos. Econ.* **2010**, *4*, 58–103.

23. Moore, J. Ecology, Capital, and the Nature of Our Times. *J. World Syst. Anal.* **2010**, *17*, 108–147.

24. Moore, J. *Capitalism in the Web of Life: Ecology and the Accumulation of Capital*; Verso: New York, NY, USA, 2015.

25. Chew, S.C. For Nature: Deep Greening World Systems Analysis for the Twenty-First Century. *J. World Syst. Res.* **2015**, *3*, 381–402.

26. Chew, S. Ecological Relations and the Decline of Civilizations in the Bronze Age World System: Mesopotamia and Harrapa 2500 BC—1700 BC. In *Ecology and the World System*; Goldfrank, W., Ed.; Greenwood Press: Greenwich, CT, USA, 1999.

27. Roberts, J.T.; Grimes, P. World-Systems Theory and the Environment: A New Synthesis. In *Sociological Theory and the Environment*; Dunlap, R., Ed.; Rowman and Littlefield: Lanham, MD, USA, 2002; pp. 167–196.

28. Friedman, H. What on Earth is the Modern World-System? Food Getting and Territory in the Modern Era and Beyond. *J. World Syst. Res.* **2000**, *6*, 480–515.

29. Wallerstein, I. *Kondratieff Up or Down. Review II*; Spring: New York, NY, USA, 1979.

30. Wallerstein, I. *The End of the World as We Know It*; The University of Minnesota Press: Minneapolis, MN, USA, 1999.

31. Habermas, J. *Toward a Rational Society: Student Protest, Science and Politics*; Beacon Press: Boston, MA, USA, 1970.

32. Frank, A.G. Transitional Ideological Modes: Feudalism, Capitalism, and Socialism. *Crit. Anthropol.* **1991**, *11*, 171–188.

33. Frank, A.G.; Gills, B.K. World System Cycles, Crises, and Hegemonial Shifts. *Review* **1992**, *15*, 621–688.

34. Frank, A.G. Bronze Age World System Cycles. *Curr. Anthropol.* **1993**, *34*, 383–429.

35. Frank, A.G., Ed.; *The World System: 500 or 5000 Years*; Routledge: New York, NY, USA, 1993.

36. Frank, A.G. *ReOrient: Global Economy in the Asian Age*; University of California Press: Berkeley, CA, USA, 1998.

37. Modelski, G. *World Cities*; Faros: Washington, DC, USA, 2003.

38. Modelski, G.; Thompson, W. The Evolutionary Pulse of the World System: Hinterland Incursion and Migrations 4000 BC to AD 1500. In *World System Theory in Practice*; Kardulias, N., Ed.; Rowman and Littlefield: Lanham, MD, USA, 1999; pp. 241–274.

39. Thompson, W. C-Waves, Center-Hinterland Contact and Regime Change in the Ancient Near East: Early Impacts of Globalization. In Proceedings of the International Studies Association Annual Meetings, Los Angeles, CA, USA, 23–26 March 2000.

40. Thompson, W. Trade Pulsations, Collapse, and Reorientation in the Ancient World. In Proceedings of the International Studies Association Annual Meetings, Chicago, IL, USA, 24–27 March 2001.

41. Chase-Dunn, C.; Hall, T. *Rise and Demise: Comparing World-Systems*; Westview Press: Boulder, CO, USA, 1997.

42. Wallerstein, I. *The Modern World-System Vols 1–3*; Academic Press: New York, NY, USA, 1974.

43. Wallerstein, I. The West, Capitalism, and the Modern World System. *Review* **1992**, *15*, 561–620.

44. Beaujard, P. The Indian Ocean in Eurasian and African World-Systems Before the Sixteenth Century. *J. World Hist.***2005**, *16*, 411–465.

45. Beaujard, P. Evolution and Temporal Delimitations of Possible Bronze Age World-Systems in Western Asia, Africa and the Mediterranean. In *Interweaving Worlds: Systemic Interactions in Eurasia 7th to 1st Millennia BC*; Wilkinson, T., Ed.; Oxbow Press: Oxford, UK, 2009.

46. Beaujard, P. From Three Possible Iron-Age World-Systems to a Single Afro-Eurasian World-System. *J. World Hist.***2010**, *21*, 1–43.

47. Steinberg, T. Down to Earth: Nature, Agency, and Power in History. *Am. Hist. Rev.* **2002**, *107*, 798–820.

48. Wilkinson, T.J. *Town and Country in SouthEastern Anatolia*; Oriental Institute: Chicago, IL, USA, 1990.

49. Desborough, V.R. *The Greek Dark Ages*; Ernest Benn: London, UK, 1972.

50. Snodgrass, A.M. *The Dark Age of Greec*; Edinburgh University Press: Edinburgh, UK, 1971.

51. Snodgrass, A.M. *Archaic Greece*; MacMillan: London, UK, 1980.

52. Snodgrass, A.M. The Coming of the Iron Age in Greece: Europe's Earliest Bronze/Iron Transition. In *Bronze-Iron Age Transition in Europe*; BAR International Series No. 483;

Sorensen, M.L., Thomas, R., Eds.; Archeopress: Oxford, UK, 1989.

53. Braudel, F. *The Mediterranean and the Mediterranean World in the Age of Philip II*; Fontana: London, UK, 1972; Volume 1.

54. Braudel, F. *The Structure of Everyday Life*; Harper and Row: New York, NY, USA, 1981; Volume 1.

55. Braudel, F. *The Wheels of Commerce*; Harper and Row: New York, NY, USA, 1982; Volume 2.

56. Braudel, F. *The Perspective of the World*; Harper and Row: New York, NY, USA, 1984; Volume 3.

57. Braudel, F. *The Identity of France*; Harper and Row: New York, NY, USA, 1989; Volume 1–2.

58. Braudel, F. *Memory and the Mediterranean*; Alfred Knopf: New York, NY, USA, 2001.

59. Kristiansen, K. The Emergence of the European World System in the Bronze Age: Divergence, Convergence, and Social Evolution During the First and Second Millennia BC in Europe. *Sheff. Archaeol. Monogr.* **1993**, *6*, 7–30.

60. Kristiansen, K. *Europe before History*; Cambridge University Press: Cambridge, UK, 1998.

61. Kristiansen, K.; Larsson, T. *The Rise of Bronze Age Society Travels, Transmission, and Transformation*; Cambridge University Press: Cambridge, UK, 2005.

62. Kohl, P. The Ancient Economy, Transferable Technologies, and the Bronze Age World System: A View from the NorthEastern Frontiers of the Ancient Near East. In *Centre and Periphery in the Ancient World*; Rowlands, M., Mogens,

L., Kristian, K., Eds.; Cambridge University Press: Cambridge, UK, 1987.

63. Childe, G. *What Happened in History*; Penguin: Harmondsworth, UK, 1942.

64. Childe, G. The Urban Revolution. *Town Plan. Rev.* **1950**, *21*, 3–17.

65. Bell, B. The Dark Ages in Ancient History I: The First Dark Age in Egypt. *Am. J. Archaeol.* **1971**, *75*, 1–20.

66. Bell, B. Climate and History of Egypt. *Am. J. Archaeol.* **1975**, *79*, 223–279.

67. Perlin, J. *A Forest Journey*; Harvard University Press: Cambridge, UK, 1989.

68. Williams, M. *Deforesting the Earth: From Prehistory to Global Crisis*; University of Chicago Press: Chicago, IL, USA, 2003.

69. Rowton, M.B. The Woodlands of Ancient Western Asia. *J. Near East. Stud.* **1967**, *26*, 261–277.

70. Wilcox, G.H. Timber and Tress: Ancient Exploitation in the Middle East. In *Trees and Timber in Mesopotamia*; Bulletin on Sumerian Agriculture 6; Postgate, J.N., Powell, M.A., Eds.; Cambridge University: Cambridge, UK, 1992.

71. Lal, B.B. *The Earliest Civilization of South Asia: Rise, Maturity, and Decline*; Aryan Books International: New Delhi, India, 1997.

72. Behre, K.E. Some Reflections on Anthropogenic Indicators and the Record of Prehistoric Occupation Phases in Pollen Diagrams. In *Man's Role in the Shaping of the Eastern Mediterranean Landscape*; Bottema, S., Entjesbieburg, G.,

van Zeist, W., Eds.; Balkema: Rotterdam, The Netherlands, 1990.

73. Neumann, J.; Parpola, S. Climate Change and 11–10th Century Eclipse of Assyria and Babylonia. *J. Near East. Stud.* **1987**, *46*, 161–182.

74. Weiss, H.; Bradley, R. Archaeology: What Drives Societal Collapse? *Science* **2001**, *26*, 609–610.

75. Bentaleb, I.; Caratini, C.; Fontungne, M.; Morzadec-Kerfourn, M.; Pascal, J.; Tissot, C. Monsoon Regime Variations During the Late Holocene in SouthWestern India. In *Third Millennium BC Climate Change and Old World Collapse*; Dalfes, H., Ed.; Springer-Verlag: Heidelberg, Germany, 1997.

76. Ratnagar, S. *Encounters: The Westerly Trade of the Harappan Civilization*; Oxford University Press: New Delhi, India, 1981.

77. Fagan, B. *The Long Summer*; Basic Books: New York, NY, USA, 2004.

78. Issar, A. Climate Change and History during the Holocene in the Eastern Mediterranean Region. In *Water, Environment, and Society in Times of Climatic Change*; Issar, A., Brown, N., Eds.; Kluwer: Hague, The Netherlands, 1998.

79. Fairbridge, R.O.; Erol, O.; Karaca, M.; Yilmaz, Y. Background to Mid-Holocene Climate Change in Anatolia and Adjacent Regions. In *Third Millenium BC Climate Change and Old World Collapse*; Dalfes, H., Ed.; Springer-Verlag: Heidelberg, Germany, 1997.

80. Agrawal, D.P.; Sood, R.K. Ecological Factors and the Harappan Civilization. In *Harappan Civilization:*

Contemporary Perspective; Possehl, G., Ed.; Oxford University Press: New Delhi, India, 1982; pp. 223–231.

81. Possehl, G. *Ancient Cities of the Indus*; Vikas: New Delhi, India, 1979.

82. Possehl, G. The Harappan Civilization: A Contemporary Perspective. In *Harappan Civilization*; Possehl, G., Ed.; Oxford University Press: New Delhi, India, 1982.

83. Enzel, Y.; Ely, L.L.; Mishra, S.; Ramesh, R.; Amit, R.; Lazar, B.; Rajaguru, S.N.; Baker, V.R.; Sander, A. High Resolution Holocene Environmental Changes in the Thar Desert, Northwest India. *Science* **1999**, *2*, 125–128.

84. Matthews, R. Zebu: Harbinger of Doom in Bronze Age Western Asia. *Antiquity* **2002**, *76*, 438–446.

85. Hiebert, F. Bronze Age Central Eurasian Cultures in their Steppe and Desert Environments. In *Environmental Disaster and the Archaeology of Human Response*; Bawden, G., Reycraft, R., Eds.; University of New Mexico Press: Albuquerque, NM, USA, 2000.

86. Krementski, C. The Late Holocene Environmental and Climate Shift in Russia and Surrounding Lands. In *Third Millenium BC Climate Change and Old World Collapse*; Dalfes, H., Ed.; Springer-Verlag: Heidelberg, Germany, 1997.

87. Mellink, M. The Early Bronze Age in Western Anatolia: Aegean and Asiatic Correlations. In *End of the Early Bronze Age in the Aegean*; Cadogan, G., Ed.; Brill: Leiden, The Netherlands, 1986.

88. Butzer, K.W. Socio Political Discontinuity in the Near East c. 2200 BCE. Scenarios from Palestine and Egypt. In *Third Millenium BC Climate Change and Old World Collapse*; Dalfes, H., Ed.; Springer-Verlag: Heidelberg, Germany, 1997.

89. Harrison, T. Shifting Patterns of Settlement in the Highlands of Central Jordan during the Early Bronze Age. *Bull. Am. Sch. Orient. Res.* **1997**, *306*, 1–38.

90. Jameson, M.; Runnels, C.; Van Andel, T.; Munn, M. *A Greek Countryside: The Southern Argolid from Prehistory to the Present Day*; Stanford University Press: Stanford, CA, USA, 1994.

91. Watrous, L.V. Review of the Aegean Prehistory III: Crete from Earliest Prehistory through the Protopalatial Period. *Am. J. Archaeol.* **1994**, *98*, 695–753.

92. McGovern, P. Central TransJordan in Late Bronze Age and Early Iron Ages: An Alternative Hypothesis of Socioeconomic Collapse. In *Studies in the History and Archaeology of Jordan 3*; Hadidi, A., Ed.; Routledge and Kegan Pail: London, UK, 1987.

93. Bovarski, E. First Intermediate Period Private Tombs. In *Encyclopedia of Ancient Egypt*; Bard, K., Ed.; Routledge: New York, NY, USA, 1998.

94. Brinkman, J.A. Ur: The Kassite Period and the Period of Assyrian Kings. *Orientalis* **1968**, *38*, 310–348.

95. Knapp, A.B. Thalassocracies in the Bronze Age Eastern Mediterranean Trade: Making and Breaking a Myth World. *World Archaeol.* **1993**, *24*, 332–347.

96. Sheratt, S. The Growth of the Mediterranean Economy in the Early First Millennium BC. *World Archaeol.* **1993**, *24*, 361–378.

97. Sheratt, S. Sea Peoples and the Economic Structure of the late 2nd Millennium in the Eastern Mediterranean. In *Mediterranean Peoples in Transition: 13th to Early 10th Century BCE*; Gitin, S., Mazar, A., Sternleds, E., Eds.;

Jerusalem Archaeological Society: Jerusalem, Palestine, 1998; pp. 292–313.

98. Sheratt, S. Circulation of Metals and the End of the Bronze Age in the Eastern Mediterranean. In *Metals Make the World Go Round*; Pare, C., Ed.; Oxbow Books: Oxford, UK, 2000; pp. 82–98.

99. Toynbee, A.J. *A Study of History IV and V*; Oxford University Press: Oxford, UK, 1939.

100. Harding, A., Ed.; *Climatic Change in Later Prehistory*; Edinburgh University Press: Edinburgh, UK, 1982.

101. Carter, V.; Dale, T. *Topsoil and Civilization*; University of Oklahoma Press: Norman, France, 1974.

102. Zangger, E. The Environmental Setting. In *Sandy Pylos*; Davis, J., Ed.; University of Texas Press: Austin, TX, USA, 1998.

103. Runnels, C.N. Environmental Degradation in Ancient Greece. *Sci. Am.* **1995**, *272*, 96–99.

104. Van Andel, T.; Runnels, C.; Pope, O. Five Thousand Years of Land Use and Abuse in the Southern Argolid Greece. *Hesperia* **1986**, *55*, 103–128.

105. Blintiff, J. Erosion in the Mediterranean Lands: Reconsideration of Pattern, Process, and Methodology. In *Past and Present Soil Erosion*; Bell, M., Boardman, J., Eds.; Oxbow: Orford, UK, 1992.

106. Marinatos, S. The Volcanic Eruption of Minoan Crete. *Antiquity* **1939**, *13*, 425–439.

107. Chadwick, J. *The Mycenaean World*; Cambridge University Press: New York, NY, USA, 1976.

108. Warren, P.M. Minoan Palaces. *Sci. Am.* **1985**, *253*, 94–103.

109. Carpenter, R. *Discontinuity in Greek Civilization*; Cambridge University Press: Cambridge, UK, 1968.

110. Drews, R. *The End of the Bronze Age*; Princeton University Press: Princeton, NJ, USA, 1993.

111. Lamb, H.R. Carpenter's Discontinuity in Greek Civilization. *Antiquity* **1967**, *41*, 33–34.

112. Bryson, R.A.; Lamb, H.H.; Donley, D.L. Drought and the Decline of Mycenae. *Antiquity* **1974**, *48*, 46–50.

113. Bryson, R.A.; Padoch, C. On Climates of History. *J. Interdiscip. Hist.* **1980**, *10*, 583–597.

114. Morris, I. *Burial and Ancient Society: The Rise of the Greek City-State*; Cambridge University Press: Cambridge, UK, 1987.

115. Morris, I. Tomb Cult and the Greek Renaissance: The Past in the Present 8th Century BC. *Antiquity* **1988**, *62*, 750–761.

116. Morris, I. *Archaeology as Cultural History: Words and Things in Iron Age Greece*; Blackwell: Malden, MA, USA, 2000.

117. Whitley, J. *Style and Society in Dark Age Greece: The Changing Face of Pre-Literate Society 1100—700 BC*; Cambridge University Press: Cambridge, UK, 1991.

118. Harrison, A.B.; Nigel, S. After the Palace: The Early History of Messinia. In *Sandy Pylos*; Davis, J., Ed.; University of Texas Press: Austin, TX, USA, 1998.

119. Small, D. Handmade Burnished Ware and Prehistoric Aegean Economics. *J. Mediterr. Archaeol.* **1990**, *3*, 3–25.

120. Rutter, J. Cultural Novelties in the Post Palatial Aegean World: Indices of Vitality or Decline. In *The Crisis Years:*

The 12th Century BC; Ward, W., Joukowsky, M., Eds.; Kendall Hunt: Dubuque, IA, USA, 1989.

121. Deger-Jalkotzy, S. The Last Mycenaeans and their Successors Updated. In *Mediterranean Peoples in Transition: Thirteenth to Early Tenth Centuries BCE: In Honor of Professor Trude Dothan*; Gitin, S., Mazar, A., Stern, E., Eds.; Israel Exploration Society: Jerusalem, Palestine, 1998; pp. 114–128.

122. Muhly, J.D. The role of the Sea People of Cyprus during the LC III Period. In *Cyprus at the Close of the Late Bronze Age*; Karageorghis, V., Muhly, J., Eds.; Zavallis: Nicosia, Cyprus, 1984.

123. Stanislawski, D. Dark Age Contributions to the Mediterranean Way of Life. *Ann. Assoc. Am. Geogr.* **1973**, *63*, 397–410.

124. McNeill, J.R.; McNeill, W. *The Human Web*; Norton: New York, NY, USA, 2003.

125. Heichelheim, F.M. *An Ancient Economic History*; A.W. Sijthoff: Leiden, The Netherlands, 1968; Volume 1.

126. Polanyi, K. *The Livelihood of Man*; Academic Press: New York, NY, USA, 1977.

127. Imamura, K. *Prehistoric Japan: New Perspectives on Insular East Asia*; University of Hawaii Press: Honolulu, HI, USA, 1996.

128. Zhimin, A. Effect of Prehistoric Cultures of the Lower Yangtze River on Ancient Japan. *Kaogu* **1984**, *5*, 439–558.

129. De Bary, T.W., Lee, P.H., Eds.; *Sources of Korean Tradition*; Columbia University Press: NewYork, NY, USA, 1997.

130. McCune, S. *Korea's Heritage: A Regional and Social Geography*; C.E. Tuttle: Tokyo, Japan, 1956.

131. Tongko, L. Study on Eastern Movement of Japanese. *Kaogu* **1971**, *5*, 439–558.

132. Matsumura, Y. Temporal Distribution of Cereal Remains of Asian Neolithic. *Kikan Koukogaku* **1991**, *37*, 33–35.

133. Takakura, M. The Route of the Arrival of Rice. *Kikan Koukogaku* **1991**, *37*, 40–45.

134. An, Z.M. Chinese Prehistoric Agriculture. *J. Archaeol.* **1988**, *28*, 589–593.

135. Gettens, R.J.; Clarke, R.S.; Chase, W.T. Two Early Chinese Bronze Weapons with Meteoritic Iron Blades. In *Freer Gallery of Art, Occasional Papers 4: 1–11*; Freer Gallery of Art: Washington, DC, USA, 1971.

136. Li, Z. The development of iron and steel technology in ancient China. *Kaogu Xue Bao* **1975**, *2*, 1–22.

137. Li, Z. Studies on the Iron Blade of a Shang Dynasty Bronze Yüeh-axe Unearthed at Kao-ch'eng, Hupei, China. *Kaogu Xue Bao* **1976**, *2*, 17–34.

138. Yuan, J.; Zhang, X. Shang-period Tombs Excavated in Pinggu County, Beijing. *Beijing Munic. Cult. Relics Off.* **1977**, *11*, 1–8.

139. Hua, J. Meteoritic Iron, Meteoritic Iron Artifacts, and the Invention of Iron-Smelting. *KJSW* **1982**, *9*, 17–22.

140. Huang, Z. On the Problem of the First Smelting of Iron and Use of Iron Implements in China. *Wen Wu* **1976**, *8*, 62–70.

141. Huang, Z. Ancient Culture of the Lower Yangtze River and Ancient Japan. *Kaogu* **1990**, *4*, 375–384.

142. Wagner, D.B. The Dating of the Chu Graves of Changsha: The Earliest Iron Artifacts in China? *Acta Orient.* **1987**, *48*, 111–156.

143. Wagner, D.B. *Iron and Steel in Ancient China*; E.J. Brill: New York, NY, USA, 1993.

144. Wagner, D.B. *The State and Iron Industry in Han China*; NIAS: Copenhagen, Denmark, 2001.

145. Zou, H. Stone-chamber Tumulus Sites at Wufengshan in Wuxian County, Jiangsu. *Nianjian* **1984**, *1*, 105–106.

146. Eckert, C.J.; Lee, K.; Lew, Y.; Robinson, M.; Wagner, E. *Korea, Old and New: A History*; Korea Institute: Seoul, Korea, 1990.

147. Habu, J.; Hall, M.E. Climate Change, Human Impacts on the Landscape, and Subsistence Specialization: Historical Ecology and Changes in Jomon Hunter-Gatherer Lifeways. In *The Historical Ecology of Small Scale Economies*; Victor, D.T., Waggoner, J., Eds.; University of Florida Press: Gainesville, FL, USA, 2012.

148. Guo, Y.; Mo, D.; Mao, L.; Wang, S.; Li, S. Settlement Distribution and its Relationship with Environmental Changes from the Neolithic to Shang-Zhou Dynasties in Northern Shandong, China. *J. Geogr. Sci.* **2013**, *23*, 679–694.

149. Yasuda, Y. Climate Change and the Origin and Development of Rice Cultivation in the Yangtze River Basin, China. *Ambio* **2008**, *2008*, 502–506.

150. Mao, L.J.; Mo, D.W.; Zhou, K.S.; Guo, W.M.; Jia, Y.F.; Yang, J.H.; Deng, H.; Shi, C.X.; Jia, J.Y. Rare Earth Elements and the Environmental Significance of the Dark Brown Soil in Liyang Plain, Hunan Province, Cina. *Acta Sci. Circumst.* **2009**, *29*, 1561–1568.

151. Guo, Y.; Mo, D.; Mao, L.; Jin, Y.; Guo, W.; Mudie, P.J. Settlement Distribution and its Relationship with Environmental Changes from the Paleolithic to Shang-Zhou period in Liyang Plain, China. *Quat. Int.* **2014**, *321*, 29–36.

152. Wang, X.; Chen, F.; Zhang, J.; Yang, Y.; Li, J.; Hasi, E.; Zhang, C.; Xia, D. Climate, Desertification, and the Rise and Collapse of China's Historical Dynasties. *Hum. Ecol. Interdiscip. J.* **2010**, *38*, 157–172.

153. Huang, C.C.; Su, H. Climate Change and Zhou Relocations in Early Chinese History. *J. Hist. Geogr.* **2009**, *35*, 297–310.

154. Ouyang, X.; Davis, R.L. *Historical Records of the Five Dynasties*; Columbia University Press: New York, NY, USA, 2004.

155. Huang, C.C.; Zhao, S.; Pang, J.; Zhou, Q.; Chen, S.; Li, P.; Mao, L.; Ding, M. Climatic Aridity and the Relocations of the Zhou Culture in the Southern Loess Plateau of China. *Clim. Chang.* **2003**, *61*, 361–378.

156. Chen, Y.; James, S.; Shu, G.; Irina, O.; Albert, K. Socio-economic Impacts on Flooding: A 4000-Year History of the Yellow River, China. *J. Hum. Environ.* **2012**, *41*, 682–698.

8

CHAPTER

Is Economic Development Promoting Monetary Integration in East Asia?

Kentaro Kawasaki[1,*,†] and Zhi-Qian Wang[2]

[1] *Faculty of Business Administration, Toyo University, 5-28-20, Hakusan, Bunkyo-ku, Tokyo 112-8606, Japan*

[2] *Faculty of Commerce and Management, Hitotsubashi University, 2-1 Naka, Kunitachi, Tokyo 186-8601, Japan*

ABSTRACT

This paper tries to investigate whether there exist international integrated markets among East Asian economies, by employing the Generalized Purchasing Power Parity (G-PPP) model, then, it would help to suggest whether the East Asian region is the Optimum Currency Area (OCA) or not. The empirical results in this paper suggest that holding the G-PPP among nine Asian countries (China, Indonesia, Japan, Korea, Malaysia, the Philippines, Singapore, Thailand and Vietnam) becomes more applicable in 2000–2013 than of that in 1984–1997. In the period of "globalization," which is characterized by expansion of world trade, increase of international capital flows, and development of information and communications technologies, Asian economic development has been promoting not only economic integrations but also constructing the stable linkages of real exchange rates. Therefore, it would help to adopt regional coordination for monetary policies to assure the feasibility of a possible monetary union.

Keywords: OCA, exchange rate, M-TAR, co-integration with thresholds adjustment

JEL Classification: F31; F33; F36

1. INTRODUCTION

It is well known that each of the East Asian countries considered here experienced rapid economic growth across two separate periods of development. The first period of rapid growth was called "The East Asian miracle." There were eight high-performing Asian economies (HPAEs): three ASEAN countries, four newly-industrializing countries (NIEs), and Japan, whose economy grew faster than almost all other economies from the mid-1960's until the early 1990's. Most of their economic achievements, in particular a rapid increase in GDP per capita, were based on maintaining macroeconomic stability with sound financial markets, providing government-backed supports for key industries, and maintaining sound fiscal and public policies. Although each country promoted to develop "internationalized" industries by expanding exports of manufacturing, the "localized" monetary environment played important roles in supporting the rapid growth of local infant industries.

The second period of growth has been experienced in the twenty-first century. It can be described as a century of "globalization," which is characterized by the expansion of world trade, the increase of international capital flows, and the development of information-communication technologies. These new growth factors led to spillover effects on developing countries in East Asia. Hence, this recent economic growth promoted an economic integration across the East Asian countries. Therefore, the question arises as to whether economic growth also promotes the monetary integration by moving away from monetary "localization" to monetary "regionalization".

This paper investigates this issue by employing the Generalized Purchasing Power Parity (G-PPP) model, which considers that countries that satisfy the criterion for an Optimum Currency Area (OCA) should share a common stochastic trend in their real exchange rates, which can be defined as the function of the national income process. Our empirical results suggest the existence of integrated markets among the region's economies. It allows us to consider whether the region represents an OCA. By adopting the non-linear co-integration method into Enders and Hurn's (1994) [1] original and well-known G-PPP model, our empirical analysis suggests that a consideration of G-PPP among nine Asian countries is more relevant in 2000–2013 than in the previous period of 1984–1997. This means that Asian economic development has been promoting not only economic integration but also monetary integration, where the stability of real exchange rates among regional currencies also enhances the efficiency of market transactions. Therefore, further economic integration potentially contributes to the coordination of regional monetary/financial policies, thus assuring the feasibility of a monetary union.

The rest of this paper is organized as follows. Section 2 provides the brief reviews of earlier studies on the necessity of monetary cooperation and on the OCA in East Asia. Section 3 gives the details of the G-PPP model. Section 4 provides explanations of the empirical strategy and its results. Section 5 is saved for the concluding remarks.

2. MONETARY COOPERATION IN EAST ASIA

The economic growth in East Asian area stood out as far back as 50 years ago. Since the 1960s, East Asia had been in a period of high growth; this led to Korea, Taiwan, Hong Kong, and Singapore being billed "The Four Tigers". In the 1980s, the Southeast Asian area—including Malaysia, Indonesia, and Thailand—achieved a high growth rate. The excellent performance of the East Asian economy was considered "The East Asian Miracle" by the World Bank. The myth of economic growth there, however, was broken by the unexpected incident that has since come to be known as the Asian currency crisis.

In the aftermath of the 1997 Asian currency crises, some policymakers and academics proposed surveillance over the intra-regional exchange rates of East Asian currencies, to prevent future crises. In accordance with these proposals, the Chiang Mai Initiative (CMI) was established as a safety net for a liquidity crisis by the members of the Association of Southeast Asian Nations (ASEAN), Japan, China, and Korea (ASEAN+3) in 2000. Concurrently, the finance deputy ministers of the ASEAN+3 countries executed the Economic Review and Policy Dialogue (ERPD) to oversee the macroeconomic performance of each member country.

The objective of entering into a currency swap arrangement is to manage crises; therefore, the CMI exerts its effect only in cases of an actual currency crisis. On the other hand, the ERPD is simply a surveillance system that focuses on the performance of each country's macroeconomic variables (e.g., GDP and inflation rate), as well as the soundness of its financial sector. Therefore, it is necessary to incorporate intra-regional exchange rates into the surveillance process in order to enhance foreign exchange surveillance of the ASEAN+3 countries, which may result in lowering the probability of a future crisis. The monetary authorities are expected to establish a surveillance system to monitor fluctuations and misalignments of each ASEAN+3 currency. The exchange rates to monitor include intra-regional exchange rates, as well as the one *vis-à-vis* the US dollar.

In line with the need to establish a system for monitoring fluctuations in intra-regional exchange rates, Williamson (2000) [2], Ogawa and Ito (2002) [3], Kuroda and Kawai (2003) [4], and Ogawa (2004) [5] have suggested the introduction in the East Asian area of a common basket system. Given that a common currency basket system could inhibit foreign exchange volatility and contribute to stabilizing trade balance within the East Asian area, the monetary authority of East Asian countries are expected to adopt a common currency basket system. Furthermore, some positive results have been achieved in terms of CMI multi-lateralization (CMIM) and the ASEAN+3 Macroeconomic Research Office (AMRO), after the commencement of regional monetary cooperation in East Asia.

Within the context mentioned above, Kawasaki (2012) [6] employed the G-PPP model to conclude that a common currency basket would be a desirable step toward creating a common currency area in East Asia. With respect to the economic integration in East Asia, this paper investigates whether East Asian countries have been more or less integrated in the first decade of the twenty-first century than the period before Asian currency crisis. Furthermore, recognizing the importance of intra-regional foreign exchange stabilization, this paper also extends Kawasaki (2012) [6] to identify which ASEAN member countries are suitable to form a common currency area with Japan, China, and Korea.

3. THE GENERALIZED PURCHASING POWER PARITY MODEL

The G-PPP model was developed by Enders and Hurn's (1994) [1], which extends from a simple Purchasing Power Parity (PPP) model. Enders and Hurn's (1994) [1] argue that changes in a bilateral exchange rate depend not only on changes in the relative prices between the related two countries but also on those in relative prices among other countries, such as trade partners. As

Mundell (1961) [7] pointed out, countries that have close economic relationships with each other can share factor mobility in their national income processes. The real exchange rates can be defined as a function of countries' income process; hence, the real exchange rates among countries which share factor mobility will be also highly correlated. Therefore, Enders and Hurn's (1994) [1] considered that countries that share factor mobility should exhibit a common stochastic trend in their real exchange rates, which can satisfy the criterion for the OCA. Kawasaki (2012) [6] shows the theoretical background of G-PPP model by extending the two-country and two-commodity model proposed in Obsteld and Rogoff (1996) [8]. As domestic labor mobility equalizes the productivity growth in tradables with that of non-tradables, international factor mobility between two countries would equalize the productivity growth in both two countries. Therefore, the nominal exchange rate between two countries would be equal to the relative PPP. The real exchange rates are constants over time; hence, the nominal exchange rate can be fixed between two countries. In consequence, the condition for the PPP to hold between the two countries is regarded as a sufficient condition for the OCA 1.

Here, following the theoretical background of the G-PPP model proposed by Kawasaki (2012) [6], we assume that m countries (1, 2,..., j,..., m) are expected to compose a common currency area. Country j has a trade relationship with n countries, and a strong trade relationship with m – 1 countries that are expected to compose the common currency area. The real effective exchange rate of country j can be expressed as follows:

$$\begin{aligned} ree_j = \zeta_j \cdot \left(\beta_{j,1} re_{j,1} + \beta_{j,2} re_{j,2} + \cdots + \beta_{j,m} re_{j,m}\right) \\ + \left(1-\zeta_j\right) \cdot \left(\beta_{j,m+1} re_{j,m+1} + \beta_{j,m+2} re_{j,m+2} + \cdots + \beta_{j,n} re_{j,n}\right) \end{aligned} \quad (1)$$

where $re_{j,i}$ is real exchange rate between country i and country j in logarithm. Then, ζ_j is the trade weight of the group countries that are expected to compose a common currency area, and $\beta_{j,i}$ is the trade weight of country j with country $\left(\sum_{i=1,i\neq j}^{m} \beta_{j,i} = 1, \sum_{i=m+1}^{n} \beta_{j,i} = 1\right)$.

For simplicity, we focus on the group of countries that is expected to adopt a common currency and the country m + 1 that is not expected to share a common currency with the other countries. Then the real effective exchange rate of country $j$can be rewritten as follows:

$$ree_j = \omega_{j,1} re_{j,1} + \omega_{j,2} re_{j,2} + \cdots + \omega_{j,m} re_{j,m} + \omega_{j,m+1} re_{j,m+1} \quad (2)$$

where $\omega_{j,i}$ is the trade weight of country j with country $\left(\sum_{i=1,i\neq j}^{m+1} \omega_{j,i} = 1\right)$.

Since $\omega_{j,m+1} = 1 - \omega_{j,1} - \omega_{j,2} - \omega_{j,3} - \cdots - \omega_{j,m}$, the real effective exchange rate of country j can be expressed as follows:

$$\begin{aligned} ree_j = {} & \omega_{j,1}\left(re_{j,1} - re_{j,m+1}\right) + \omega_{j,2}\left(re_{j,2} - re_{j,m+1}\right) + \cdots \\ & + \omega_{j,m-1}\left(re_{j,m-1} - re_{j,m+1}\right) + \omega_{j,m}\left(re_{j,m} - re_{j,m+1}\right) + re_{j,m+1} \end{aligned} \quad (3)$$

Given $re_{j,k} = re_{j,n} - re_{k,n}$, 2, then we can express the real effective exchange rate of country j as below:

$$ree_j = \omega_{j,1} re_{m+1,1,t} + \cdots + \omega_{j,m} re_{m+1,m,t} - re_{m+1,j,t} \quad (4)$$

Therefore, the real effective exchange rate of other countries country one, country two, ..., and country m + 1 can be expressed as follows:

$$
\begin{aligned}
ree_{1,t} &= -re_{m+1,1,t} + \omega_{1,2} re_{m+1,2,t} + \cdots + \omega_{1,m} re_{m+1,m,t} S \\
ree_{2,t} &= \omega_{2,1} re_{m+1,1,t} - re_{m+1,2,t} \cdots + \omega_{2,m} re_{m+1,m,t} \\
&\vdots \\
ree_{m,t} &= \omega_{m,1} re_{m+1,1,t} + \cdots + \omega_{m,m-1} re_{m+1,m-1,t} - re_{m+1,m,t} \\
ree_{m+1,t} &= \omega_{m+1,1} re_{m+1,1,t} + \cdots + \omega_{m+1,m-1} re_{m+1,m-1,t} + \omega_{m+1,m} re_{m+1,m,t}
\end{aligned}
$$

The real effective exchange rate of m + 1 countries can be expressed in a vector as follows:

$$
\mathbf{ree}_t = \Omega \cdot \mathbf{re}_t \tag{5}
$$

where Ω is a matrix, which defines the trade weights, and re is the real exchange rate of country j *vis-à-vis* its trading partners (m countries).

$$
\underset{(m+1)\times m}{\Omega} = \begin{bmatrix} -1 & \omega_{1,2} & \cdots & \omega_{1,m-1} & \omega_{1,m} \\ \omega_{2,1} & -1 & \cdots & \omega_{2,m-1} & \omega_{2,m} \\ \vdots & \vdots & \ddots & \vdots & \vdots \\ \omega_{m,1} & \omega_{m,2} & \cdots & \omega_{m,m-1} & -1 \\ \omega_{m+1,1} & \omega_{m+1,2} & \cdots & \omega_{m+1,m-1} & \omega_{m+1,m} \end{bmatrix} \text{ and}
$$

$$
\mathbf{re} = \left(re_{m+1,1}, re_{m+1,2}, re_{m+1,3}, \cdots, re_{m+1,m-1}, re_{m+1,m} \right)'
$$

As Enders and Hurn (1994) [1] discussed, within a common currency area the fundamental macroeconomic variables share common trends, and a G-PPP based on real macroeconomic variables suggests that certain groupings of real exchange rates share the same stochastic trends. Therefore, the real effective exchange rates within a currency area will share a common stochastic trend because the fundamental variables are sufficiently interrelated. Using the common trends representation developed in Stock and Watson (1988) [13], the real effective exchange rates can be expressed by the sum of a stationary component and a non-stationary component. That is:

$$\mathbf{ree}_t = \mathbf{r\bar{e}e}_t + \mathbf{r\tilde{e}e}_t \tag{6}$$

where $\mathbf{r\bar{e}e}$ represents a stationary component and $\mathbf{r\tilde{e}e}$ represents a non-stationary component.

Since the stationary component $\mathbf{r\bar{e}e}$, which represents the logarithm of the real effective exchange rate, can be expected to converge toward zero over the long run, the real effective exchange rate then can be described as the non-stationary component $\mathbf{r\tilde{e}e}$ only 3. As described in Stock and Watson (1988) [13], in terms of the common trends representation, $m + 1$ non-stationary variables can be described as $m + 1$ stochastic trends. We can rewrite the real effective exchange rates as follows:

$$\mathbf{ree} = \mathbf{r\tilde{e}e} = \mathbf{\Phi} \cdot \mathbf{w} \tag{7}$$

where Φ is a (m+1)×(m+1) matrix, and w is a $(m + 1)$ vector of which the vector is characterized by a random walk with non-stationary stochastic trends.

Based on Equations (5) and (7), we can obtain:

$$\mathbf{\Phi} \cdot \mathbf{w}_t = \mathbf{\Omega} \cdot \mathbf{re}_t \tag{8}$$

Here, we define a nonzero matrix Ψ which is given by (m+1)×(m+1) components, and then by substituting it into Equation (8), we can rewrite Equation (8) as follows:

$$\mathbf{\Psi} \cdot \mathbf{\Phi} \cdot \mathbf{w}_t = \mathbf{\Psi} \cdot \mathbf{\Omega} \cdot \mathbf{re}_t \tag{9}$$

If Ψ·Φ·w is expected to be equal to zero over the long run, then Ψ·Φ should not be a full rank because w that was defined as a random walk with non-stationary stochastic trends is a nonzero vector. The rank condition of $\Psi \cdot \Phi$ will be expected as follows:

$$\mathrm{rank}(\Psi \cdot \Phi) = \mathrm{rank}(\Phi) < m$$

As long as the rank condition to be held, there exists a nonzero matrix Ψ with which we can obtain the following equation:

$$\Psi \cdot \Phi = 0 \tag{10}$$

Under the circumstance given by $\Psi \cdot \Phi \cdot w=0$, we can rewrite Equation (9) as follows:

$$\mathbf{\Psi} \cdot \mathbf{\Omega} \cdot \mathbf{re} = \mathbf{Z} \cdot \mathbf{re} = 0 \tag{11}$$

where Z is defined as $Z=\Psi \cdot \Omega$.

If we can find a matrix Z for which the rank condition satisfies $\mathrm{rank}(Z)<m$, then we can obtain $Z \cdot re=0$ that there exists at least one linear combination of the real exchange rate co-integrating over the long run.

4. EMPIRICAL ANALYSIS OF A COMMON CURRENCY AREA

4.1. Empirical Methodology

As mentioned above, the G-PPP model assumes that there are common factors among the bilateral real exchange rates of these countries exhibiting strong economic relationships. Therefore, if we can detect an equilibrium relationship among the real exchange rates over the long run, these countries (with real exchange rates that share common trends), might be defined as representing a common currency area.

Ogawa and Kawasaki (2003) [14] employed the methodology of the Johansen test as elaborated by Johansen and Juselius (1990) [15] to identify whether there exist co-integration relationships among the real exchange rates of East Asian currencies over the long run. As is well known, the Johansen approach is designed to identify a co-integration relationship under the assumption of linear composition. In other words, the short-term instability converges to the long-term equilibrium level linearly. Therefore, when we identify whether combinations satisfy the condition of stationarity over the long run, some of them will be rejected due to the assumption of linear convergence. Here, we employ the momentum threshold autoregressive (M-TAR) model developed by Enders and Granger (1998) [16] to investigate the property of real exchange rates.

It is well known that many macroeconomic variables display an asymmetric adjustment process. The TAR model suggested by Enders and Granger (1998) [16] allows for asymmetric adjustment processes and can capture the key aspects of any "sharp" or "deep" movements in a series. The TAR model with high order processes can be expressed as below:

$$\Delta X_t = I_t \rho_1 (X_{t-1} - \tau) + (1 - I_t) \rho_2 (X_{t-1} - \tau) + \sum_{i=1}^{p} \alpha_i \Delta X_{t-1} + \varepsilon_t$$

$$\rho_1 < 0, \rho_2 < 0,\ I_t = \begin{cases} 1 & if \quad X_{t-1} \geq \tau \\ 0 & if \quad X_{t-1} < \tau \end{cases}, \tag{12}$$

where ρ_1 and ρ_2 indicate adjustment process respectively, $I_t \rho_1$ is regarded as the appreciation correcting coefficient, (1−It)ρ2 is regarded as the depreciation correcting coefficient, and the nonzero value τ is a threshold.

From Equation (12) we could detect whether there exists a long-term equilibrium relationship among the real exchange rate as far as the threshold value τ is given. It is also clear that autoregressive decay depends on the level value of Xt−1. As another alternative adjustment specification, Enders and Granger (1998) [16] indicated that it is useful to allow the autoregressive decay depending on the previous period's change in Xt−1 instead of on the level value. Therefore, the M-TAR model can also be given as follows:

$$\Delta X_t = I_t \rho_1 X_{t-1} + (1 - I_t)\rho_2 X_{t-1} + \sum_{i=1}^{r} \alpha_i \Delta X_{t-1} + \varepsilon_t$$

$$\rho_1 < 0, \rho_2 < 0 \quad I_t = \begin{cases} 1 & if \quad \Delta X_{t-1} \geq 0 \\ 0 & if \quad \Delta X_{t-1} < 0 \end{cases} \tag{13}$$

The M-TAR model suggests that there exists little autoregressive decay for positive ΔXt−1, but a significant decay for negative ΔXt−1 as far as the prior condition |ρ1|<|ρ2|, and *vice versa*.

Based on the theoretical model of G-PPP, we can express the co-integration relationship of Z·re=0 with the *m* + 1 real exchange rates as follows:

$$re_{USD,EUR,t} = \beta_1 \cdot re_{USD,1,t} + \beta_2 \cdot re_{USD,2,t} + \cdots + \beta_m \cdot re_{USD,m,t} + \nu_t \tag{14}$$

where reUSD,EUR,t is the anchor exchange rate, reUSD,i,t for which *i* is given by i=1, 2, 3, ⋯, m is the individual I(1) components of real exchange rate, βi for which *i* is given by i=1, 2, 3, ⋯, m is estimated parameters, and v_t is the disturbance term which is considered serially correlated.

As the two-step methodology entails using the Ordinary least-squares (OLS) to estimate a long-term equilibrium relationship, we also focus on the disturbance term to conduct a co-integration test.

However, the error correction model to identify the adjustment process is not symmetric, but asymmetric 4.

4.2. Data

The real exchange rate used in our empirical analysis is based on the nominal exchange rate and the consumer price index (CPI) from the *International Financial Statistics* of the IMF 5. The sample periods are from January 1984 to June 1997 and from January 2000 to June 2013. The possible candidates for a common currency area include six ASEAN countries (Singapore, Indonesia, Thailand, Malaysia, the Philippines, and Vietnam) and Japan, China, and Korea (ASEAN6+3). However, Vietnam is excluded from the first sample period (January 1984 to June 1997) and the inclusion of China begins in January 1987 due to data constraints. Since the United States and the euro area are important trading partners of ASEAN6+3, we employ the real exchange rate of the euro *vis-à-vis* the US dollar as an anchor exchange rate in our empirical analysis 6. The nominal exchange rates of the US dollar and the euro are also based on the *International Financial Statistics* of the IMF. The CPI of the euro area from January 1984 to June 1997 is calculated based the member of European Currency Unit (ECU), and that of the second sample period (January 2000 to June 2013) is from DataStream.

4.3. Analytical Results

For estimating the co-integration relationship over the long run, the estimation results of OLS coefficients for asymmetric co-integration and M-TAR unit root test were summarized in Table 1, Table 2, Table 3 and Table 4 7. Table 1 and Table 3 which show the results of the OLS estimation only include the combinations which all independent variables indicate significant at 5% significance level. In Table 2 and Table 4, which show the results of the M-TAR unit root test, the color filled columns suggests that two coefficients of adjustment process in the error correction model indicate significant at 2.5% significance level.

In the sample period from January 2000 to June 2013, there exist 502 possible candidates that contain nine, eight, seven, six, five, four, three, or two countries in the common currency area, and that selected from nine Asian currencies. Seventy-eight combinations were found that all coefficients for independent variables are statistically significant (Table 1). Out of the 78 combinations, 27 combinations were found that both coefficients for the M-TAR unit root test indicate statistically significant at 2.5% significance level (Table 2).

On the other hand, in the sample period from January 1984 to June 1997, of the 247 combinations of 8 currencies, 38 combinations were found that all OLS coefficient estimators indicate statistically significant (Table 3). For six of 38 combinations, adjustment coefficients the M-TAR unit root test are statistically significant (Table 4). The empirical results of this paper are summarized in Table 5.

Our empirical study suggests three features. First, in recent years, the ASEAN6+3 countries might come closer to OCA than before. Because that there exist 28 co-integration relationships among currencies of ASEAN6+3 countries in the period from January 2000 to June 2013, while only six combinations were found as a possible currency union in the period from January 1984 to June 1997. Even if we ignore the VND as a candidate for the member states of currency union, we could find 16 combinations contain co-integration relationship among the currencies of the original ASEAN5+3 countries in the period from January 2000 to June 2013 8.

Table 1. OLS Estimation for Asymmetric Integration (January 2000–June 2013).

No.	Combination	Upper: D.F. / Lower: D.W.	SGD	IDR	THB	MYR	PHP	VND	JPY	CNY	KRW
97031	CNY KRW SGD IDR	155	−0.994 ****	0.275 ****	1.224 ****	—	−1.231 ****	0.644 ****	—	0.708 ***	0.404 ****
	THB VND PHP	0.470	(0.198)	(0.069)	(0.213)	—	(0.116)	(0.162)	—	(0.282)	(0.074)
97009	JPY CNY KRW SGD	155	−0.873 ****	—	1.821 ****	—	−1.523 ****	0.603 ****	−0.092	0.729 **	0.411 ****
	THB VND PHP	0.500	(0.248)	—	(0.170)	—	(0.088)	(0.168)	(0.060)	(0.343)	(0.096)
96065	CNY KRW SGD	156	−1.089 ****	—	1.783 ****	—	−1.578 ****	0.598 ****	—	1.028 ****	0.509 ****
	THB VND PHP	0.536	(0.206)	—	(0.169)	—	(0.081)	(0.169)	—	(0.284)	(0.072)
96061	CNY KRW SGD	156	−1.090 ****	0.642 ****	—	−0.668 ****	−0.447 ****	—	—	1.876 ****	0.621 ****
	IDR MYR PHP	0.443	(0.218)	(0.062)	—	(0.252)	(0.061)	—	—	(0.223)	(0.084)
96059	CNY KRW SGD	156	−1.371 ****	0.256 ****	1.503 ****	—	−1.224 ****	—	—	1.572 ****	0.437 ****
	IDR THB PHP	0.504	(0.182)	(0.072)	(0.210)	—	(0.121)	—	—	(0.189)	(0.077)
96058	CNY KRW SGD	156	−1.308 ****	0.817 ****	−0.675 ****	—	—	0.618 ****	—	0.906 ***	0.544 ****
	IDR THB VND	0.363	(0.256)	(0.060)	(0.151)	—	—	(0.212)	—	(0.369)	(0.095)
96057	CNY KRW SGD	156	−1.427 ****	0.843 ****	−0.418 ****	−0.734 ***	—	—	—	1.933 ****	0.607 ****
	IDR THB MYR	0.445	(0.244)	(0.063)	(0.118)	(0.282)	—	—	—	(0.249)	(0.096)
96056	JPY IDR THB	156	—	0.307 ****	1.616 ****	−0.639 ****	−1.210 ****	0.444 ****	−0.263 ****	—	—
	MYR VND PHP	0.398	—	(0.076)	(0.208)	(0.155)	(0.125)	(0.092)	(0.048)	—	—
96050	JPY KRW THB	156	—	—	1.866 ****	−0.330 **	−1.520 ****	0.662 ****	−0.235 ****	—	0.246 ****
	MYR VND PHP	0.401	—	—	(0.186)	(0.153)	(0.091)	(0.116)	(0.054)	—	(0.079)
96044	JPY KRW SGD	156	−0.408 ****	—	1.847 ****	—	−1.541 ****	0.837 ****	−0.165 ****	—	0.282 ****
	THB VND PHP	0.448	(0.119)	—	(0.171)	—	(0.089)	(0.128)	(0.050)	—	(0.075)

No.	Combination	Upper: D.F. / Lower: D.W.	Explanatories								
			SGD	IDR	THB	MYR	PHP	VND	JPY	CNY	KRW
96037	JPY KRW SGD	156	−0.693 ****	0.790 ****	−0.547 ****	—	—	0.816 ****	−0.158 ***	—	0.337 ****
	IDR THB VND	0.297	(0.152)	(0.067)	(0.184)	—	—	(0.160)	(0.066)	—	(0.094)
96032	JPY CNY IDR	156	—	0.316 ****	1.802 ****	−0.953 ****	−1.166 ****	—	−0.311 ****	0.481 ****	—
	THB MYR PHP	0.399	—	(0.078)	(0.208)	(0.215)	(0.128)	—	(0.048)	(0.130)	—
96030	JPY CNY SGD	156	0.699 **	—	—	1.838 ****	−1.039 ****	2.527 ****	−0.293 ****	−2.884 ****	—
	MYR VND PHP	0.290	(0.340)	—	—	(0.414)	(0.123)	(0.250)	(0.088)	(0.396)	—
96023	JPY CNY SGD	156	−0.761 ****	0.280 ****	1.905 ****	—	−1.256 ****	—	−0.193 ****	0.636 ****	—
	IDR THB PHP	0.402	(0.200)	(0.078)	(0.213)	—	(0.128)	—	(0.052)	(0.176)	—
96012	JPY CNY KRW	156	—	0.776 ****	−0.599 ****	—	—	0.910 ****	−0.254 ****	−0.693 ****	0.219 **
	IDR THB VND	0.252	—	(0.070)	(0.189)	—	—	(0.200)	(0.066)	(0.218)	(0.105)
96002	JPY CNY KRW	156	−0.789 ***	0.763 ****	—	−1.083 ****	—	—	−0.260 ****	1.269 ****	0.354 ****
	SGD IDR MYR	0.369	(0.321)	(0.064)	—	(0.293)	—	—	(0.060)	(0.283)	(0.097)
95125	SGD THB MYR	157	−0.928 ****	—	2.383 ****	0.653 ****	−1.893 ****	0.808 ****	—	—	—
	VND PHP	0.500	(0.183)	—	(0.137)	(0.220)	(0.071)	(0.107)	—	—	—
95119	KRW IDR MYR	157	—	0.547 ****	—	−0.388 ***	−0.784 ****	0.964 ****	—	—	0.456 ****
	VND PHP	0.295	—	(0.064)	—	(0.168)	(0.061)	(0.105)	—	—	(0.070)
95116	KRW IDR THB	157	—	0.951 ****	−1.030 ****	−0.686 ****	—	0.838 ****	—	—	0.455 ****
	MYR VND	0.302	—	(0.062)	(0.133)	(0.201)	—	(0.136)	—	—	(0.090)
95115	KRW SGD MYR	157	−0.776 ****	—	—	1.028 ****	−1.020 ****	1.627 ****	—	—	0.839 ****
	VND PHP	0.290	(0.208)	—	—	(0.244)	(0.060)	(0.111)	—	—	(0.059)

No.	Combination	Upper: D.F. / Lower: D.W.	Explanatories								
			SGD	IDR	THB	MYR	PHP	VND	JPY	CNY	KRW
95111	KRW SGD IDR	157	−0.538 ****	0.549 ****	—	—	−0.708 ****	1.112 ****	—	—	0.448 ****
	VND PHP	0.346	(0.124)	(0.056)	—	—	(0.062)	(0.109)	—	—	(0.066)
95107	KRW SGD IDR	157	−0.791 ****	0.890 ****	−0.848 ****	—	—	1.017 ****	—	—	0.434 ****
	THB VND	0.329	(0.149)	(0.053)	(0.135)	—	—	(0.137)	—	—	(0.085)
95082	CNY KRW IDR	157	—	0.924 ****	−1.154 ****	—	—	1.138 ****	—	−0.639 ****	0.400 ****
	THB VND	0.285	—	(0.061)	(0.127)	—	—	(0.200)	—	(0.227)	(0.098)
95081	CNY KRW IDR	157	—	0.992 ****	−0.732 ****	−1.362 ****	—	—	—	1.073 ****	0.492 ****
	THB MYR	0.314	—	(0.063)	(0.115)	(0.288)	—	—	—	(0.221)	(0.103)
95077	CNY KRW SGD	157	−1.435 ****	—	2.006 ****	—	−1.548 ****	—	—	1.814 ****	0.533 ****
	THB PHP	0.573	(0.188)	—	(0.162)	—	(0.084)	—	—	(0.183)	(0.075)
95074	CNY KRW SGD	157	−1.293 ****	0.599 ****	—	—	−0.447 ****	—	—	1.697 ****	0.595 ****
	IDR PHP	0.381	(0.208)	(0.061)	—	—	(0.062)	—	—	(0.216)	(0.085)
95072	CNY KRW SGD	157	−1.823 ****	0.839 ****	—	−0.669 ***	—	—	—	1.884 ****	0.505 ****
	IDR MYR	0.424	(0.225)	(0.065)	—	(0.292)	—	—	—	(0.258)	(0.095)
95071	CNY KRW SGD	157	−1.668 ****	0.795 ****	−0.398 ****	—	—	—	—	1.734 ****	0.575 ****
	IDR THB	0.384	(0.230)	(0.061)	(0.120)	—	—	—	—	(0.241)	(0.097)
95070	JPY THB MYR	157	—	—	2.289 ****	−0.435 ****	−1.578 ****	0.449 ****	−0.322 ****	—	—
	VND PHP	0.448	—	—	0.131	(0.154)	(0.091)	(0.096)	(0.047)	—	—
95069	JPY IDR MYR	157	—	0.778 ****	—	−0.690 ****	−0.415 ****	0.605 ****	−0.200 ****	—	—
	VND PHP	0.312	—	(0.053)	—	0.182	(0.085)	(0.105)	(0.055)	—	—

No.	Combination	Upper: D.F. / Lower: D.W.	Explanatories								
			SGD	IDR	THB	MYR	PHP	VND	JPY	CNY	KRW
95067	JPY IDR THB	157	—	0.312 ****	1.842 ****	−0.382 ***	−1.147 ****	—	−0.311 ****	—	—
	MYR PHP	0.308	—	(0.081)	(0.216)	(0.155)	(0.133)	—	(0.050)	—	—
95064	JPY SGD THB	157	−0.410 ****	—	2.294 ****	—	−1.609 ****	0.566 ****	−0.254 ****	—	—
	VND PHP	0.478	(0.124)	—	(0.128)	—	(0.091)	(0.110)	(0.046)	—	—
95047	JPY KRW IDR	157	—	0.711 ****	−0.666 ****	—	—	0.470 ****	−0.240 ****	—	0.353 ****
	THB VND	0.213	—	(0.069)	(0.193)	—	—	(0.149)	(0.068)	—	(0.099)
95034	JPY CNY THB	157	—	—	2.139 ****	—	−1.595 ****	0.762 ****	−0.282 ****	−0.497 ****	—
	VND PHP	0.434	—	—	(0.120)	—	(0.091)	(0.160)	(0.045)	(0.160)	—
95033	JPY CNY THB	157	—	—	2.497 ****	−0.733 ****	−1.543 ****	—	−0.373 ****	0.474 ****	—
	MYR PHP	0.444	—	—	(0.124)	(0.218)	(0.093)	—	(0.047)	(0.137)	—
95031	JPY CNY IDR	157	—	0.706 ****	—	—	−0.561 ****	1.157 ****	−0.148 ****	−0.878 ****	—
	VND PHP	0.311	—	(0.046)	—	—	(0.077)	(0.168)	(0.053)	(0.176)	—
95030	JPY CNY IDR	157	—	0.870 ****	—	−0.973 ****	−0.210 ****	—	−0.258 ****	0.540 ****	—
	MYR PHP	0.303	—	(0.054)	—	(0.261)	(0.079)	—	(0.057)	(0.158)	—
95022	JPY CNY SGD	157	−0.635 ****	—	2.526 ****	—	−1.583 ****	—	−0.271 ****	0.623 ****	—
	THB PHP	0.458	(0.205)	—	(0.130)	—	(0.094)	—	(0.049)	(0.182)	—
95019	JPY CNY SGD	157	−0.554 ***	0.842 ****	—	—	−0.264 ****	—	−0.159 ***	0.533 ***	—
	IDR PHP	0.261	(0.244)	(0.056)	—	—	(0.079)	—	(0.064)	(0.215)	—
95009	JPY CNY KRW	157	—	0.611 ****	—	—	−0.479 ****	—	−0.144 ***	0.481 ****	0.346 ****
	IDR PHP	0.193	—	(0.067)	—	—	(0.087)	—	(0.060)	(0.147)	(0.093)

No.	Combination	Upper: D.F. / Lower: D.W.	Explanatories: SGD	IDR	THB	MYR	PHP	VND	JPY	CNY	KRW
95001	JPY CNY KRW	157	−1.373 ****	0.721 ****	—	—	—	—	−0.187 ****	1.182 ****	0.360 ****
	SGD IDR	0.311	(0.291)	(0.066)	—	—	—	—	(0.059)	(0.293)	(0.100)
94125	IDR MYR VND	158	—	0.834 ****	—	−0.580 ****	−0.631 ****	0.674 ****	—	—	—
	PHP	0.292	—	(0.053)	—	(0.186)	(0.064)	(0.107)	—	—	—
94122	IDR THB MYR	158	—	1.158 ****	−0.700 ****	−0.884 ****	—	0.498 ****	—	—	—
	VND	0.301	—	(0.050)	(0.125)	(0.212)	—	(0.127)	—	—	—
94117	SGD IDR VND	158	−0.642 ****	0.813 ****	—	—	−0.557 ****	0.832 ****	—	—	—
	PHP	0.330	(0.140)	(0.045)	—	—	(0.066)	(0.114)	—	—	—
94113	SGD IDR THB	158	−0.926 ****	1.067 ****	−0.517 ****	—	—	0.710 ****	—	—	—
	VND	0.323	(0.157)	(0.043)	(0.127)	—	—	(0.133)	—	—	—
94107	KRW IDR VND	158	—	0.468 ****	—	—	−0.839 ****	0.898 ****	—	—	0.484 ****
	PHP	0.258	—	(0.056)	—	—	(0.057)	(0.103)	—	—	(0.069)
94103	KRW IDR THB	158	—	0.857 ****	−1.188 ****	—	—	0.719 ****	—	—	0.515 ****
	VND	0.252	—	(0.057)	(0.129)	—	—	(0.136)	—	—	(0.091)
94087	CNY IDR VND	158	—	0.762 ****	—	—	−0.712 ****	1.251 ****	—	−0.910 ****	—
	PHP	0.314	—	(0.042)	—	—	(0.057)	(0.168)	—	(0.179)	—
94086	CNY IDR MYR	158	—	0.961 ****	—	−0.766 ****	−0.461 ****	—	—	0.536 ****	—
	PHP	0.266	—	(0.053)	—	(0.272)	(0.060)	—	—	(0.167)	—
94083	CNY IDR THB	158	—	1.099 ****	−0.918 ****	—	—	1.109 ****	—	−1.024 ****	—
	VND	0.292	—	(0.045)	(0.118)	—	—	(0.209)	—	(0.216)	—

No.	Combination	Upper: D.F. / Lower: D.W.	SGD	IDR	THB	MYR	PHP	VND	JPY	CNY	KRW
94082	CNY IDR THB	158	—	1.185 ****	−0.484 ****	−1.047 ****	—	—	—	0.421 ***	—
	MYR	0.285	—	(0.051)	(0.109)	(0.298)	—	—	—	(0.185)	—
94078	CNY SGD THB	158	−1.056 ****	—	2.873 ****	—	−1.969 ****	—	—	1.093 ****	—
	PHP	0.519	(0.206)	—	(0.123)	—	(0.068)	—	—	(0.175)	—
94075	CNY SGD IDR	158	−0.809 ****	0.926 ****	—	—	−0.364 ****	—	—	0.770 ****	—
	PHP	0.284	(0.225)	(0.045)	—	—	(0.069)	—	—	(0.196)	—
94057	CNY KRW SGD	158	−2.027 ****	0.795 ****	—	—	—	—	—	1.704 ****	0.480 ****
	IDR	0.372	(0.209)	(0.063)	—	—	—	—	—	(0.249)	(0.096)
94055	JPY THB VND	158	—	—	2.148 ****	—	−1.583 ****	0.349 ****	−0.284 ****	—	—
	PHP	0.378	—	—	(0.123)	—	(0.093)	(0.091)	(0.046)	—	—
94052	JPY IDR VND	158	—	0.680 ****	—	—	−0.534 ****	0.468 ****	−0.165 ****	—	—
	PHP	0.225	—	(0.049)	—	—	(0.083)	(0.103)	(0.056)	—	—
94039	JPY SGD IDR	158	−0.735 ****	0.801 ****	—	—	—	0.428 ****	−0.296 ****	—	—
	VND	0.277	(0.156)	(0.056)	—	—	—	(0.120)	(0.050)	—	—
94030	JPY KRW IDR	158	—	0.780 ****	—	—	−0.265 ****	—	−0.213 ****	—	0.143 **
	PHP	0.202	—	(0.044)	—	—	(0.060)	—	(0.058)	—	(0.072)
94026	JPY KRW SGD	158	1.238 ****	—	—	—	−0.449 ****	—	−0.534 ****	—	0.606 ****
	PHP	0.085	(0.129)	—	—	—	(0.111)	—	(0.071)	—	(0.091)
94013	JPY CNY IDR	158	—	0.877 ****	—	−1.206 ****	—	—	−0.365 ****	0.469 ****	—
	MYR	0.314	—	(0.055)	—	(0.250)	—	—	(0.042)	(0.158)	—

No.	Combination	Upper: D.F. / Lower: D.W.	SGD	IDR	THB	MYR	PHP	VND	JPY	CNY	KRW
						Explanatories					
94007	JPY CNY SGD	158	−0.759 ****	0.846 ****	—	—	—	—	−0.267 ****	0.459 **	—
	IDR	0.266	(0.244)	(0.058)	—	—	—	—	(0.057)	(0.221)	—
93076	IDR THB VND	159	—	1.067 ****	−0.854 ****	—	—	0.280 ***	—	—	—
		0.221	—	(0.047)	(0.125)	—	—	(0.122)	—	—	—
93075	IDR THB MYR	159	—	1.173 ****	−0.423 ****	−0.542 ****	—	—	—	—	—
		0.246	—	(0.052)	(0.107)	(0.202)	—	—	—	—	—
93067	SGD IDR VND	159	−1.213 ****	1.037 ****	—	—	—	0.526 ****	—	—	—
		0.280	(0.147)	(0.044)	—	—	—	(0.131)	—	—	—
93065	SGD IDR THB	159	−0.461 ****	1.128 ****	−0.285 **	—	—	—	—	—	—
		0.236	(0.142)	(0.045)	(0.130)	—	—	—	—	—	—
93063	KRW MYR PHP	159	—	—	—	2.262 ****	−0.821 ****	—	—	—	0.801 ****
		0.130	—	—	—	(0.154)	(0.075)	—	—	—	(0.091)
93059	KRW THB MYR	159	—	—	−0.599 ****	1.908 ****	—	—	—	—	1.065 ****
		0.089	—	—	(0.185)	(0.289)	—	—	—	—	(0.119)
93046	CNY THB PHP	159	—	—	2.670 ****	—	−2.049 ****	—	—	0.342 ****	—
		0.347	—	—	(0.126)	—	(0.072)	—	—	(0.103)	—
93035	CNY SGD IDR	159	−1.509 ****	1.039 ****	—	—	—	—	—	0.929 ****	—
		0.317	(0.196)	(0.043)	—	—	—	—	—	(0.209)	—
93025	JPY THB PHP	159	—	—	2.439 ****	—	−1.528 ****	—	−0.350 ****	—	—
		0.346	—	—	(0.101)	—	(0.096)	—	(0.045)	—	—

No.	Combination	Upper: D.F. / Lower: D.W.	Explanatories: SGD	IDR	THB	MYR	PHP	VND	JPY	CNY	KRW
93022	JPY IDR PHP	159	—	0.814 ****	—	—	−0.260 ****	—	−0.231 ****	—	—
		0.208	—	(0.041)	—	—	(0.060)	—	(0.058)	—	—
93020	JPY IDR MYR	159	—	0.884 ****	—	−0.585 ****	—	—	−0.343 ****	—	—
		0.251	—	(0.056)	—	(0.140)	—	—	(0.042)	—	—
92036	VND PHP	160	—	—	—	—	−1.212 ****	1.918 ****	—	—	—
		0.160	—	—	—	—	(0.086)	(0.096)	—	—	—
92033	THB PHP	160	—	—	2.984 ****	—	−2.098 ****	—	—	—	—
		0.351	—	—	(0.085)	—	(0.072)	—	—	—	—
92030	IDR PHP	160	—	0.938 ****	—	—	−0.444 ****	—	—	—	—
		0.206	—	(0.028)	—	—	(0.041)	—	—	—	—
92028	IDR MYR	160	—	1.152 ****	—	−1.101 ****	—	—	—	—	—
		0.233	—	(0.054)	—	(0.149)	—	—	—	—	—
92027	IDR THB	160	—	1.101 ****	−0.626 ****	—	—	—	—	—	—
		0.211	—	(0.045)	(0.078)	—	—	—	—	—	—
92022	SGD IDR	160	−0.715 ****	1.099 ****	—	—	—	—	—	—	—
		0.228	(0.084)	(0.043)	—	—	—	—	—	—	—

Note: SGD denotes the Singapore dollar, IDR denotes the Indonesian rupiah, THB denotes the Thai baht, MYR denotes the Malaysian ringgit, VND denotes the Vietnamese dong, PHP denotes the Philippine peso, JPY denotes the Japanese yen, CNY denotes the Chinese yuan, and KRW denotes the Korean won. Explained variable for all estimations is the euro real exchange rates against the US dollar. D.F. denotes the degree of freedom and D.W. denotes the Durbin Watson statistics. ****, ***, **, and * indicate significance at the 1%, 2.5%, 5%, and 10% levels in two-tailed test, respectively. Standard error is in parentheses.

Table 2. M-TAR Unit Root Test for Residuals from Co-integration Estimation (January 2000–June 2013).

No.	Combination	Upper: D.F. Lower: D.W.	Lag(s)	Coefficient (with S.E.) (Upper: Z-Plus) (Lower: Z-Minus)			No.	Combination	Upper: D.F. Lower: D.W.	Lag(s)	Coefficient (with S.E.) (Upper: Z-Plus) (Lower: Z-Minus)		
97031	CNY KRW SGD IDR	159	0	−0.288	(0.068)	****	96037	JPY KRW SGD	159	0	−0.139	(0.061)	***
	THB VND PHP	2.0499		−0.163	(0.077)	**		IDR THB VND	1.9364		−0.153	(0.057)	****
97009	JPY CNY KRW SGD	149	5	−0.265	(0.088)	****	96032	JPY CNY IDR	159	0	−0.247	(0.069)	****
	THB VND PHP	2.0194		−0.210	(0.092)	***		THB MYR PHP	2.0749		−0.137	(0.068)	**
96065	CNY KRW SGD	149	5	−0.285	(0.087)	****	96030	JPY CNY SGD	159	0	−0.167	(0.055)	****
	THB VND PHP	2.0209		−0.201	(0.098)	**		MYR VND PHP	1.9598		−0.114	(0.062)	*
96061	CNY KRW SGD	159	0	−0.237	(0.075)	****	96023	JPY CNY SGD	159	0	−0.254	(0.063)	****
	IDR MYR PHP	2.0587		−0.203	(0.067)	****		IDR THB PHP	2.1121		−0.123	(0.073)	*
96059	CNY KRW SGD	151	4	−0.236	(0.081)	****	96012	JPY CNY KRW	159	0	−0.108	(0.057)	*
	IDR THB PHP	1.9952		−0.200	(0.088)	***		IDR THB VND	1.8988		−0.136	(0.053)	***
96058	CNY KRW SGD	159	0	−0.150	(0.069)	**	96002	JPY CNY KRW	159	0	−0.150	(0.068)	**
	IDR THB VND	1.9631		−0.204	(0.061)	****		SGD IDR MYR	1.9875		−0.204	(0.064)	****
96057	CNY KRW SGD	159	0	−0.239	(0.080)	****	95125	SGD THB MYR	159	0	−0.367	(0.072)	****
	IDR THB MYR	2.0237		−0.209	(0.064)	****		VND PHP	1.9960		−0.123	(0.074)	*
96056	JPY IDR THB	159	0	−0.263	(0.069)	****	95119	KRW IDR MYR	159	0	−0.202	(0.063)	****
	MYR VND PHP	2.0355		−0.128	(0.066)	*		VND PHP	1.9990		−0.101	(0.055)	*
96050	JPY KRW THB	159	0	−0.280	(0.070)	****	95116	KRW IDR THB	159	0	−0.158	(0.059)	****
	MYR VND PHP	1.9604		−0.119	(0.066)	*		MYR VND	1.9165		−0.140	(0.060)	***
96044	JPY KRW SGD	159	0	−0.318	(0.072)	****	95115	KRW SGD MYR	159	0	−0.128	(0.056)	***
	THB VND PHP	1.9479		−0.133	(0.069)	*		VND PHP	1.9194		−0.162	(0.061)	****

No.	Combination	Upper: D.F. Lower: D.W.	Lag(s)	Coefficient (with S.E.) (Upper: Z-Plus) (Lower: Z-Minus)			No.	Combination	Upper: D.F. Lower: D.W.	Lag(s)	Coefficient (with S.E.) (Upper: Z-Plus) (Lower: Z-Minus)		
95111	KRW SGD IDR	159	0	−0.221	(0.067)	****	95067	JPY IDR THB	159	0	−0.194	(0.063)	****
	VND PHP	1.9888		−0.131	(0.060)	**		MYR PHP	2.0663		−0.112	(0.058)	*
95107	KRW SGD IDR	159	0	−0.174	(0.063)	****	95064	JPY SGD THB	159	0	−0.292	(0.074)	****
	THB VND	1.9469		−0.155	(0.060)	***		VND PHP	1.9595		−0.181	(0.073)	***
95082	CNY KRW IDR	159	0	−0.147	(0.058)	***	95047	JPY KRW IDR	159	0	−0.108	(0.051)	**
	THB VND	1.9160		−0.136	(0.057)	***		THB VND	1.9371		−0.097	(0.051)	*
95081	CNY KRW IDR	159	0	−0.135	(0.061)	**	95034	JPY CNY THB	159	0	−0.307	(0.073)	****
	THB MYR	1.9319		−0.173	(0.060)	****		VND PHP	1.9329		−0.133	(0.067)	**
95077	CNY KRW SGD	151	4	−0.249	(0.089)	****	95033	JPY CNY THB	159	0	−0.258	(0.077)	****
	THB PHP	1.9746		−0.249	(0.094)	****		MYR PHP	1.9975		−0.181	(0.067)	****
95074	CNY KRW SGD	159	0	−0.184	(0.071)	***	95031	JPY CNY IDR	159	0	−0.182	(0.063)	****
	IDR PHP	2.0784		−0.193	(0.062)	****		VND PHP	1.9755		−0.129	(0.058)	**
95072	CNY KRW SGD	159	0	−0.237	(0.079)	****	95030	JPY CNY IDR	159	0	−0.131	(0.062)	**
	IDR MYR	2.0864		−0.195	(0.062)	****		MYR PHP	1.9863		−0.159	(0.058)	****
95071	CNY KRW SGD	159	0	−0.172	(0.074)	***	95022	JPY CNY SGD	159	0	−0.242	(0.074)	****
	IDR THB	2.0385		−0.205	(0.060)	****		THB PHP	1.9936		−0.211	(0.070)	****
95070	JPY THB MYR	159	0	−0.290	(0.074)	****	95019	JPY CNY SGD	159	0	−0.129	(0.056)	***
	VND PHP	1.9712		−0.154	(0.069)	**		IDR PHP	2.0536		−0.128	(0.055)	***
95069	JPY IDR MYR	159	0	−0.173	(0.066)	****	95009	JPY CNY KRW	159	0	−0.081	(0.048)	*
	VND PHP	1.9840		−0.134	(0.057)	***		IDR PHP	2.0529		−0.106	(0.049)	**

No.	Combination	Upper: D.F. Lower: D.W.	Lag(s)	Coefficient (with S.E.) (Upper: Z-Plus) (Lower: Z-Minus)			No.	Combination	Upper: D.F. Lower: D.W.	Lag(s)	Coefficient (with S.E.) (Upper: Z-Plus) (Lower: Z-Minus)		
95001	JPY CNY KRW	159	0	−0.121	(0.066)	*	94082	CNY IDR THB	159	0	−0.140	(0.060)	***
	SGD IDR	2.0386		−0.176	(0.055)	****		MYR	1.9609		−0.143	(0.056)	***
94125	IDR MYR VND	159	0	−0.185	(0.060)	****	94078	CNY SGD THB	159	0	−0.370	(0.079)	****
	PHP	2.0103		−0.105	(0.057)	*		PHP	2.0317		−0.170	(0.071)	***
94122	IDR THB MYR	159	0	−0.191	(0.062)	****	94075	CNY SGD IDR	159	0	−0.163	(0.056)	****
	VND	1.9694		−0.114	(0.057)	**		PHP	2.0921		−0.117	(0.059)	**
94117	SGD IDR VND	159	0	−0.186	(0.062)	****	94057	CNY KRW SGD	159	0	−0.198	(0.074)	****
	PHP	2.0371		−0.142	(0.061)	***		IDR	2.0991		−0.178	(0.059)	****
94113	SGD IDR THB	159	0	−0.156	(0.063)	***	94055	JPY THB VND	159	0	−0.221	(0.068)	****
	VND	1.9969		−0.166	(0.059)	****		PHP	1.9667		−0.149	(0.065)	***
94107	KRW IDR VND	159	0	−0.147	(0.055)	****	94052	JPY IDR VND	159	0	−0.120	(0.052)	***
	PHP	2.0132		−0.105	(0.056)	*		PHP	2.0247		−0.096	(0.052)	*
94103	KRW IDR THB	159	0	−0.117	(0.054)	**	94039	JPY SGD IDR	159	0	−0.106	(0.061)	*
	VND	1.9321		−0.132	(0.055)	***		VND	1.9752		−0.159	(0.054)	****
94087	CNY IDR VND	159	0	−0.209	(0.060)	****	94030	JPY KRW IDR	159	0	−0.086	(0.051)	*
	PHP	2.0056		−0.104	(0.060)	*		PHP	1.9903		−0.111	(0.048)	***
94086	CNY IDR MYR	159	0	−0.127	(0.055)	***	94026	JPY KRW SGD	135	12	−0.087	(0.035)	***
	PHP	2.0313		−0.137	(0.058)	***		PHP	2.0056		−0.056	(0.032)	*
94083	CNY IDR THB	159	0	−0.134	(0.062)	**	94013	JPY CNY IDR	159	0	−0.136	(0.067)	**
	VND	1.9273		−0.156	(0.055)	****		MYR	1.9560		−0.161	(0.056)	****

No.	Combination	Upper: D.F. Lower: D.W.	Lag(s)	Coefficient (with S.E.) (Upper: Z-Plus) (Lower: Z-Minus)			No.	Combination	Upper: D.F. Lower: D.W.	Lag(s)	Coefficient (with S.E.) (Upper: Z-Plus) (Lower: Z-Minus)		
94007	JPY CNY SGD IDR	159	0	−0.097	(0.057)	*	93025	JPY THB PHP	159	0	−0.197	(0.065)	****
		2.0087		−0.161	(0.055)	****			1.9810		−0.143	(0.062)	***
93076	IDR THB VND	159	0	−0.120	(0.051)	***	93022	JPY IDR PHP	159	0	−0.090	(0.053)	*
		1.9707		−0.100	(0.051)	*			2.0066		−0.112	(0.048)	***
93075	IDR THB MYR	159	0	−0.126	(0.056)	**	93020	JPY IDR MYR	159	0	−0.132	(0.058)	***
		1.9707		−0.119	(0.052)	***			1.9727		−0.114	(0.052)	**
93067	SGD IDR VND	159	0	−0.117	(0.062)	*	92036	VND PHP	159	0	−0.074	(0.043)	*
		2.0408		−0.158	(0.054)	****			1.9578		−0.081	(0.045)	*
93065	SGD IDR THB	159	0	−0.138	(0.055)	***	92033	THB PHP	159	0	−0.264	(0.068)	****
		2.0275		−0.101	(0.051)	**			2.0242		−0.108	(0.059)	*
93063	KRW MYR PHP	141	9	−0.078	(0.043)	*	92030	IDR PHP	159	0	−0.119	(0.050)	***
		1.9068		−0.091	(0.041)	**			2.0481		−0.087	(0.049)	*
93059	KRW THB MYR	135	12	−0.065	(0.038)	*	92028	IDR MYR	159	0	−0.172	(0.063)	****
		1.9757		−0.067	(0.039)	*			2.0614		−0.087	(0.046)	*
93046	CNY THB PHP	159	0	−0.256	(0.065)	****	92027	IDR THB	159	0	−0.120	(0.052)	***
		2.0123		−0.102	(0.060)	*			1.9935		−0.093	(0.049)	*
93035	CNY SGD IDR	159	0	−0.183	(0.068)	****	92022	SGD IDR	159	0	−0.116	(0.058)	**
		2.1130		−0.143	(0.055)	***			2.0476		−0.112	(0.048)	***

Note: ****, ***, **, and * indicate significance at the 1%, 2.5%, 5%, and 10% levels in single-tailed test, respectively. Standard error is in parentheses. D.F. denotes the degree of freedom and D.W. denotes the Durbin Watson statistics.

Table 3. OLS Estimation for Asymmetric Integration (January 1984–June 1997).

No.	Combination	Upper: D.F.	Explanatories							
		Lower: D.W.	SGD	IDR	THB	MYR	PHP	JPY	CNY	KRW
8705	JPY CNY KRW IDR	119	—	0.946 ****	−1.556 ****	−1.092 ****	0.664 ****	0.188 ****	0.192 ****	−0.879 ****
(97012)	THB MYR PHP	0.407	—	(0.305)	(0.323)	(0.264)	(0.121)	(0.071)	(0.057)	(0.160)
8626	CNY KRW IDR	120	—	1.346 ****	−1.651 ****	−0.723 ****	0.508 ****	—	0.104 **	−0.603 ****
(96068)	THB MYR PHP	0.314	—	(0.271)	(0.329)	(0.230)	(0.108)	—	(0.048)	(0.124)
8610	JPY CNY KRW	120	—	—	−1.165 ****	−1.137 ****	0.747 ****	0.299 ****	0.290 ****	−1.032 ****
(96018)	THB MYR PHP	0.441	—	—	(0.308)	(0.273)	(0.122)	(0.064)	(0.049)	(0.157)
8606	JPY CNY KRW	120	−0.710 ****	—	—	−1.194 ****	0.802 ****	0.302 ****	0.166 ***	−0.935 ****
(96009)	SGD MYR PHP	0.467	(0.164)	—	—	(0.263)	(0.124)	(0.063)	(0.064)	(0.161)
8551	KRW SGD IDR	157	−0.483 ****	0.973 ****	−0.791 ****	0.751 ****	—	—	—	0.250 **
(95106)	THB MYR	0.352	(0.088)	(0.077)	(0.196)	(0.192)	—	—	—	(0.123)
8547	CNY SGD IDR	121	−0.809 ****	1.306 ****	−1.173 **	—	0.472 ****	—	−0.133 ****	—
(95093)	THB PHP	0.224	(0.216)	(0.292)	(0.563)	—	(0.111)	—	(0.047)	—
8544	CNY KRW IDR	121	—	0.818 ****	—	−1.055 ****	0.240 ***	—	0.245 ****	−0.902 ****
(95085)	MYR PHP	0.334	—	(0.273)	—	(0.241)	(0.103)	—	(0.042)	(0.119)
8531	JPY SGD IDR	157	−0.200 ***	0.679 ****	−0.595 ****	0.503 ****	—	−0.269 ****	—	—
(95056)	THB MYR	0.285	(0.085)	(0.083)	(0.131)	(0.132)	—	(0.043)	—	—
8525	JPY KRW SGD	157	−0.490 ***	—	0.687 ****	—	0.316 ****	−0.578 ****	—	−0.619 ****
(95042)	THB PHP	0.124	(0.191)	—	(0.136)	—	(0.120)	(0.044)	—	(0.094)
8510	JPY CNY KRW	121	—	—	—	−1.452 ****	0.511 ****	0.273 ****	0.368 ****	−1.245 ****
(95014)	MYR PHP	0.491	—	—	—	(0.274)	(0.111)	(0.067)	(0.047)	(0.155)

No.	Combination	Upper: D.F. / Lower: D.W.	SGD	IDR	THB	MYR	PHP	JPY	CNY	KRW
			Explanatories							
8509	JPY CNY KRW	121	—	—	−1.556 ****	—	0.456 ****	0.144 ***	0.167 ****	−0.391 ****
(95012)	THB PHP	0.262	—	—	(0.312)	—	(0.107)	(0.056)	(0.042)	(0.035)
8470	IDR THB MYR	158	—	0.981 ****	−0.928 ****	0.694 ****	−0.202 ****	—	—	—
(94123)	PHP	0.356	—	(0.082)	(0.109)	(0.149)	(0.060)	—	—	—
8460	KRW SGD THB	158	−1.476 ****	—	2.054 ****	—	0.486 ****	—	—	−1.156 ****
(94098)	PHP	0.138	(0.254)	—	(0.126)	—	(0.173)	—	—	(0.122)
8445	CNY KRW MYR	122	—	—	—	−0.730 ****	0.301 ****	—	0.269 ****	−0.806 ****
(94070)	PHP	0.296	—	—	—	(0.222)	(0.104)	—	(0.043)	(0.118)
8444	CNY KRW THB	122	—	—	−1.263 ****	—	0.406 ****	—	0.154 ****	−0.369 ****
(94068)	PHP	0.227	—	—	(0.298)	—	(0.108)	—	(0.043)	(0.035)
8441	CNY KRW IDR	122	—	0.943 ****	—	−0.679 ****	—	—	0.198 ****	−0.673 ****
(94063)	MYR	0.306	—	(0.273)	—	(0.182)	—	—	(0.038)	(0.068)
8432	JPY IDR THB	158	—	0.668 ****	−0.810 ****	0.568 ****	—	−0.314 ****	—	—
(94047)	MYR	0.289	—	(0.084)	(0.094)	(0.131)	—	(0.040)	—	—
8431	JPY SGD MYR	158	−0.651 ****	—	—	0.919 ****	0.241 ***	−0.459 ****	—	—
(94045)	PHP	0.137	(0.112)	—	—	(0.086)	(0.100)	(0.045)	—	—
8428	JPY SGD IDR	158	−0.729 ****	0.805 ****	—	—	0.323 ****	−0.259 ****	—	—
(94040)	PHP	0.274	(0.094)	(0.052)	—	—	(0.083)	(0.044)	—	—
8420	JPY KRW IDR	158	—	0.808 ****	−0.414 ****	—	—	−0.324 ****	—	−0.198 ***
(94027)	THB	0.267	—	(0.079)	(0.112)	—	—	(0.041)	—	(0.084)

No.	Combination	Upper: D.F.	Explanatories							
		Lower: D.W.	SGD	IDR	THB	MYR	PHP	JPY	CNY	KRW
8418	JPY KRW SGD	158	−0.268 ***	—	—	0.787 ****	—	−0.461 ****	—	−0.246 ***
(94024)	MYR	0.140	(0.104)	—	—	(0.104)	—	(0.045)	—	(0.101)
8353	IDR THB MYR	159	—	1.060 ****	−1.070 ****	0.668 ****	—	—	—	—
(93075)		0.344	—	(0.081)	(0.104)	(0.154)	—	—	—	—
8346	KRW MYR PHP	159	—	—	—	1.472 ****	−0.417 ****	—	—	−0.551 ****
(93063)		0.171	—	—	—	(0.070)	(0.089)	—	—	(0.107)
8345	KRW THB PHP	159	—	—	1.558 ****	—	−0.331 ****	—	—	−1.669 ****
(93061)		0.134	—	—	(0.102)	—	(0.111)	—	—	(0.093)
8343	KRW IDR PHP	159	—	0.969 ****	—	—	−0.226 ****	—	—	−0.445 ****
(93058)		0.277	—	(0.032)	—	—	(0.066)	—	—	(0.080)
8341	KRW IDR THB	159	—	1.236 ****	−0.602 ****	—	—	—	—	−0.242 ***
(93055)		0.329	—	(0.068)	(0.129)	—	—	—	—	(0.098)
8338	KRW SGD THB	159	−0.896 ****	—	1.896 ****	—	—	—	—	−1.279 ****
(93051)		0.133	(0.151)	—	(0.116)	—	—	—	—	(0.116)
8332	CNY IDR MYR	123	—	−1.173 ****	—	1.031 ****	—	—	0.306 ****	—
(93041)		0.237	—	(0.228)	—	(0.078)	—	—	(0.049)	—
8319	JPY THB MYR	159	—	—	−0.797 ****	1.287 ****	—	−0.497 ****	—	—
(93023)		0.184	—	—	(0.111)	(0.111)	—	(0.038)	—	—
8316	JPY IDR THB	159	—	0.921 ****	−0.594 ****	—	—	−0.331 ****	—	—
(93019)		0.287	—	(0.064)	(0.084)	—	—	(0.042)	—	—

No.	Combination	Upper: D.F. / Lower: D.W.	SGD	IDR	THB	MYR	PHP	JPY	CNY	KRW
8311	JPY KRW PHP	159	—	—	—	—	0.213 ****	−0.760 ****	—	−0.596 ****
(93013)		0.099	—	—	—	—	(0.073)	(0.029)	—	(0.086)
8309	JPY KRW THB	159	—	—	0.482 ****	—	—	−0.609 ****	—	−0.713 ****
(93010)		0.115	—	—	(0.090)	—	—	(0.038)	—	(0.086)
8308	JPY KRW IDR	159	—	0.579 ****	—	—	—	−0.356 ****	—	−0.407 ****
(93009)		0.208	—	(0.051)	—	—	—	(0.042)	—	(0.064)
8305	JPY CNY MYR	123	—	—	—	0.749 ****	—	−0.301 ****	0.217 ****	—
(93005)		0.162	—	—	—	(0.079)	—	(0.053)	(0.053)	—
8223	IDR THB	160	—	1.386 ****	−0.828 ****	—	—	—	—	—
(92027)		0.361	—	(0.032)	(0.092)	—	—	—	—	—
8217	KRW MYR	160	—	—	—	1.386 ****	—	—	—	−0.812 ****
(92019)		0.130	—	—	—	(0.072)	—	—	—	(0.097)
8212	CNY MYR	124	—	—	—	0.915 ****	—	—	0.350 ****	—
(92013)		0.200	—	—	—	(0.083)	—	—	(0.053)	—
8208	CNY KRW	124	—	—	—	—	—	—	0.223 ****	−0.431 ****
(92009)		0.275	—	—	—	—	—	—	(0.039)	(0.023)

Note: SGD denotes the Singapore dollar, IDR denotes the Indonesian rupiah, THB denotes the Thai baht, MYR denotes the Malaysian ringgit, PHP denotes the Philippine peso, JPY denotes the Japanese yen, CNY denotes the Chinese yuan, and KRW denotes the Korean won. Explained Variable for all estimations is the euro real exchange rates against the US dollar. D.F. denotes the degree of freedom and D.W. denotes the Durbin Watson statistics. ****, ***, **, and * indicate significance at the 1%, 2.5%, 5%, and 10% levels in two-tailed test, respectively. Standard error is in parentheses.

Table 4. M-TAR Unit Root Test for Residuals from Co-integration Estimation (January 1984–June 1997).

No.	Combination	Upper: D.F. Lower: D.W.	Lag(s)	Coefficient (with S.E.) (Upper: Z-Plus) (Lower: Z-Minus)			No.	Combination	Upper: D.F. Lower: D.W.	Lag(s)	Coefficient (with S.E.) (Upper: Z-Plus) (Lower: Z-Minus)		
8705	JPY CNY KRW IDR	121	1	−0.227	(0.077)	****	8509	JPY CNY KRW	121	1	−0.103	(0.058)	*
(97012)	THB MYR PHP	1.9850		−0.262	(0.081)	****	(95012)	THB PHP	1.9638		−0.228	(0.072)	****
8610	JPY CNY KRW	123	0	−0.189	(0.076)	***	8470	IDR THB MYR	159	0	−0.209	(0.059)	****
(96018)	THB MYR PHP	1.7700		−0.257	(0.084)	****	(94123)	PHP	1.8554		−0.122	(0.072)	*
8606	JPY CNY KRW	123	0	−0.165	(0.078)	**	8460	KRW SGD THB	157	1	−0.080	(0.037)	**
(96009)	SGD MYR PHP	1.7918		−0.314	(0.085)	****	(94098)	PHP	1.9861		−0.079	(0.047)	*
8551	KRW SGD IDR	159	0	−0.206	(0.059)	****	8445	CNY KRW MYR	121	1	−0.130	(0.063)	**
(95106)	THB MYR	1.8744		−0.121	(0.070)	*	(94070)	PHP	1.9668		−0.236	(0.072)	****
8547	CNY SGD IDR	121	1	−0.115	(0.057)	**	8444	CNY KRW THB	121	1	−0.093	(0.052)	*
(95093)	THB PHP	1.9851		−0.132	(0.065)	**	(94068)	PHP	1.9690		−0.211	(0.071)	****
8544	CNY KRW IDR	121	1	−0.155	(0.070)	**	8441	CNY KRW IDR	121	1	−0.122	(0.066)	*
(95085)	MYR PHP	1.9651		−0.255	(0.072)	****	(94063)	MYR	1.9581		−0.260	(0.069)	****
8531	JPY SGD IDR	159	0	−0.144	(0.054)	****	8432	JPY IDR THB	159	0	−0.133	(0.054)	***
(95056)	THB MYR	1.8646		−0.134	(0.063)	**	(94047)	MYR	1.8741		−0.155	(0.064)	***
8526	JPY KRW SGD	145	7	−0.076	(0.044)	*	8431	JPY SGD MYR	145	7	−0.080	(0.041)	*
(95044)	MYR PHP	1.9545		−0.190	(0.044)	****	(94045)	PHP	1.9681		−0.193	(0.045)	****
8525	JPY KRW SGD	145	7	−0.093	(0.039)	***	8428	JPY SGD IDR	159	0	−0.149	(0.053)	****
(95042)	THB PHP	1.9795		−0.120	(0.044)	****	(94040)	PHP	1.8383		−0.118	(0.062)	*
8510	JPY CNY KRW	121	1	−0.205	(0.080)	***	8420	JPY KRW IDR	159	0	−0.149	(0.051)	****
(95014)	MYR PHP	1.9962		−0.401	(0.090)	****	(94027)	THB	1.8387		−0.108	(0.062)	*

No.	Combination	Upper: D.F. Lower: D.W.	Lag(s)	Coefficient (with S.E.) (Upper: Z-Plus) (Lower: Z-Minus)			No.	Combination	Upper: D.F. Lower: D.W.	Lag(s)	Coefficient (with S.E.) (Upper: Z-Plus) (Lower: Z-Minus)		
8418	JPY KRW SGD	145	7	−0.086	(0.044)	*	8316	JPY IDR THB	159	0	−0.156	(0.053)	****
(94024)	MYR	1.9382		−0.176	(0.046)	****	(93019)		1.8746		−0.119	(0.065)	*
8353	IDR THB MYR	159	0	−0.191	(0.057)	****	8311	JPY KRW PHP	145	7	−0.087	(0.035)	***
(93075)		1.8563		−0.138	(0.071)	*	(93013)		2.0032		−0.082	(0.041)	**
8346	KRW MYR PHP	155	2	−0.088	(0.043)	**	8309	JPY KRW THB	131	14	−0.083	(0.041)	**
(93063)		2.0047		−0.127	(0.049)	***	(93010)		1.9759		−0.125	(0.049)	***
8345	KRW THB PHP	131	14	−0.145	(0.043)	****	8308	JPY KRW IDR	157	1	−0.124	(0.047)	****
(93061)		2.0071		−0.120	(0.053)	**	(93009)		1.9779		−0.106	(0.053)	**
8343	KRW IDR PHP	157	1	−0.192	(0.053)	****	8305	JPY CNY MYR	121	1	−0.074	(0.044)	*
(93058)		2.0106		−0.106	(0.063)	*	(93005)		1.9948		−0.142	(0.061)	***
8341	KRW IDR THB	157	1	−0.211	(0.054)	****	8223	IDR THB	157	1	−0.226	(0.056)	****
(93055)		2.0148		−0.125	(0.075)	*	(92027)		2.0177		−0.135	(0.081)	*
8338	KRW SGD THB	131	14	−0.129	(0.041)	****	8217	KRW MYR	155	2	−0.073	(0.038)	*
(93051)		1.9866		−0.145	(0.053)	****	(92019)		2.0166		−0.093	(0.042)	**
8332	CNY IDR MYR	121	1	−0.096	(0.052)	*	8212	CNY MYR	121	1	−0.090	(0.051)	*
(93041)		2.0009		−0.235	(0.072)	****	(92013)		1.9974		−0.156	(0.063)	***
8319	JPY THB MYR	145	7	−0.108	(0.049)	**	8208	CNY KRW	121	1	−0.118	(0.059)	**
(93023)		1.9852		−0.254	(0.055)	****	(92009)		1.9663		−0.237	(0.072)	****

Note: SGD denotes the Singapore dollar, IDR denotes the Indonesian rupiah, THB denotes the Thai baht, MYR denotes the Malaysian ringgit, PHP denotes the Philippine peso, JPY denotes the Japanese yen, CNY denotes the Chinese yuan, and KRW denotes the Korean won. D.F. denotes the degree of freedom and D.W. denotes the Durbin Watson statistics. ****, ***, **, and * indicate significance at the 1%, 2.5%, 5%, and 10% levels in two-tailed test, respectively. Standard error is in parentheses.

Table 5. Summary of Empirical Results (Candidates for member states of the Common Currency Union).

The Number of Countries		No.	SGD	IDR	THB	MYR	PHP	VND	JPY	CNY	KRW
(January 2000–June 2013)											
7		97009	X	–	X	–	X	X	X	X	X
6		96061	X	X	–	X	X	–	–	X	X
		96059	X	X	X	–	X	–	–	X	X
		96057	X	X	X	X	–	–	–	X	X
		96037	X	X	X	–	–	X	X	–	X
5		95116	–	X	X	X	–	X	–	–	X
		95115	X	–	–	X	X	X	–	–	X
		95107	X	X	X	–	–	X	–	–	X
		95082	–	X	X	–	–	X	–	X	X
		95077	X	–	X	–	X	–	–	X	X
		95074	X	X	–	–	X	–	–	X	X
		95072	X	X	–	X	–	–	–	X	X
		95071	X	X	X	–	–	–	–	X	X
		95069	–	X	–	X	X	X	X	–	–
		95064	X	–	X	–	X	X	X	–	–
		95033	–	–	X	X	X	–	X	X	–
		95022	X	–	X	–	X	–	X	X	–
		95019	X	X	–	–	X	–	X	X	–
4		94117	X	X	–	–	X	X	–	–	–
		94113	X	X	X	–	–	X	–	–	–
		94086	–	X	–	X	X	–	–	X	–
		94082	–	X	X	X	–	–	–	X	–
		94078	X	–	X	–	X	–	–	X	–
		94057	X	X	–	–	–	–	–	X	X
		94055	–	–	X	–	X	X	X	–	–
3		93035	X	X	–	–	–	–	–	–	X
		93025	–	–	X	–	X	–	X	–	–
(January 1984–June 1997)											
7	8705	(97012)	–	X	X	X	X	–	X	X	X
6	8610	(96018)	–	–	X	X	X	–	X	X	X
5	8525	(95042)	X	–	X	–	X	–	X	–	X
	8510	(95014)	–	–	–	X	X	–	X	X	X
4	8432	(94047)	–	X	X	X	–	–	X	–	–
3	8338	(93051)	X	–	X	–	–	–	–	–	X

Note: "X" denotes the candidate for the member states of a possible common currency union.

Second, in the case that the common currency union contains more than four countries, the possible currency union should include the Japanese yen as a key currency when the samples from January 1984 to June 1997 were applied. On the other hand, the ASEAN6 countries could form a common currency union with Japan, China, and/or Korea, in the sample period from January 2000 to June 2013. Therefore, not only Japan but also "the plus three" countries might affect significant impacts on the possible common currency union.

Third, our empirical results suggest the combination of Singapore, Indonesia, Philippines, and Vietnam (94117), and the combination of Singapore, Indonesia, Thailand, and Vietnam (94113) could form a currency union without "the plus three" countries. This might reflect the recent economic integration which is deepening with the intra-industrial trade or the horizontal trade; the regional integration might not be only dominated by the large economies such as Japan or China or by the developed economies such as Japan or Korea. This might suggest that the possible currency union might be deepening not as "vertical integration" but as "horizontal integration".

4.4. Discussion

The results can be explained by the recent developments of economic integration in ASEAN6+3. Since the beginning of 2000, on the basis of high economic growth in the East Asian area, intra-regional trade and investment has become more vigorous than ever before, and real economic integration within the area is in progress. Foreign direct investment via intra-regional multinational firms has also given rise to a manufacturing network within the East Asian area. The intra-regional trade volumes of ASEAN6+3 have been increasing steadily since the early 2000s and reached approximately one-half of its total trade volume in recent years. Through this manufacturing network, advanced economies, such as Japan and Korea, have tended to export their low-added-value products to developing countries, and process these products while incurring low labor costs. In contrast, most of the developing countries in East Asia—such as China and Thailand—act as the "workshops" of developed economies by taking on low-added-value work and re-exporting the end products to advanced and other developing economies in the East Asian area. The added-profit trade—which includes processing and assembly—has been a typical economic growth model among most developing East Asian countries, and it is obvious that each country's economic growth is deeply involved in the manufacturing network. Through the integration of real economies, multinational firms have been optimizing their supply chains, information technologies, and capital flows.

Another aspect of the difference between the growth periods of 1984–1997 and 2000–2013 is related to exchange rate regimes or policies. Most of the monetary authorities in East Asian countries had adopted the *de facto* dollar peg system before the Asian Crisis in 1997, and switched to the floating system after the crisis. In some cases, countries adopted a basket beg system to fix their currencies. Although the East Asian countries could promote exports and investments to/from the US under the fixed exchange rates regimes, they had faced with significant fluctuations in exchange rates against the other trade partner's currencies, such as the Japanese yen, the German mark and the sterling pound. Since the dependencies of East Asian economies are not only on the US economy, but also on other developed economies, a more flexible exchange rate regime, such as the floating or the basket peg, would help the East Asian countries develop their economies in "the globalization era", as the countries expand their trade partners across the world.

Based on our empirical analysis and our conclusions on economic integration, East Asia is now closer than ever to exhibiting the conditions for a common currency. However, the integration of the financial markets in this region is still under development. As the Chinese economy has been growing rapidly, the RMB has become more popular as a currency of settlement for export and import in this area. However, the capital investments across the region are still mostly the dollar-denominated investments because the local financial markets are fragile against liquidity risks, systemic risks, and sovereign risks. This means that the agents in this area still have to manage exchange rate risks of the dollar fluctuations when they invest their local money in the regional economy. In order to utilize the available local/regional savings as a growth engine, the fragile local markets need to be interlinked with the regional financial center. Further regional monetary cooperation or political collective actions should play important roles in developing and integrating the regional financial market. This would contribute to forming a common currency union in this region.

5. CONCLUSIONS

Since the 1960s, economic integration within the East Asia area has been implemented through the use of corporate initiatives, in what has been referred to as "functioning integration". East Asian multi-national production networks have been established through the expansion of Japanese enterprises—as well as those of newly industrialized economies—into ASEAN and China. The trade volumes within the East Asian area are one-half its total trade volume worldwide. FTAs among the East Asian countries have been enacted since the 2000s, and internal trade among them will increase as more FTAs are formulated. However, the exchange rate—one of the key factors affecting trade volume—might be a destabilizing factor in intra-regional trade transactions. In line with the need to stabilize the foreign exchange rate within the East Asian area, the monetary authorities of East Asian countries need to cooperate with each other on their foreign exchange policy. As a measurement to stabilize the foreign exchange rate, the monetary authorities of East Asian countries need to create a common currency basket. Some of the previous studies argued that a common currency basket can rectify currency overvaluation or undervaluation, and is more suitable for East Asian countries to create a common currency area.

In this paper, we investigate whether East Asian countries are suitable candidates for forming a common currency area by employing the G-PPP model and by testing for co-integration with asymmetric error correction. Comparing the pre- and post-period of the Asian currency crisis, some East Asian countries tend to converge. In particular, after the crisis the member countries of ASEAN are converging either around themselves or around the three largest economies of Japan, China, and Korea.

The results of our empirical analysis suggest that East Asian countries are more suitable today for creating a common currency area based on the G-PPP model in the first decade of the twenty-first century than before the Asian currency crisis. It implies that East Asian economic development has been promoting trade transactions and monetary regionalization. In the next decade, a stable real exchange rate among East Asian countries is expected to promote the efficiency of market transactions and economic integration.

Furthermore, to evaluate which East Asian countries are more applicable for creating a common currency area appropriately, in future research, we need to improve the anchor exchange rate by reference to a currency basket calculated by including all the trading partners of ASEAN6+3.

ACKNOWLEDGMENTS

This study is conducted as a part of the Project "Research on Currency Baskets" undertaken at Research Institute of Economy, Trade and Industry (RIETI).dx. The authors are grateful for helpful comments and suggestions by Ganeshan Wignaraja (Asian Development Bank Institute) as a discussant of the 14th conference of East Asian Economic Association, 1–2 November 2014, and Discussion Paper seminar participants at RIETI.

AUTHOR CONTRIBUTIONS

Kentaro Kawasaki and Zhi-Qian Wang conceived and designed the experiments; Zhi-Qian Wang performed the experiments; Kentaro Kawasaki and Zhi-Qian Wang analyzed the data; Kentaro Kawasaki contributed analysis tools; Kentaro Kawasaki and Zhi-Qian Wang wrote the paper.

CONFLICTS OF INTEREST

The authors declare no conflict of interest.

NOTES:

[1]Recently, there are several empirical studies to investigate the OCA issue to employ the G-PPP approach, such as Wilson and Choy (2007) [9], Sun and Sinons (2011) [10], and de Truchis and Keddad (2013) [11]. Especially, Keddad (2013) [12] has investigated this issue considering applying the Asian currency baskets.

[2]The real exchange rate between country *j* and country *k* can also be expressed as follows: rej,k=−ren,j+ren,k.

[3]The stationary component $r\bar{e}e$ can be given by E($r\bar{e}e$)=0 over the long run.

[4]For more detail, see Enders and Siklos (2001) [17].

[5]The CPI data of China is based on the *International Financial Statistics* of IMF, as well as the AMU database in the Research Institute of Economy, Trade and Industry (RIETI).

[6]In a strict sense, the anchor exchange rate in this empirical analysis should be a currency basket, which includes all the

trading partners of ASEAN6+3. Here for simplicity, we use the exchange rate of euro to the US dollar instead of the currency basket. In our future research, we intend to calculate the currency basket along with data accumulation.

[7]With respect to the property of real exchange rate of each currency, the M-TAR unit root test revealed that the PPP does not hold over the long run in both sample periods. The estimation results of OLS coefficients and M-TAR unit root test are not reported completely because of space limitations but are available upon request. Lag orders are based on the Akaike information criteria (AIC) and the Schwartz Bayes information criteria (SBIC).

[8]Since the sample period in the recent years includes nine currencies and covers larger sample currencies than in the sample period from 1984 to 1997, we cannot compare the two sample periods without careful consideration and further conclude that the currencies of the recent sample period are more cointegrated.

REFERENCES

1. Enders, W.; Hurn, S. Theory and tests of generalized purchasing power parity: Common trends and real exchange rates in the Pacific Rim. *Rev. Int. Econ.* **1994**, *2*, 179–190.

2. Williamson, J. *Exchange Rate Regimes for Emerging Markets: Reviving the Intermediate Option*; Institute for International Economics: Washington, DC, USA, 2000.

3. Ogawa, E.; Ito, T. On the desirability of a regional basket currency arrangement. *J. Jpn. Int. Econ.* **2002**, *16*, 317–334.

4. Kuroda, H.; Kawai, M. Strengthening regional financial cooperation in East Asia. Available

online: https://www.mof.go.jp/pri/research/discussion_paper/ron061.pdf (accessed on 30 September 2006).

5. Ogawa, E. Regional monetary cooperation in East Asia against asymmetric responses to the US dollar depreciation. *J. Korean Econ.* **2004**, *5*, 43–72.

6. Kawasaki, K. Are the ASEAN plus three countries coming closer to an optimum currency area? *China Econ. Policy Rev.* **2012**.

7. Mundell, R.A. A theory of optimum currency areas. *Am. Econ. Rev.* **1961**, *51*, 657–665.

8. Obstfeld, M.; Rogoff, K. *Fundations of International Macroeconomics*; The MIT press: Cambridge, MA, USA, 1996.

9. Wilson, P.; Choy, K.M. Prospects for enhanced exchange rate cooperation in East Asia: Some preliminary findings from Generalized PPP theory. *Appl. Econ.* **2007**, *39*, 981–995.

10. Sun, W.; Simons, G. Monetary integration in East Asia: Evidence from real effective exchange rates. *Rev. Int. Econ.***2011**, *19*, 865–876.

11. De Truchis, G.; Keddad, B. Southeast Asian monetary integration: New evidences from fractional cointegration of real exchange rates. *J. Int. Financ. Mark. Inst. Money* **2013**, *26*, 394–412.

12. Keddad, B. Exchange rate coordination in Asia under regional currency basket systems. *Econ. Bull.* **2013**, *4*, 2913–2929.

13. Stock, J.H.; Watson, M.W. Testing for common trends. *J. Am. Stat. Assoc.* **1988**, *83*, 1097–1107.

14. Ogawa, E.; Kawasaki, K. *Possibility of Creating a Common Currency Basket for East Asia*; JBICI Discussion Paper Series; Japan Bank for International Cooperation: Tokyo, Japan, 2003.

15. Johansen, S.; Juselius, K. Maximum likelihood estimation and inference on cointegration (with applications to the demand for money). *Oxf. Bull. Econ. Stat.* **1990**, *52*, 169–210.

16. Enders, W.; Granger, C.W.J. Unit root tests and asymmetric adjustment with an example using the term structure of interest rates. *J. Bus. Econ. Stat.* **1998**, *16*, 304–311.

17. Enders, W.; Siklos, P.L. Cointegration and threshold adjustment. *J. Bus. Econ. Stat.* **2001**, *19*, 166–176.

9

CHAPTER

The Chinese Political Dissidents in Exile: Struggle for a Sustainable and Relevant Movement

Jie Chen

Political Science and International Relations, University of Western Australia, Perth, Australia

ABSTRACT

The overseas Chinese democracy movement started in the early 1980s and comprised of the networks, organisations and campaigns of those mainland Chinese activists, in exile mostly in the West, particularly the United States. These dissidents were mainly Democracy Wall (1978-79) veterans, the Tiananmen Square event (1989) student leaders and intellectuals, and other activists who became politicised while studying or living abroad. This paper investigates the reflection and readjustment of the political exiles to halt the decline of their movement over the past decade, to make it more sustainable and relevant to both their host nations and conditions in China in the new century. While the movement has little direct role to play in China's democratization or its host states' policies towards China, the exile community has become more flexible and adaptable in both strategic direction and tactical approaches, with more efforts to: intervene and support new social contention in China, establish specialized campaign agencies, experiment with new models of organizational development, influence domestic and international public opinions, and rejuvenate solidarity with the evolving civil societies in Taiwan and Hong Kong on the basis of shared political values more than "one China" sentiment. The significance of these new dynamics, in terms of the movement's survival and impact, can only be appreciated by breaking free from state-centric perspectives which have already been challenged in the literature on transnational social movements and exile politics.

Keywords: Overseas Chinese Democracy Movement, Dissidents, Exile Politics, Tiananmen Event, Civil Society

1. INTRODUCTION

The overseas Chinese democracy movement (OCDM) started in the 1980s and consisted of the networks, organisations and campaigns of those mainland Chinese activists, in exile mostly in the West, particularly in the United States (US). These dissidents were mainly Democracy Wall (1978-79) veterans, the Tiananmen Square event (1989) student leaders and intellectuals, and other activists who became politicised while studying or living abroad. Through lobbying, publicity, conferencing, training, protests and many other contentious activities, they advocate liberal democratic values to systematically expose the fundamental flaws in the system of the party-state in China and struggle for its ending.

Based on primary sources and field research, this paper investigates the struggle of the Chinese political dissidents in exile to arrest their declining movement, to make it more sustainable and relevant to both their host nations and democratization of China in the new century. First, the paper presents the historical context and accounts for the wax and wane of OCDM. Second, it offers a general analysis of the reflection and tactical readjustment on the part of the democracy activists under the more challenging circumstances. In the subsequent sections, the paper examines the discernible efforts or trends emanating from the movement which are related and mutually reinforcing, epitomizing a new direction of the movement. They include attempts to: intervene in the Rights Defending Movement within China; extend financial and spiritual support fordomestic activists; undertake new experiment in organizational development; adopt more diverse and creative ways to influence public opinion; and rejuvenate solidarity with the other societies of Greater China, particularly Taiwan. The conclusion sheds broad light on whither the movement goes in light of these new trends.

2. WAX AND WANE OF THE MOVEMENT

Inspired by the suppressed Democracy Wall Movement in Beijing (1978-79), Wang Bingzhang, a medical graduate of McGill University (Canada), initiated in New York in December 1983 the Chinese Alliance for Democracy (CAD), the first overseas political opposition organization of mainland Chinese background since 1949. This single *spark* was followed by a *prairie* fire from June 1989, when the exodus of Tiananmen students and intellectuals, and agitation caused by the Beijing crackdown, led to a climax of political activism in the Chinese diaspora communities worldwide. These new comers to the OCDM scene founded the Federation for a Democratic China (FDC) in Paris in September 1989, which subsequently established branches in 25 countries, boasting 3000 members. CAD also expanded, reaching a similar number of members and setting up branches in dozens of countries well beyond North America by the end of 1989, while maintaining secret contact points inside China. By the early 1990s, there emerged a robust global sphere of overseas Chinese dissident politics. Their active networking, campaigning and lobbying penetrated Chinatowns and university campuses, and interacted with the Western governments, parliaments, international media and social groups. However, from the late 1990s, the movement started to lose its momentum, stagnating and declining in its visibility and influence, even though between 50 and 60 new organizations had been formed (Chen, 2014: pp. 446-448). Shrinking rank and file of the established OCDM groups was particularly observable. Xue (2013), the CAD president (2011-15), estimated the remaining membership of the organization as around 200 (2013). Sheng (2013), the current FDC president, believed her organization still retained about 100 active members. Other indicators of the movement's low tide were the much smaller turnout at conferences and protest rallies, financial difficulties, deteriorating reputation of the organizations and activists, and abandoning of the cause by some well-known activists in favour of careers in business, academia and religion (Zhou, 2010: p. 78).

The downward trajectory was caused by a conjunction of structural circumstances and problematic agency. The international environment started to become more arduous for the movement from the mid-1990s. The Western nations started to abandon their Tiananmen sanctions against China. The new century has seen the OCDM fighting even more of an uphill battle. China's international economic and diplomatic prowess continued to grow, forging strategic partnerships with major Western powers. China's indispensable roles in a host of newly salient global economic, environmental and security issues, such as transnation alterrorism, financial stability, Korean nuclear crisis, and climate change, made the Western nations more muted on the country's human rights record (He, 2013). Meanwhile, political transformation in Taiwan weakened the movement. Before democratisation of its own authoritarian political system which started from the late 1980s, the Republic of China (ROC) on Taiwan functioned as an ideological rival to the People's Republic on the mainland and treated Wang and his followers as honourable anti-communist warriors. During the 1980s-90s, the Kuomintang regime in Taipei was the biggest financial sponsor of the movement. Enthusiasm started to dwindle from the late 1990s, due to political de-Sinification, cross-straits rapprochement and Taipei's attempt to capitalize on China's phenomenal economic growth. Another cooling effect on OCDM arose from the changing political dynamics in the Chinese diaspora communities in the West. More and more migrants and students have changed their attitude towards Beijing, from universal condemnation or shunning of the regime due to its political repression to embracing it, for the sake of economic and career benefit, or as a result of Beijing's success in its soft power campaigns in Chinatowns worldwide. Diasporic attraction to the homeland has also been encouraged by Beijing's own united front initiatives which include offering business and employment opportunities, and organizing tour groups, targeting both the students abroad and the diaspora community at large.[1] Marginalization of the political exiles in the overseas Chinese communities significantly weakened their grassroots support base. It must be further noted that the Chinese government's perfection of its border control policy has exacerbated the overseas activists' attempt to develop opposition cells within China. They have been banned from visiting China and the post-handover Hong Kong. For those Democracy Wall veterans and Tiananmen student leaders and intellectuals, they typically have never been able to visit China ever since they left the country, irrespective of their residential status abroad including foreign citizenship, and regardless of the circumstances in which they left the country. In the exile community, a popular saying is that while they have found a haven of freedom under foreign skies, they have lost the land of China, or "gaining the sky, losing the ground". Some adventurous exile dissidents tried to sneak into China, only to be seized upon landing, followed by interrogation and expelling.

Evolution of OCDM reflects the interaction between the changing structural environment and the activists' agency. In the discourse of transnational social movements, the roles of social activists or political entrepreneurs are posited as among the crucial factors which condition the movements' effective development. The significance of "actor characteristics" is such that activists with effective transcultural communication and campaign skills, and dense exchanges and close solidarity between the various organizations, are among the enabling elements for the movements(Keck & Sikkink, 1998: pp. 28-29) . In OCDM, over the years prominent roles were played by former beneficiaries of the party-state (such as Chen Yizhi, and Wan Runnan), or Democracy Wall veterans (such as Wei Jingsheng, Xu Wenli, and Wang Xizhe), or the 1989 student heroes from the Tiananmen Square such as Wuer Kaixi, Wang Dan and Liu Gang, or the emerging professional lobbyist-kind of activists who first came to the US to study or migrate but successfully recreated themselves as formidable activists (such as Yang Jianli and Fu Xiqiu). These democracy activists have different styles and knowledges which complemented each other, though many older ones do not have the sort of effective transcultural communication and campaign skills. What became debilitating for the movement was the dearth of another enabling element mentioned in the theory, namely comradely solidarity. For many years from the mid-1990s, the movement was plagued by chronic infighting and factionalism within and between dissident organizations. There was little dispute over fundamental political ideals, and hostilities were chiefly caused by clashing egos of the activists, self-interests and allegations of corruption. Rowena He (2013) , a Harvard researcher of Tiananmen event, argued that the splits, infighting, and inter-personal bitterness within the community of exiled dissidents arose partially from their domestic political socialization experiences in China that focused on struggles against nature and the people, rather than conflict resolution and leadership. Another debilitating factor she suggested was the traumas suffered by the dissidents before leaving China, claiming that she "observed signs and behaviour of post-traumatic stress disorder among almost every single exiled dissident whom I have encountered over the years, in both their personal and public lives" (2014, p. 175). Wang Dan (2012: p. 348) , a renowned Tiananmen student leader now in exile, also attributed the infighting mainly to the beliefs, values and attitudes adopted by the activists in their early political education. *He candidly admitted that while they had embarked on a pro-democracy path, many exile activists including himself had hardly shaken off all the legacies of the communist political culture which heavily influenced their formative years. Thus they saw the political world in* black-or-white fashion, treating fellow travellers with different opinions as enemies, and were unable to use defined procedures and civil dialogue to settle conflicts. Thus different opinions often led to attacks and split. This trend was compounded by a ubiquitous fear of Beijing's infiltration through an increasing number of informants and agents, which often caused mutual suspicion among some activists. Yan Jiaqi, the first president of FDC and a well-learned political scientist, said that factionalism and infighting were normal in the ranks of political activism in exile, and that the overseas dissident movements from the Soviet Union and Eastern Europe, and even the Solidarity movement within Poland, were no exceptions either (Yan, 2008) . This may well be true?and one can also cite the bitter infighting and split in the overseas movements of the much earlier Russian Bolsheviks and Sun Yat-sen's republican revolution, it is undeniable that the phenomenon had caused reputational harm to OCDM, enduring personal tension among some of the leading activists, and disillusionment among the Western and Taiwanese supporters and funders. The problematic agency and a worsening structural environment mentioned earlier became mutually reinforcing to cause the movement to lose its momentum.

Today even the most dedicated OCDM veterans would not deny that the movement has overall declined compared to its climax reached during the immediate post-Tiananmen years.[2] However, the history of OCDM is not a story of total disarray. New developments have been emerging and become salient during the recent decade, demonstrating a trend of reflection and adaptation of the activists in reaction to the arduous political environment and debilitating impacts caused by the intra-movement problems. Consequently, the movement appears to have gained a new lease of life by becoming organizationally and tactically more diverse, creative and society-oriented, as discussed in the following sections.

3. ASSESSMENT, REFLECTION AND READJUSTMENT

A balanced and broad analytical framework is necessary to appreciate the meaning of the new trends. In the more vocal negative commentaries of the OCDM since the 20th anniversary of the Tiananmen event, the naysayers mostly single out the movement's declining impact on the China policies of the host states and China's own political development. An editorial in the Beijing-based Global Times claims that overseas democracy activists used to be confident in the overthrow of the Chinese political system but have now become marginalized in the West-China diplomatic chessboard. In fact they have become the smallest pieces in the board with negligible influence over the Western states' policies towards China (Chan, 2013). This official line is shared by a veteran CNN correspondent who covered the Tiananmen event and China's international relations. He believes that OCDM was influential in the 1990s, when the exile dissidents effectively used the Congressional debate to present their proposals to force changes in China as a condition to retain its most favoured nation (MFN) status and secure permanent normal trade relations (PNTR) with the US. Activists also benefited from the role of the then Assistant Secretary of State Winston Lord (1993-1997), who emphasized human rights due to his personal engagement with the student activists at Beijing University during his ambassadorial time in China (1985-89). However, the Clinton administration's decision to delink the annual decision-making on China's MFN status from its human rights record in 1995, and grant PNTR to China in 1999, deprived the dissidents of key campaign leverages. It is further argued that exile dissidents today are manipulated by the Western political forces for their own domestic politicking despite the more consistent support from a few politicians like Nancy Pelosi (the Democratic Leader of the US House of Representatives), caught in an American debate, not China's.[3] Dismissing the significance of OCDM, a former Asia policy adviser to President Obama simply said that dissidents in exile needed to be someone like Kim Dae-jung, who already had his own popular powerbase in the homeland (South Korea) before exile in the US (1982-85), so that Washington could find them more usable for its own geopolitical goals.[4] None of the exile Chinese dissidents was ever a major figure in the national politics. Nor has any become an undisputed leader in the overseas Chinese communities. Such critiques, however, are state-centric. Based on numerous case studies, Goddeer concludes that activities undertaken in exile politics are multifaceted, and its objectives and efficacy must be judged accordingly. Three fields are highlighted: the changing of policy (in both the home and the host land), the informing and influencing of public opinion, and the development of new ideas(Goddeeris, 2007: p. 397, 402) .

To influence and change state policies remains important to the dissidents and they are making greater efforts. For example, regular testimonies at the US Congressional hearings are characterized by more professional presentations on diverse issues including one-child policy as well as other human rights and democracy issues. Dialogue with the Canadian foreign policy officials has been held once or twice a year, though such engagement with the Australian parliament has become sporadic. At the meetings of the United Nations Human Rights Council (UNHRC) in Geneva in 2013-14, activists expressed sharply critical views in the scrutiny of China's Universal Periodic Review report and its bidding for the council's membership (Friends of FDC, 2014-15) . Wei Jingsheng, chairman of the Overseas Chinese Democracy Coalition and an old hand in the Congressional and UN lobbying, maintains his optimism, arguing that even in the post-PNTR Congress, there are still opportunities to influence for the pro-active dissidents like himself. He has claimed that in her meeting with him in late September 2015, Pelosi said that when she met President Xi Jinping a few days earlier, she considered Wei's opinions and thus did not mince her words in criticizing China's human rights abuses. Wei (2015) believes that in a relationship of mutual use with the Western politicians, the dissidents' cause can be advanced.

It has become much harder, however, for the dissidents to influence the US administration and Western governments in general due to the changing strategic environment mentioned earlier. Those naysayers' assessments of OCDM's position are not far from the mark. As Wei himself has admitted, the UN Commission on Human Rights (predecessor of UNHRC) used to function as a key forum where member states frequently debated and condemned China's political repression. Exile dissidents enjoyed the opportunities to unnerve the Chinese delegates by attempting to mobilise votes to pass resolutions aimed at investigating human rights conditions in China. However, when the Commission was transformed to UNHRC in 2006, Beijing had already commanded sophisticated maneuvering tactics to stave off the forum's diplomatic pressure. Dissidents may still use the Council's periodical China review and annual meetings to expose the rights abuses and make moral appeals, but can no longer realistically contemplate the tactic of vote mobilisation to pressurize China (Wei, 2014) .

Goddeeris' positive view of the efficacy of the exiles' campaigns to change state policies is in fact based on the study of states much smaller than China, including the East European states and Cuba. He also includes the better-resourced governments in exile as well as exile political movements. Challenges confronting the Chinese activists are substantially more arduous. This point can be more poignantly made by looking at China's own region, where exile activists from South Korea, Taiwan and the Philippines during the 1970s-80s benefited from the fact that the US administration and Congress had far more influence over their home states than Washington has ever had over Beijing. This ensured the relative effectiveness of their lobbying work.

The Chinese dissident circles seem to be encouraged by the recent talks in the foreign policy communities in the US and some of its Asian allies suggesting a major readjustment of their relations with China. China's aggressive behaviour in territorial disputes in East and South China Seas, and the escalating cyber hacking reportedly conducted from the country, may cause high tension with the West. However, if the dissidents assume that this may escalate into a Cold War—kind of containment of China so that they would receive substantial support from the West, their minds should be more measured. In an era characterised by comprehensive economic, financial and social integration between the West and China, it is anyone's guess whether the US and its allies would be interested in a strategy of across-the-board rivalry.

Still, Goddeeris' idea of dissidents' multifaceted activities and impacts point to useful benchmarks beyond the state realm. This idea is more elaborately presented in Wapner's (1996: pp. 1-16)theorization of world civic politics, which opens up a new horizon in assessing the scope and impacts of transnational activism. It argues that the notion of political influence should be broadened so that in addition to their work on the policies of states, the impact of transnational social movements must be assessed from a different but related dimension, namely the attempt by activists to create or manipulate shifts in public opinion and shape the conduct of behaviour by working directly within and across national societies. By disseminating new ideas and information through awareness-raising programs towards the general public, enlivening public debates, and cooperating with and influencing other non-state actors, transnational activists attempt to lead the society to change independently of state policies. Though civic politics may eventually lead to a change in state policies, this may not be the goal or immediate objective of activists. Wapner's idea is grounded on the work of large international environmental NGOs such as Greenpeace and World Wildlife Fund, which enjoy UN consultative status and operate their own offices inside China. Since they have encountered frustrations in trying to influence China's policies and the UN's approaches towards China on the issues of conservation and environmental protection, hence the necessity to also assess their work from the perspective of civic politics,[5] it is then only natural that the exile dissidents, who target China on the core political issues without the slightest chance to set up branches in China, should not be belittled due to an apparent lack of influence over the party-state, or any other state for that matter.

Ideas of Goddeeris and Wapner are capitalized on in this investigation of the OCDM's intensified activities beyond the state policy arena in the recent decade. Their ideas, however, only serve as a broad guide to organize my empirical observations of the OCDM's proliferating strands of activism, beyond a narrow focus on the dissidents' interactions with, and impacts on, the state. This borrowing in broad sense is because the complex Chinese exile movement is not the sort of cases used in Goddeeris' generalization. Also, as a diaspora-based transnational movement which is focused on one country, the OCDM is different from the typical transnational social movement analysed by Wapner which comprises of cause-oriented international groups with multinational membership.

First, one must discern any influence on public sentiment from the dissidents' activities in the state policy arena. Lobbying campaigns at the various parliaments, and the shaming and exposing of Beijing at the UN agencies, may not sway state policies, but the wide media publicity thus generated may influence public opinion.[6] Second, and more importantly, due analytical weight must be given to the kind of OCDM activities which are of general developmental nature or mainly target at the society and public opinion both inside and outside China. The overall deteriorating operational environment at the state and diaspora levels, and the rise of new social contention in China such as the Rights Defending Movement, have forced the exile activists to soul- searching, reflection, and readjustment over the past decade. If they were ever trying to ready themselves to change or even take over the political regime in China, only to find their revolutionary bubble burst in the 1990s, they have now become more nuanced and practical. The new consensus is that the movement must be prepared for a long-term, more effective and sustainable struggle, making itself more geared towards China's complex process of democratization and the Western and Taiwanese socio-political reality. Niche roles must be identified, with a closer focus on the sort of activities which their fellow travellers inside China cannot undertake, rather than lamenting at their own perennial exile.[7] As a result, the OCDM organizations have started to strengthen the activities aimed at sustaining the morale of domestic social activists and enhancing their campaigns, swaying the public opinion of the realities of China, preserving and cultivating fresh activist resources, and capitalizing on new political awakening in the mature civil societies in Taiwan and Hong Kong. More use has been made of online platforms and social media (including the China-based Weibo and We Chat) to mitigate the debilitating effects of decreased organizational membership. Though perennial exile has weakened the overseas activists' personal touch of socio-political transformation in China, dense connections with domestic activists and the use of advanced technology ensure that they can easily receive accurate information from China and determinate it quickly and widely, against the odds posed by China's internet blocking devices.[8]Generally the OCDM activities have become more creative and diverse, showing new dynamics as reflected in the endeavours presented in the following sections.

These developing trends have coincided with much decreased incidents of infighting within the movement, another result of lesson-learning as well as fatigue. Reconciliation or ceasefire is epitomized, for example, by the regular meetings of an Overseas Coordinating Committee of the Chinese Democracy Movement which was formed in 1999 to coordinate commemoration of the 20th anniversary of the Tiananmen event. Initiated by 15 organizations, it now boasts a membership of more than 50. Although this has by no means filled the cracks and resolved personal bitterness caused by factional infighting, the Committee functions like a looser UN of the movement. It has become a forum to synchronize the global Tiananmen commemorations through web-based conferences and discuss general issues of the movement (Xue, 2015). Meanwhile, in 2012, to celebrate the 30th anniversary of China Spring magazine, the predecessor of CAD, many activists joined to release a Convention of Overseas Chinese Democracy

Movement (http://news.boxun.com/news/gb/party/2012/06/201206080254.shtml#.UOg-WXfYGSo) which calls for comradely solidarity and mutual respect.

4. SUPPORT FOR DOMESTIC SOCIO-POLITICAL CONTENTION

Supporting and instigating political opposition within China has been the OCDM's imbedded duty. However, activists have met mounting practical difficulties. In China, attempts to establish political parties (such as China Liberal Democratic Party in 1992, and China Democracy Party in 1998), and dissidents calling for explicit systemic reform of the party-state (such as Charter 08 movement), have been severely punished with long jail terms. Also, to liaise and collaborate with such revolutionary elements inside China would often necessitate clandestine visits to the country by the exile dissidents, an act which has become infeasible and risky, as shown in the jailing or expelling of a number of dissidents who sneaked into the country by using pseudonyms. On the other hand, OCDM could become irrelevant if the leading dissidents overseas were stuck to their Tiananmen or Democracy Wall idealism. China marched forward in their exile years, with new social cleavages and new waves of protest movements developing over the past decade. Spearheaded by rights lawyers, the so-called Rights Defending Movement has operated within China's existing legal and political mechanisms and tried to use them to defend citizens' rights in the issue fields of low politics, including food safety, land acquisition, environmental protection, housing affordability, educational opportunities, factory workers' rights and conditions, and gender equality. The authorities' tolerance started to become thinner since 2013 after some rights lawyers tried to initiate a New Citizens Movement, a platform trying to steer the Rights Defending Movement to a clearer advocacy for civil society, constitutional rights, rule of law and public declaration of the national leaders' private property. However, while the Xi Jinping administration started a nationwide crackdown on rights lawyers in mid-2015, overall the Rights Defending Movement has been more feasible and effective in organization and mobilization under the current political circumstances in China, than outright attempts to stage real political opposition.

Dissidents in exile saw the new socio-political contention as opening a fresh window for their own struggle and broadened their domestic focus. Their task has become to disseminate to China the international experiences of non-violent social movements and strive to ideationally connect the Rights Defending Movement to the track of struggle for democracy. Supporting this movement also helps in broadening the dissidents' united front with transnational human rights movements. At a time when exile politics has become a rarity in the world, OCDM can only realistically forge solidarity with transnational activists whose concern with China are mostly based on a rights frame, not wholesale regime change. This tactical moderation also makes the OCDM more acceptable to the Western funding bodies which often do not like to jeopardize their governments' China engagement policies by funding radical exile groups.

The OCDM organizations' engagement in the Rights Defending Movement is characterized by a strenuous effort to internationalize the struggle, such as bringing out the activists for protest rallies in the UN or for training sessions overseas. What's particularly revealing of this new momentum of OCDM is that some former Tiananmen heroes in exile have moderated their political tones by pursuing more modest and feasible programs. For example, Chai Ling, the chief commander of a Tiananmen Square Protection Headquarters of 1989, founded All Girls Allowed in 2010 to campaign on the wellbeing of rural women and injustices in family planning. Han Dongfang, the founder of Beijing Workers Autonomous Union in 1989, has moved on to promote a collective bargaining mechanism to improve the rights and working conditions of the Chinese workers within the official trade union system (Boxun News, 2013b) . Even Wei Jingsheng, the veteran democracy fighter known to be radical, has also started to advocate the Chinese workers' collective bargaining rights, claiming that this would raise workers' income, thus expanding the Chinese market for the benefit of both its own economy and Western business (Wei Jingsheng Foundation, 2015) .

Reflecting the above trend, extending more tangible financial and spiritual support to domestic activists has become a distinct sector in OCDM. The number of participating organizations has increased, including some whose mandate is to specifically provide such support. Also, recipients in China are no longer just traditional political dissidents, but increasingly also rights lawyers. For many years, China Spring (and its successor magazine Beijing Spring), was the main financial supporter for domestc fellow travellers through honorarium. Other groups started their own systematic financial support for the victims of political persecutionin more recent years, including FDC's "ten dollar humanitarian donation program" (initiated in 2004). More significantly, new support groups have emerged, created by those dissidents who stayed out of scandolous factional in fighting which besieged the larger OCDM groups, thus attracting more donors. For example, Zhou Fengsuo, a leader of the 1989 Student Congress in Beijing, established Humanitarian China in San Francesco in 2007. The organi- zation provided financial support to around 100 prisoners of conscience and their families in dire financial stress in 2014 alone, including more than US$10,000 to the family of Ilham *Tohti, a Uighur scholar jailed for life for criticizing Beijing's policy towards minorities* (CK, 2015a) . Sun Liyong, a former police officer in Beijing who spent seven years in jail due to hisrole in Tiananmen movement, now heads the Sydney-based Support Network for the Persecuted in China, which he founded in 2005 to provide financial assistance to the families of those jailed for their political or religious beliefs, ranging from US$600 to US$1,000 in each case.Sun (2015) vividly spoke of the morale boosting effect of this work, arguing that cash aid to the families of those frontline dissidents helped the wives to meet their jailed husbands, enabled their children to go to school, and improved the quality of the prisoners' meals. International humanitarian assistance made the wives, children and parents of the jailed democracy fighters regard them as heroes, and made the heroes feel that they were far from isolated. Assistance in the overseas settlement of the domestic activists and their families is another humanitarian endeavour of the OCDM groups. Such activities include offering cash and accommodation to the new arrivals in the US, and the more complex operation to secure a transit to a Western country of the Chinese activists who have escaped to Thailand, a key escape route after Hong Kong's handover to China. This operation includes helping the escapees to apply for refugee status from the Bangkok office of The UN High Commissioner for Refugees (UNHCR) and avoid harassment by the Thai authorities.[9]

Activists languishing in jailal so have their morale boosted by the awards they receive, some of which also include cash. Throughout the 1980s-90s, a Chinese Democratic Education Foundation based in San Fancesco was the only institution giving such awards. It was started by some former Rightists who eventually settled in the US, and the awardees included democracy activists from Taiwan, Hong Kong as well as the mainland China. With a former Tiananmen activist Fang Zheng as its president, the foundation has focused on Chinese dissidents, intellectuals and rights lawyers over the past decade (http://www.cdef.org/). Meanwhile, the practice of giving awards and prizes to domestic dissidents and rights lawyers has become a major pursuit of the OCDM at large. The proliferating awards, their founders and starting years include: China Youth Human Rights Award (Wang Dan and other Tiananmen student leaders, 2001), Free Spirit Award (Independent Federation of Chinese Students and Scholars, 2001), Wei Jingsheng Chinese Democracy Champion Prize (The Wei Jingsheng Foundation, 2004), Human Rights Fighter Award (Asia-Pacific Human Rights Foundation, 2005), Freedom Pioneer Award (Beijing Spring, 2007),

Make a Better China Award (The Qi's Cultural Foundation, 2008), Oskar Award for Chinese Freedom and Human Rights (a group of US-based dissidents, 2014), and Citizen Power Award (Initiatives for China, 2015). From their own experiences in China, those exile activists like Wei Jingsheng, who won the Olaf Palmer Prize in 1994, understand that such glory is important to keep up the spirit of the jailed dissidents and rights defenders.

5. NEW EXPERIMENTS IN ORGANIZATIONAL DEVELOPMENT

This dynamic is manifested by the formation of new kind of dissident organizations and fresh trials in the organizational development of some traditional membership-based groups. This diversification is not exactly a synonym for "multi-mountainism", a usual negative reference to the split and tension in the dissident camps. It is more about tactics to suit changing circumstances and self-conscious pursuit of emerging activists to find their special positions.

Apart from some of the aforementioned organizations specializing in financial support and award giving, professional lobbyist agencies have also emerged in the OCDM. These agencies, such as Initiatives for China (founded 2007), and China Aid (2002), were formed by activists who were disillusioned with the inefficacy and decline of the traditional groups, and sought to find their own niche roles in the movement. They tend to adopt creative approaches in their campaigns. For example, they recruited daughters of several Chinese prisoners of conscience to testify before the US Congress and speak at the UN, hence a human touch in their advocacy (Hiatt, 2013a). Meanwhile, specialized democracy training institutions have sprung up, including Civil Society Institute (Las Vegas, 2015), China Democracy School (Melbourne, 2011), New School for Democracy (Taipei, 2011), and the Tiananmen University of Democracy (San Francesco, 2014). The last two online universities were the initiatives of former protest leaders in Tiananmen Square. The New

School for Democracy, which has Wang Dan as chairman of the board of directors, and Wang Juntao, a board member, offers courses in both political theories and practical operations such as knowledge and skills of working through the UN human rights mechanisms (http://idemocracy.asia/).The Tiananmen University of Democracy, headed by Feng Congde, is a resumption of a similar institution established on the Tiananmen Square shortly before the massacre in 1989. It is now offering courses taught by the renowned democratization scholar Larry Diamond. While enrolments for the courses in Wang's school are mostly from Taiwan and the mainland, the overwhelming majority of attendants at Feng's are mainland Chinese youth who manage to overcome the official internet blocking system (CK, 2015b) .

New momentum in organizational rejuvenation is also seen in some traditional membership-based OCDM groups, with their often controversial approaches to recruit members and raise funding. Their focus is to capitalize on an increasing large number of Chinese visitors, students and even illegal migrants over the past ten years who seek permanent residence in a Western country, particularly the US, by applying for political refugee status. Joining an OCDM organization and participating in its activities would enhance such application. This offers lucrative "refugee business" opportunities to the cash-strapped and membership-depleted organizations which nonetheless can provide legal and political assistance. This practice has been spearheaded by the various China Democracy Parties (CDP). After the original CDP was crushed in China in 1998, hundreds of activists and members were arrested and received long-term imprisonment, with a combined time in prison totaling a thousand years (Yan, 2010) . The harsh treatment of these daring dissidents created a unique moral aura for CDP, and association with this party might help a Chinese visitor, student or illegal migrant boost their chance to apply for the US green card on the ground of fear of persecution once returning home. Subsequently no less than four CDPs were set up overseas, all headquartered in New York, each claiming to be the legitimate inheritor of the original, competing against each other in "refugee business" by using the CDP brand. This practice has caused much controversy, regarding the perceived opportunism of both new members and their helpers, fraudulent dealings and profiteering. However, it is also true that under the current circumstances, this approach has served a number of useful purposes. It has brought in some fresh and younger members for the parties, increased the attendants of protest rallies, and helped cover the expenses of activities. Irrespective of the motivations of those who have joined a dissident organization and paid large sum of fees for assistance to achieve political credentials to boost their refugee status claim, they must go through the required systematic educational and training programs on democracy, with lectures given by bona fide dissidents including the real CDP founders in exile, and participate in various protest rallies. Even though new party members may disappear as soon as they receive permanent residential status of the US, this does not happen en masse as in the mid-1990s, when some Western governments' mass granting of permanent residence to all Chinese students and visitors who left China before Tiananmen event or shortly afterwards led to an instant evaporation of large number of members and followers of the major OCDM groups. Under the current circumstances, refugee status processing is based on individual cases, and some party members, particularly those who do have earlier experiences of political persecution in China, have stayed on in the parties. The National Committee of Democratic Party of China, founded in 2010 as the newest variant of CDP, has made good use of its new recruits to contribute to the cause. One of its regular activities is that each week the chairman Wang Juntao, a veteran dissident and one of the "black hands" accused of organizing the Tiananmen Square demonstrations, has been taking around 20 new members (mostly young Chinese students) to stage a protest rally in the Times Square in New York. The themes are focused on particular events in China such as jailing of a rights lawyer or crackdown on a mass rally. All participating members in this program, or "Jasmine Revolution" as officially called by the party, would make speeches in public expressing their understanding of the relevant events and condemning the Chinese government. While such activities may be part of an attempt to boost their chances with a US green card, the participants do feel exercised in a democratic process. A special feat is that, of the ten Chinese students abroad who released a declaration in May 2015 condemning the Tiananmen massacre, seven came from Wang's party, having learned crucial facts from those Tiananmen survivors in exile. This was the first time such a public statement was made by elements of the 1980s-90s generations who were the main carriers of the officially imposed culture of Tiananmen amnesia. Wang's affinitive and charismatic personality, and his prioritizing of personal connections and infrastructural development over political idealism in party-building, seems to open up a new path for traditional membership-based groups. Boasting a membership of 560, the party had donated a total of US$52,700 to domestic activists by 2014.[10]

6. MORE DIVERSE AND CREATIVE WAYS TO INFLUENCE PUBLIC OPINION

To influence public opinion, targeting both the international audiences and overseas and domestic Chinese communities, remains a major mission of OCDM. It is not only about challenging the state narrative of key historical events in the Chinese political history and propagating a democratic vision for the country, but also providing alternative information and opinions of the current political affairs in China, including events in Tibet and Xinjiang. Activists' endeavours in that regard have become more diverse and creative in recent years. Importance of their voice, expressed in various ways as elaborated in the following, can be read from a broad context where Beijing's propaganda machine has rapidly infiltrated the international community in recent years, with news and commentary produced in Beijing rebroadcast through overseas Chinese print media and community radio stations that have been bought up, and through foreign language news services established by Beijing itself (Fitzgerald, 2014; Shambaugh, 2015).

Leading dissidents have maintained their vigour in awareness-raising campaigns at the general community level through speech tours of various institutions including universities and schools. In fact, as a result of advancement in study and career, some members of the exile community have become established academics in Western universities, thus occupying crucial positions to shape the perceptions of their students regarding the Chinese politics and host states' policies towards China. Meanwhile, more activists have appeared in the Chinese language programs and websites of major international broadcasting corporations, particularly Voice of America (both radio and television), Radio Free Asia, Deutsche Welle, Radio France, and the Falun Gong's print media and television channel, by way of regular colums and interviews. Interactive platforms often feature robust dialogue between the activists and readers and calling-in listeners based in China. Furthermore, opinion pieces penned by dissidents have regularly appeared in the mainstream media outlets such as The New York Times, The Washington Post, and The Wall Street Journal. This is partly because veterans like Wei Jingsheng are considered by the media as indispensable commentators on some political events in China, and partly because the new generation, English-fluent and lobbying-oriented activists are more media savvy.

Publication of books from the dissident community has become more diverse and mature. Thus apart from memoirs of those renowned Tiananmen heroes, which often celebrate their own historic roles, an increasing number of recent books are authored by lesser-known activists who want to tell their suffering in the hands and jails of the Chinese party-state. These more ordinary stories are often more appealing and contagious to the readers who can easily identify with the authors' experiences due to their own lived experiences in China or their parents', hence a more significant impact from the books. For example, Qi (2010, 2011, 2014) a woman from Sichuang, has published three books detailing her ten years in labour campus in the 1960s-70s due to the crime of "counter-revolution", her experience of living like a dog after release caused by under-employment and poverty, and her crime's impacts on her parents and siblings. In her book, Sun (2011), a woman from Shanghai, tells the story of her three-year imprisonment due to her activities in support of Beijing students in June 1989, social estrangement and official harrassment after release, and the resultant misery in everyday family life. The afore mentioned Sun (2009), who supported the Tiananmen student movement as a policeman in Beijing, has presented a vivid human account of political prisoners, common prisoners and prison officers based on his own seven years inprison in the 1990s. The human story of political dissent is also told by Fred Hiatt, the editorial page editor of The Washington Post. With the arrangement by Initiatives for China, Hiatt came to know Ti-Anna Wang, the daughter of Wang Bingzhang, founder of CAD. Because of his frustration with the declining international support for OCDM, Wang started to talk and write loosely about the need of violent revolution. In June 2002, he was kidnapped in Vietnam-China border and abducted to China, in a joint operation of the two governments' agents. He was sentenced to life imprisonment in February 2003, under the charges of "terrorism" and "espionage". Targeting the middle-school-aged readers, Hiatt' (2013b) spart fiction is based on Ti-Anna's personal struggle to rescue her father.

Street protest activities remain a major method to sway public perceptions, and new tactics have been emerging. One is Operation Sparrow, a campaign launched by Initiatives for China which seeks to create international spotlight on the practice of forced eviction and land grabbing perpetrated mainly by the local governments in China for commercial redevelopment. The operation exposes to the international community the numerous cases of violent demolition of citizens' houses and acquisition of farmers' land without consent or proper compensation. Under the operation, many victims and petitioners have been coming to the US and staging regular rallies and exhibitions in front of the UN headquarters since 2012, with banners and photos, telling the world what happened to their properties, how they were illegally detained and tortured when seeking justice against the local authorities benefiting from land sales (Boxun News, 2013a) . As if to apply the ancient Chinese petition method of blocking the emperor's carriage to plead him to correct the unlawful acts by local officials, two Sparrow petitioners blocked Xi Jinping's motorcade on 25 September 2015, when the visiting Chinese president was heading to the State Department. The two women rushed through police lines, ran towards the motorcade and threw themselves in front of two limousines, one believed to be Xi's. Under the broad public glare, a Chinese official, believed to be Xi's secretary or aide, took petition letters from the adventurous protesters. The videos of this saga went viral on You Tube (Initiatives for China, 2015) .

Street performance art is also experiemented in other protest rallies in recent years. In the annual rallies to commemorate the June 4 event, performances showing tanks crushing students have been staged. For 28 days in September 2013, in Times Square, Wang Juntao was sitting in a makeshift cage with moveable bars to mark the 10th year of Wang Bingzhang's imprisonment back in China. Dissidents have chosen the Oskar Awards ceremony day to present their own Oskar Award for Chinese Freedom and Human Rights. They staged the show at a spot as close as possible to the official ceremony in order to attract attention, and the award object is a replica of the original Oscar statuette except with shackles around it (Boxun News, 2014) .

7. REJUVENATING SOLIDARITY WITH OTHER SOCIETIES OF GREATER CHINA

As discussed earlier, Taiwan's role in OCDM has undergone a metmophasis, from ardent support to detachment. However, while the state of Taiwan has been washing its hands off the mainland dissidents, the latter have come to realize the potentials of the society in Taiwan. Wang Dan started to live and work in Taiwan as a teacher at various universities since 2010, joining Wuer Kaxi, another prominent Tiananmen student leader who settled on the island in the mid-1990s. Even though it has been challenging for these activists to manoeuvre through Taiwan's chronic partisan quagmire, they have found ready platforms in the recent waves of the thousands of mainland students enrolling in Taiwanese universities. If teacher Wang is an ideal person to pass the knowledge of Tiananmen to those mainland students who are also witnessing democracy in action in a Chinese society, political fugitive Wuer Kaixi's campaign for the 2016 legislative elections as an independent candidate may serve as a living democratic demonstration to the mainlanders.

More significantly, from 2011-12, the maturing civil society in Taiwan has started to pick up what the state and main political parties have left out in terms of solidarity with OCDM. Some social activists and Democratic Progressive Party legislators rooted in social movements started to argue that care for democracy and human rights in China does not have to hinge on one's attitude towards "one China" unification. Having signed and nationalised international laws on human rights, Taiwan should support China's democratisation from the standpoint of universal values. In addition, activists and students perceive China as a looming challenge to Taiwan's own human rights standards as well as a security threat. If political restrictions and censorship on Taiwanese citizens visiting or living in China is no longer news, then China's penetration in Taiwan's society and economy, a result of the Ma administration's black-box dealing with the mainland, is seen to also erode freedom of speech and rights conditions on the island itself. The Sunflower Student Movement of March-April 2014, when hundreds of university students and other civic activists occupied the chamber of the Legislative Yuan to protest the Ma administration's secretive trade deals with Beijing, showed that China could no longer be avoided even for those elements of the Taiwanese society who are least attached to the historical "one China" sentiment. Thus supporting China's democratisation is to care for the survival of Taiwan's own democracy. Instead of treating the Chinese dissidents as anti-communist warriors or avoiding them just because of their lack of support for Taiwan independence, they should be assisted as fellow travellers for the shared universal values and Taiwan's political well being, and those dissidents jailed in China should be dealt with simply as prisoners of conscience as defined by international laws, from a perspective free of historical and cultural obsession with China. It was with such new sentiment that a Taiwan Association for China Human Rights (TACHR) was founded in May 2011 (Yang, 2015), and the well-established Taiwan Association for Human Rights (TAHR), which avoided China-related cases all along, has also started to campaign for rights conditions in China (Wei, C. F., 2015). This demonstrates to the world that the Taiwanese people, having achieved democratization themselves, still care about the lack of political freedom in other countries, just as activists in the West assisted democracy fighters in Taiwan, including political exiles from the island, during the years of the Kuomintang's authoritarian regime.

This emerging sentiment has opened a new window of opportunity for OCDM. Mainland dissidents have started to proactively tap Taiwan's civil society as a new resource. As a result of their joint campaigns with TACHR and TAHR, resolutions have been adopted in the Legislative Yuan expressing concerns with the Chinese prisoners of conscience. Initiatives for China chose Taipei as the site for itsannual Interethnic Interfaith Leadership Conference in April 2014, when the Sunflower Student Movement was unfolding. The Taiwanese activists were invited from the front line to exchange ideas with the rights defenders fetched from the mainland and provide first-hand training of the methods used in peaceful social movements including how to handle the police(Chen, 2015) . Though some tactics taught by the Taiwanese activists were not totally applicable across the strait, capitalizing on the island's advanced civil society to help the mainland activists is a creative approach of OCDM, at a time when generous ideological and financial support from any Taiwanese governemnt seems distant history. Another encouraging development is that, initiated by Wang Dan but systematically organized by TACHR and a range of Taiwanese student and social groups, an annual Tiananmen memorial service has been held in Taipei's Freedom Square since 2011. The author's personal observation suggests that over the years the attendants increased from a few hundreds to close to a thousand, easily the largest overseas Tiananmen memorial rally second only to the annual June 4 vigils held in Hong Kong's Victoria Park.

On the other hand, the continuing memorial service in Hong Kong fails to conceal the former colony's declining role in lending direct support for the mainland's democratization. The 1997 hand over meant that Hong Kong's position as the Chinese political exiles' nearest operational base to the mainland since the late Qing dynasty was largely lost. Furthermore, despite the existence of a small network of hard-core OCDM supporters, the recent decade has witnessed the rise of a strong localist political consciousness, particularly among the young generations who no longer have the sort of proclivity to identify with political development on the mainland like their parents. Most of them are more interested in resisting Beijing'serosion of political freedom and obstruction of full democratization in Hong Kong, in order to maintain its international and pluralistic identity.

However, the mainland dissidents' perceptions of Hong Kong have recently changed, due to a series of mass sit-in street protests there urging genuine universal suffrage, whereby all Hong Kong residents would have the right to vote for the post of the Chief Executive, the city's top official. In particular, during September- December 2014, in what became known as the Umbrella Movement, protestors took over downtown Hong Kong and held it for seventy-nine days. The mainland dissidents in exile profoundly valued Hong Kong's political struggle for its demonstration effect on the mainland and launched global campaigns to support it. Though few dissidents could manage to sneak into Hong Kong to join the Umbrella Movement, joint rallies were held with Hong Kong expatriates, and ideas and lessons were exchanged intensely between Hong Kong student leaders and the former Tiananmen activists. A milestonein solidarity was that the mainland dissidents used the We The People petition mechanism of the White House, whereby a petition with no less than 100,000 signatures would secure an official response from the US administration. Framing their campaign as a struggle to prevent a second Tiananmen massacre in Hong Kong, dissident groups gathered 197,001 signatures, thus the Obama administration must make a clear statement about the ongoing Umbrella Movement. Among other points in support of "the aspirations of the Hong Kong people", the official response from the White House made it clear that "We believe that the legitimacy of the Chief Executive will be greatly enhanced if the Basic Law's ultimate aim of selection of the Chief Executive by universal suffrage is fulfilled and if the election provides the people of Hong Kong a genuine choice of candidates representative of the voters' will" (White House, 2014) .

8. CONCLUSION: OCDM TOWARDS THE NORMAL?

In China's ever expanding global politico-diplomatic shadow, and living with the Western world's accommoda- tion with Beijing, the question of whither the overseas Chinese democracy movement goes has been asked by both its detractors and supporters. The OCDM has long been ruled out as a community with a major direct role to play in China's democratization or its host states' policies towards China. However, transnational activism has developed new dynamics over the recent decade. Despite the continuing intra-movement tension and controversies, the exile community has become more flexible and adaptable in both strategic direction and tactical approaches, with more energy spent on trying to intervene and support new social contention in China, establish specialized campaign organizations, experiment with new models of organizational development, influence domestic and international public opinions, and rejuvenate solidarity with the evolving civil societies in Taiwan and Hong Kong on the basis of shared political values more than "one China" sentiment. In conjunction, these dynamics will suggest that the Chinese political activism in exile has started to move towards pragmatism and professionalism, with more activists finding their niche roles to make the movement survive and to develop as well as strengthening its impact in the sphere of civic politics. The OCDM is now neither a spark nor a spreading *prairie* fire, but may have the potential to function as a kindling material under the right broad circumstances beyond the exiles' control. In hindsight, the exciting scene in the early 1990s, when the OCDM inflated by the one-off event of Tiananmen was fighting what was widely seen as a falling party-state in China, was abnormal, and the current circumstance of the movement was normal or the new normal.

NOTES

[1]For President Xi Jinping's recent speech on patriotic united front, see Xi (2015) .

[2]See, for example, Chen (2013) . Chen serves as the vice president of CAD and chief editor of Beijing Spring.

[3]Personal interview, August 2014, Perth, Australia. Interviewee wishes to remain anonymous.

[4]Personal interview, December 2014, Perth, Australia. Interviewee wishes to remain anonymous.

[5]For an elaborate analysis of transnational environment movements and China, see Chen (2012) .

[6]For a typical opinion piece penned by dissidents on China's role in UNHRC, see Yang (2013) . Yang is the founder and president of the Washington DC-based Initiatives for China.

[7]This summary of the emerging consensus among the leading dissidents is based on personal interviews in Germany, the US, and Australia, 2014-15. See also Wang (2011) .

[8]For an earlier discussion of the role of internet in transnational activism, see Yang (2009: pp. 185-208) .

[9]The arrest and deportation in November 2015 of two Chinese dissidents, Jiang Yefei and Dong Guangping, who had already been granted refugee status by UNHCR (Holmes, 2015) , suggests that as a transit stop, Thailand's position has become more ambiguous.

[10]This discussion of Wang (2014) and activities of his party is based on personal interviews and on-site observation, New York, December 2014, and email from Wang (2015) .

REFERENCES

1. Boxun News (2013a). Petitioners Association of China Forced Eviction Visited the UN to Defend Rights. (In Chinese)http://news.boxun.com/news/gb/yuanqing/2013/04/201304121323.shtml#.VmWbvWOqlm5

2. Boxun News (2013b). Workers Leader Han Dongfang on Chinese Union Movement at Duke University. (In Chinese)http://news.boxun.com/news/gb/intl/2013/04/201304281117.shtml#.VlE7fWOqlm4

3. Boxun News (2014). Shinning on the Star Track: The First Oskar Award for Chinese Freedom and Human Rights. (In Chinese) http://news.boxun.com/news/gb/intl/2014/03/201403031151.shtml#.UxSC5oXEKSo

4. Chan, R. P. (2013). Overseas Democracy Movement Must Swallow Its Own Bitter Pills. Huanqiu Shibao. (In Chinese) http://opinion.dwnews.com/news/2013-08-14/59309687.html

5. Chen, J. (2012). Transnational Civil Society in China: Intrusion and Impact. London: Edward Elgar.

6. Chen, J. (2014). The Overseas Chinese Democracy Movement after Thirty Years: New Trends at Low Tide. Asian Survey, 54, 445-470. http://dx.doi.org/10.1525/as.2014.54.3.445

7. Chen, W. J. (2013). Global Times Knows Nothing about Democracy Movement's Great Ambition. (In Chinese) http://news.boxun.com/news/gb/pubvp/2013/08/201308180817.shtml#.UhIqWT-6W1c

8. Chen, W. J. (2015). Personal Interview. April 2015, Sydney.

9. CK (2015a). Humanitarian China and China Change Joint Donations to Help Gao Yu. (In Chinese) http://www.rfa.org/mandarin/yataibaodao/meiti/ck-04292015102858.html

10. CK (2015b). Democracy Theoretician Larry Diamond Teaches at the Tiananmen University of Democracy. (In Chinese)http://www.rfa.org/mandarin/yataibaodao/renquanfazhi/ck-02052015102619.html

11. Fitzgerald, J. (2014). Why Values Matter in Australia's Relations with China. 13 June.http://www.theasanforum.org/why-values-matter-in-australias-relations-with-china/

12. Friends of FDC (2014-15). A Google Discussion Group, Various Postings.

13. Goddeeris, I. (2007). The Temptation of Legitimacy: ExilePolitics from a Comparative Perspective. Contemporary European History, 16, 395-405. http://dx.doi.org/10.1017/S0960777307003992

14. He, B. G. (2013). Working with China to Promote Democracy. The Washington Quarterly, 36, 37-53. http://dx.doi.org/10.1080/0163660X.2013.751649

15. He, R. (2014). Tiananmen Exiles: Voices of the Struggle for Democracy in China. New York: Palgrave Macmillan. http://dx. doi.org /10.1057/9781137438324

16. Hiatt, F. (2013a). Five Chinese Daughters Speak Up for Their Fathers. The Washington Post, 6 December. http://www.washingtonpost.com/opinions/fred-hiatt-five-chinese-daughters-speak-up-for-their-fathers/2013/12/05/195b6704-5df1-11e3-be07-006c776266ed_story.html

17. Hiatt, F. (2013b). Nine Days. Washington DC: Delacorte Press.

18. Holmes, O. (2015). UN condemns Thai Repatriation of Chinese Dissidents. The Guardian, 17 November. http://www.theguardian.com/world/2015/nov/17/un-condemns-thailand-repatriation-chinese-dissidents

19. Initiatives for China (2015). Two Sparrows Blocked Xi Jinping's Motorcade. Press Release, 17 November.

20. Keck, M. E., & Sikkink, K. (1998). Activists beyond Borders: Advocacy Networks in International Politics. London: Cornell University Press.

21. Qi, J. Z. (2010). The Black Wall: The True Story of Father & Daughter. Melbourne: Book Pal.

22. Qi, J. Z. (2011). Red Dog: My Days in China. Taipei: Yunchen Culture. (In Chinese)

23. Qi, J. Z. (2014). Survivors inside the Black Walls. Taipei: Xinrui Wenchuang Publisher. (In Chinese)

24. Shambaugh, D. (2015). China's Soft Power Push: The Search for Respect. Foreign Affairs, 94. https://www.foreignaffairs.com/articles/china/2015-06-16/china-s-soft-power-push

25. Sheng, X. (2013). Personal Email, September.

26. Sun, B. Q. (2011). A Woman Prisonerin Shanghai. Hong Kong: Wuqi Society Publisher. (In Chinese)

27. Sun, L.Y. (2009). Walking through the Icy Mountain. Hong Kong: Wuqi Society Publisher. (In Chinese)

28. Sun, L.Y. (2015). Personal Interview, Sydney, April.

29. Wang, C. (2011). Lessons of Twenty Years of Overseas Democracy Movement. (In Chinese) http://www.peacehall.com/news/gb/pubvp/2011/06/201106052302.shtml

30. Wang, D. (2012). Wang Dan Mémoire: From 4 June to Exile. Taipei: China Times Press. (In Chinese)

31. Wang, J. T. (2014). Personal Interview, New York, December.

32. Wang, J. T. (2015). Personal Email, July.

33. Wapner, P. (1996). Environmental Activism and World Civic Politics. Albany, NY: State University of New York Press.

34. Wei Jingsheng Foundation (2015). Wei Jingsheng Foundation News and Article Release. A891-W573. 27.

35. Wei, C. F. (2015). Former President of TAHR, Personal Interview, Taipei, May.

36. Wei, J. S. (2014). Personal Interview, Washington DC, December.

37. Wei, J. S. (2015). Personal Email, October.

38. White House (2014). Response to We the People Petition on the Protests in Hong Kong. https://petitions.whitehouse.gov/petition/support-hong-kong-democracy-and-prevent-second-tiananmen-massacre-hong-kong

39. Xi, J. P. (2015). Consolidate and Develop the Broadest Patriotic United Front. (In Chinese) http://news.xinhuanet.com/politics/2015-05/20/c_1115351358.htm

40. Xue, W. (2013). Personal Email, September.

41. Xue, W. (2015). Personal Email, October.

42. Yan, J. Q. (2008). Personal Interview, New York, July.

43. Yan, J. Q. (2010). Thousand Years' Imprisonment for China Democracy Party. 23 August. (In Chinese) http://blog.boxun.com/hero/201008/yanjiaqi99/2_1.shtml

44. Yang, G. B. (2009). The Power of the Internet in China: Citizen Activism Online. New York: Columbia University Press.

45. Yang, J. L. (2013). China Hasn't Earned a Spot on Human Rights Council. The Washington Post, 2 November. http://www.washingtonpost.com/opinions/yang-jianli-china-hasnt-earned-a-spot-on-human-rights-council/2013/11/01/a2e444da-431d-11e3-a751-f032898f2dbc_story.html

46. Yang, S. H. (2015). President of TACHR, Personal Interview, Taipei, May.

47. Zhou, Y. C. (2010). Survey of Chinese Political Movement in Exile over the Past Twenty Years. Beijing Spring, 209, 76-89. (In Chinese)

Index